Take Me to the River

Take Me to the River

AN AUTOBIOGRAPHY

AL GREEN

WITH DAVIN SEAY

CHICAGO
REVIEW
PRESS

An A Cappella Book

Cover design: Jonathan Hahn
Cover image: Charlie Gillett Archive / Redferns

This unabridged edition is reprinted by arrangement with
HarperEntertainment, an imprint of HarperCollins Publishers
This edition published in 2009 by A Cappella Books
An imprint of Chicago Review Press, Incorporated
814 North Franklin Street
Chicago, Illinois 60610
ISBN 978-1-55652-810-1
Printed in the United States of America
5 4 3 2 1

To my father,

Robert L. Greene

• • •

Davin Seay would like to dedicate his work

to his number-one soul sister, Melissa.

INTRODUCTION

It happens every time, and every time it does, I have to laugh.

I'll be standing backstage, waiting in the wings for my cue, and the MC or the promoter or the opening act will be out there, working the crowd up for the main event, the featured attraction, the one they've all marked their calendars and asked their dates and paid their tickets to see.

Me.

And over the drum rolls and all the oohs and aahs will come the oldest line in show business: "He's a man," they'll say, "who needs no introduction."

And when the curtain goes up and I walk on that stage and the band starts playing "Love and Happiness," or "Let's Stay Together," or "Call Me," or "Sha-La-La"—for just that moment, everyone actually believes that it's true.

Al Green. The Man Who Needs No Introduction.

Like I said, I have to laugh.

Because if it really was true, if everything you needed to know about Al Green could be heard on a greatest hits collection, I sure wouldn't be sitting here—the Man Who Needs No Introduction—

writing out the Introduction to the story of my life . . . and you wouldn't be reading it, either. Why bother?

But the truth is, even if you can recite the words and hum the melodies to all my songs; even if you know the chart position, the release date, and the catalog number of every track I ever cut; even if you'd been to a hundred concerts and stood backstage for an autograph at every one, you still wouldn't know who Al Green is . . . not the real Al Green.

The Al Green you see onstage or hear over the radio is about as real as a dream that might wake you up one night . . . and gone just as quick. I'm not my song sheets, or my publicity photos, or my press clippings. I'm not the stories you read or the rumors you've heard. I'm not the leading man of your romantic fantasies, a figment of your imagination, or even a golden oldie from your long-lost youth. And if that's who you want me to be, you might as well stop reading right now.

So if I'm not all that, then who am I? The truth is, introducing the real Al Green is like introducing three different people, each one with his own point of view and each one with his own side of the story. And more often than not, they're all fighting with each other, trying to call the shots and rule the roost. The Al Green onstage bears no resemblance to the Al Green in the pulpit. The Al Green who sings "You Ought to Be with Me" wants nothing to do with the one who sings "Jesus Is Waiting." That Al Green standing in the wings has got nothing in common with the Al Green kneeling in his prayer closet. Most of the time, they can't even stand living in the same skin.

People sometimes think it's strange when they hear me talking about myself in the third person—"Al Green this" or "Al Green that." And I bet they'd think it was even stranger if they knew that there's three people actually doing the talking. First, there's "Al" . . . he's the smooth, sexy one with the big, bright smile, who's never been known to resist a good-looking woman. Then there's the "Reverend Green," blood bought and born again, called out and set apart for the purposes of Jehovah God Himself. There's even just plain "Al Green," your average guy on the street, caught between his best intensions and his worst impulses, trying to let all those angels and devils do their thing without getting in each other's way, like a traffic cop or a referee.

There's Al Green, the Last of the Great Soul Men; Al Green, the Country Preacher with the common touch; and Al Green, the family man. And most of the time, you never know which Al you're going to get. And neither does he. I could be up onstage, ready to get funky, when the preacher suddenly arrives. Or I could be in the church, primed for the Holy Ghost, when the soul man shows up. I could be trying to go about my daily routine and the heavens will open wide and reveal the hidden things of God. Or I'll be seeking His face with every fiber of my being and all I'll be seeing in my mind's eye is that woman who happened to pass by while I was waiting for a red light. There's been times I've tried my best to explain some simple thing and find myself talking in tongues and other times when all I want to do is praise God and find myself singing some old blues song instead.

I've been called crazy, demon-possessed, a split personality, and worse. And maybe it's true. I know that in my life, I've heard voices, seen visions, and felt urges that came directly out of the spiritual realm, and I know that any man who sees through the veil of this world, beyond to the eternal one, becomes a stranger in the land and a prophet without honor. And I also know that any man who has tasted temptation as deeply and as often as I have is forever ruined for the routines of a regular life.

But I also believe that for all the different Al Greens in me, there's a cast of characters crowded inside of you, too. We're all pulled and tugged by God and the devil and each one of us is a battlefield for good and evil. Maybe you don't know it because you haven't yet learned to discern which part of you is looking up to heaven and which part is reaching down to hell. But I have. Maybe you've come to a place in your life where you've made peace with yourself, accepted your limitations, and learned to take the good with the bad. But I haven't.

If there's a difference between Al Green and everyone else, it's that for Al Green, it's a winner-take-all situation. The good that's in me and the bad that's in me can't live peaceably side by side. They've staked out a no-man's-land in my soul, separating the sacred and the profane. What you see is what you get, depending on who's winning the war, from day to day and from hour to hour.

Introducing Al Green begins by understanding that he's always had a choice, not just to do what's right or wrong, but to give himself over to the powerful voices that speak through him. And when you listen to Al Green's greatest hits, that's exactly what you're hearing—sin and salvation trying to sing the same song. If I can sing that song to a woman and make it sound like I'm pleading for God's mercy, you better believe I can sing that song to God and make it sound like I'm pleading for a woman's mercy. I've always known that the reason Al Green's music speaks to people is because for Al Green, the sensual and the spiritual are two sides of the same feeling, a longing that no words can describe. Everyone knows that feeling and somewhere along the line everyone does something about it—gives it over to God or gives it up for the thrill of the moment. For Al Green, it's a choice that's torn him apart. You can hear it when he sings . . . that ache that reaches all the way down to his roots.

And if you were Al Green, you'd be torn, too. Almost since I can remember, women have wanted to get next to me, and when I sing, it's like they've received a personal invitation. There's no use denying it. I've tried. It doesn't work. I might as well admit I have a gift and get on with it: I'm a soul singer and I take what comes along with the job.

But I've been gifted in other ways, too. When a sparrow sings, I hear the voice of God. When I take a walk in the forest, the trees turn themselves into the very pillars of heaven. My destiny is laid out like an open book in Scripture, and the words of prophets tell the story of my life. I love Jesus and feel his love for me like a mother loves the baby at her breast. I'm a minister of the Gospel and I give it everything I've got.

So the truth is, the Man Who Needs No Introduction actually needs many introductions. Sinner and saint. Sex symbol and sanctified soul stirrer. And even if he could tell you everything you wanted to know about those two parts of himself, there's the third part—that third person—who lives somewhere in between those unforgiving extremes. That's a whole other Al Green. He's never had a chance to say much. Until now.

One way to look at Al Green is that he's just like everyone else—only more so. I'm sure you've felt sad and confused about the different parts of your life that don't fit together, doing things that are sinful, even while you're telling yourself it's wrong. But imagine if you had a thirst for righteousness just as powerful as your gift for sin. The price of peace, the Bible says, is to embrace the one and put to death the other. It's like plucking out the eye that offends you, only for Al Green, one eye isn't going to do it. The good and bad are all tangled up inside of him, like the intertwined roots of two trees, drawing water from the same well of life. Siamese twins share the same heart: Give it to one and the other withers away. How are you going to choose?

The difference inside me is more than just the way God made me up—it's the way I was brought up. I've felt pulled in two directions ever since I could walk, and there's never been a middle ground. I believe the words of the Bible when it says that he who is not for the Lord is against Him, but for Al Green, they've always been more than just words. They're a rebuke from holy God to sinful man, and I'd be lying if I didn't say I sometimes wish it wasn't about being either for or against, that Al Green could just fit the two halves of himself back together and live in harmony.

But that's not the path I've been called to follow and I'm not alone. Black people in America have always been torn between walking with Jesus and wandering in the world, clear back to the times of slavery when we either cried out in captivity by singing the blues or held out for a better hope by singing spirituals. The church and the roadhouse have always been two stops on our long road to liberation, and we've been walking the line for hundreds of years. It's only natural that some of us lose our balance once in a while. That struggle is part of what makes us great as a people . . . and part of what makes our music so powerful. Anybody can tell you that all the great soul singers learned their best licks in the choir loft, that the church is the mother of R&B and the grandmother of rock & roll. But no one can tell you the pain of having the choice between lifting up your voice for God or taking a bow for your third encore. That's something you have to experience for yourself. Like Sam Cooke. Like Marvin Gaye. Like Al Green.

Of course, Sam and Marvin have gone on to their reward. Al Green is still here, preaching at the Full Gospel Tabernacle. That's my little church off a side street in Memphis, not too far from Graceland; that's where, year after year, millions come to pay homage at the shrine of another great singer who had to make his choice between serving God or pleasing all those folks who thought he *was* God. Make no mistake about it—if you're faced with that decision, you better think carefully.

And when you really get down to it, that's what this book—the story of Al Green—is about . . . taking that decision, making that choice, setting my face in one direction and turning my back to another. When it's all said and done, there's plenty of singers in this world, some of them not as good as me and some them a whole lot better. And a lot of them—good, bad, or indifferent—do just fine singing the songs the people shout out for, the ones they get all nostalgic about and always want to hear just one more time. There's nothing wrong with that. People need to be entertained and, on occasion, when the spirit moves me, I'll dust off a few of those oldies myself . . . like it says in that song I did a few years back: "For the Good Times."

It took me a while to figure this out, but God's not displeased with His servant Al Green for singing "Tired of Being Alone," or "Here I Am," or "I'm Still in Love with You." He wants his people to feel good, to laugh and carry on and remember what it was like when they were young. He has graciously given me the ability to bless people with some simple rhymes and melodies, and I thank Him for that.

But for Al Green, these days, it's about more than making people feel good, more than just being one of those singers that does just fine with his smooth moves and his certified solid senders. These days, the Reverend Green has his hands full, preaching a sermon on Sunday morning and teaching the Bible study on Wednesday night. He counsels the troubled and lays hands on the sick and shepherds the flock and seeks out the strays. He'd be lying if he told you that old Al—the sexy one in the leather pants and the feathered hats and the platform shoes—doesn't come around anymore to strut his stuff. And he'd be a whole more less than honest if he claimed that Reverend Green doesn't sometimes call on Al when he needs to make his point to the people. There's always been a fine line between those two, but that's the point of this whole story. It's been almost thirty years since Al Green crossed that line. And he's not looking back.

Of course, there's lots of stories about how a man will turn from his wicked, wicked ways, get right with God, and spend the rest of his days laboring to bring in the harvest. The Bible is full of them and I believe every one. But I'm not a fool. I know that being born again is the beginning of the journey, not the end. I know that our struggle is not against flesh and blood, but against prinicipalities and powers and that it's a struggle that goes on every day in the depths of my soul. God is not done with Al Green, the good, the bad, and the one in-between. God has promised that, one day, He will do for Al Green what Al Green can't do for himself: heal that divided soul and make him whole.

So in the meantime, I just wait and try to do the best I can. People sometimes ask me if I miss all the glamour and glitter of being a world-class music star. They wonder how I could give it all up to tend the needs of a handful of poor folk from the wrong side of the Memphis tracks. What I tell them is what I tell myself: God has put me in this place, made me humble, and worked me hard because one day He will lift me up. I believe that everything I've done in my life—all the suffering and the sin and standing up for Jesus, right up to writing these very words on this page—has been for a reason. God will use sexy Al to call His people to Him. He will use Reverend Green to preach to them the Good News and he will use plain old Al Green as a witness to his love and mercy. One day, and it won't be long, there's going to be no difference between Al Green singing a love song or a gospel hymn, no difference between Al Green getting funky or getting holy. God will use all things to His purpose and Al Green, tempered and tried in the refiner's fire, will lift his voice to call in the faithful from the far corners of the earth for a celebration of the Lord's goodness and mercy. You wait and see.

Like Moses on the back side of the mountain, my time is coming. God has prepared Al Green for such a day as this, when I will lift my voice like the prophets of old to reveal His glory. He gave me twenty years on the road to teach me how to reach people. He gave me twenty years in the pulpit to teach me what to say. Who knows how long He's going to give me to stand up before this generation and declare His wondrous works?

Of course, no man can declare God's purpose except He prepare the way. In the case of Al Green, that preparation has taken a lifetime. There's hardly anything you can think of I haven't seen or done, no valley I haven't walked through or mountain I haven't climbed. And now the time is at hand. I'm writing this book—the story of my life—to present my credentials: to let you know where I've come, how I got here, and where I'm going. I hope you find it entertaining because, after all, Al *loves* to entertain. And I hope you find it inspiring because—you ask my church—Reverend Green *loves* to inspire. But most of all, I hope you relate because Al Green is just an ordinary man, trying to stay true to himself.

Allow me to introduce that man. My name is Al Green.

CHAPTER 1

Most of my earliest memories, good and bad, have music in them somewhere. Music has always been my clearest channel to God, my way of touching the hem of His garment and feeling the strength of His love. I don't mean to say that when I hear a song, I'm hearing the voice of God, telling me this or that, answering my questions or setting me straight. That kind of divine encounter only comes through praise and prayer. But in music, I do hear His heartbeat and the breath of His presence. God gave me music as a special way to reach Him and, because God is everywhere, it seems that everywhere I turn, I hear music.

And not the kind of music that they pipe in elevators and supermarkets and airports, either. The music that surrounds me, way out where I live in the country, is the music of creation. I've been asked before what my earliest influences were; whether I liked Elvis or Otis, Jackie Wilson or Wilson Pickett. My answer is that I like them all, but if you really want to know what my earliest influences were, you'd have to go back to the rain on the window, the wind in the corn crop, or the water lapping on the banks of the river. That is music to my ears.

I can still remember childhood days when I'd wake up early to the sound of the birds singing in the trees and throw open the window just to catch their whistles and chirps. It made no difference to me that it was the dead of winter or that my brothers were yelling at me from the bed we shared to shut the window and stop acting like a fool. They just didn't hear what I heard. And it would be a long time before I understood in my mind what I always knew was true in my heart—God speaks through His creation and the language He uses is music to those with ears to hear.

It seems like my whole life has had a soundtrack to it, and the clearest scenes in my memory always have songs playing behind them. I remember the morning we laid my grandmother to rest as we all gathered around the fresh-dug grave, singing her off with harmonies so clear and perfect it was like the angels had come to carry her away.

I remember being on the road with the family gospel group, the Greene Brothers (I wouldn't drop that final "e" on the family name until I began my solo career). I was too young to sing, but my daddy had me along for company, riding up front with him in our old blue GMC truck. "Now, don't tell your mama," he'd say as he pulled over to some lonely juke joint by the side of the road and left me to drift off to sleep, listening to down-and-dirty blues throbbing through the warm Southern night.

It's the sound of gospel music that mixes with other sensations in my memory, like the scent of fresh-cut sawdust hanging in the revival tents as my brothers sang soft and low, or the sight of my daddy, staring straight ahead, tears rolling down his cheeks and falling onto the open Bible in his hand. I swear, even now, I can hear them plopping onto the page.

Of course, memory is an unreliable sort of thing. There's no way tears on a page could have carried over tambourines banging and voices rising higher and higher until the people jumped clear out of their seats, shouting and signifying. Or maybe it's just that you hear things differently when you're a child. To my mind, there wasn't much difference between those folks carousing in the road-house and the ones raising the roof at the revival.

I remember huddling under the covers, tuning in the radio, down low and late at night, while my brothers slept beside me, try-ing to pick up those hot and heavy sounds out of Memphis, the for-bidden fruit my mama said would rob me of my soul. I remember gathering around the old upright piano with my high school glee club, chalk dust hanging in the music room air. I remember Satur-day nights in the El Grotto Club in Detroit, singing five sets a night with Jr. Walker and the All Stars back behind me like a runaway freight train. But mostly, I remember just walking along by myself down a country road, singing a song with no words, just "sha-la-la," and making up the melody as I went along.

It can take us a lifetime to learn what little we understand about God and His creation, but sometimes it seems that in the things we know as children—those things we just accept without having to ask why or how—God reveals His true nature. Little Al Greene never had any doubt that God loved him, that He knew his name from the foundation of the universe, and that he was pre-cious in the Master's sight. It was from joy that he sang those sim-ple songs, and when he did, he could feel God's pleasure as sure as the sun on his back and the wind in his face.

The truth was, however, that there wasn't much else in my life to make me feel very special or set apart. Poverty has a way of rob-bing a child of his identity and self-worth, making him nothing more than just another mouth to feed, and, along with all the music of my childhood, I also remember a dark cloud of hardship hanging over those early days.

I couldn't tell you when I knew for sure that we were a poor family. Maybe it was that night we were all sitting around the kitchen table, staring at a lonely pot of okra and hoping that my daddy would come home soon from hunting in the fields with a rabbit or a pheasant of something—*anything*—to add to that pitiful stew. Or it might have been the time when Mama read me the Bible verse in Genesis about how God gave clothing to Adam and Eve to cover their shame and wondering then that if wearing clothes took away shame, why it was I felt so ashamed walking around in my raggedy overalls with no shoes? Or it could have been waking up at night, my four brothers in bed next to me, elbows and knees poking at me and somebody snoring and someone else talking in their sleep.

But if I had to guess, I'd say it was time when I was four years old and Christmas was coming. We got ourselves a Christmas tree and all us kids sat around it, with the older ones telling the little ones all about how Santa Claus was going to come down the chimney with gifts for everybody who'd been good. I didn't quite buy that story of a jolly old white man with a sack full of presents, but I got just as excited as everyone else thinking about what I wanted to find under that tree come Christmas Day. I only had one thing on my list: a bicycle. I could imagine myself flying down the country road so fast the wind would pin back my ears, but that morning all I found under the tree with my name on it was a bag of oranges and apples, with a few pieces of hard candy and a handful of nuts thrown in.

Right then I knew not only was there no such a person as Santa Claus, but that people don't always get what they want, even if they *have* been good all year long. It was easy enough to guess where that bag of fruit came from and I made sure Mama and Daddy saw the smile on my face when I opened it up. But deep down inside, there was no way around it: I'd wanted that bike and I could almost taste the bitterness of my disappointment.

But with that old Christmas story comes another memory, one that reminded me of the comfort I'd known all along, even at the tender age of four. That same Christmas Day, as I was walking instead of riding down the road to my great-great-grandmother's house, I heard a song coming from the Taylor's Chapel, right next door to where she lived. The congregation was singing "Silent Night," and at the sound of that carol, I was overcome. It was so beautiful, so pure and peaceful. I began to weep and I was still weeping, with a joy inexpressible, when my brothers found me and started teasing me about being such a big baby for not getting that bike. Then my daddy came along and I knew he'd feel bad about seeing me bawling like that and thinking it was all about the Christmas he couldn't afford to give us, so I dried my eyes and went in with the rest of them for a family dinner with Grandma Queeny while those words and that melody just soothed my spirit and brought calm to my four-year-old soul.

I suppose it helped, being as poor as we were, knowing that the folks around us weren't a whole lot better off. There's another memory from those days that mixes misery and mercy in my mind. It was harvesttime and it seemed like the whole community was fretful and afraid, knowing that the crop for that year was going to be meager and fetch a poor price at market. We were already barely scraping by and the time quickly came when there was finally nothing left to eat in the Greene house—not even a pot of okra. All the sweet potatoes and black-eyed peas from my mama's kitchen garden were long since gone and my daddy couldn't find a rabbit or a quail to save his life—or the lives of his hungry children.

Finally, in despair, he went to the general store in town and he took me with him. I don't know why exactly, except that maybe he thought the sight of my skinny, saucer-eyed self would help his cause. But I'll never forget standing beside him, staring up at the white clerk as my daddy drew up with all the dignity he could muster and said, "My name is Greene. I'm a sharecropper down the road at the Benton place, and the crop ain't comin' in. I've got five little boys and five little girls and no way to feed them. If you could see your way to—" And just when he got to that point of having to swallow all his pride and beg, that clerk cracked a big, wide smile and said, "Why don't you go on back there, Mr. Greene, and get what you need to feed those children? You can sign a ticket and pay me when you're able."

God had moved on the heart of that man. I could see it in his eyes and the way that he was so quick to spare my daddy from having to plead for his family. I knew, even then, that God could work through the conscience of men to accomplish His loving kindness. If we were willing, like that white clerk was on that one moment on a cold October morning, then God could use us all as vessels of His will. It's a lesson I have never forgotten.

Of course, my daddy didn't really have to introduce himself to the man behind the counter. They both knew each other, just as they both knew that my daddy was putting his request in a such formal way to make it understood that he wasn't asking for a handout, just a little help. The fact was, in Jacknash, Arkansas, everybody not only knew everybody else by their first name—they knew the first name of your daddy, your granddaddy, and his daddy before him. You couldn't help it, since there wasn't but a few dozen people in the town to start with.

That clerk probably knew every one of us Greene kids by sight, and there's no doubt he was well acquainted with Mr. Paul Benton, a gentleman farmer from an old Arkansas family, on whose farm my daddy sharecropped a few hundred acres in exchange for a roof over our heads and a percentage of the cotton, cane, soybeans, corn, or whatever else it was Mr. Benton decided to plant from one season to the next: 30 percent, 40 percent. A sharecropper did the best he could.

The Bentons were a power in the local community in and around Forrest City, where their pioneering ancestors had carved out big tracks from that flat, hard land to call their own. They were good folks as far as they could be, but like everyone else, they were caught up in a system that ground people down in a lifetime of hard labor, working just to survive and surviving just to keep on working. Paul Benton sure didn't invent tenant farming and you sure couldn't blame him for not coming up with something better. That's how it had always been down in that part of Arkansas—across the whole South, for that matter—and if a man poured out his life in sweat and blood, only to die and be buried, and all on land he would never call his own, well, that's just how things were for as long as anyone could remember.

And as long as anyone could remember, the Greene family had been sharecroppers for the Benton family. It was a tie that went back four generations and it was meant to go on for four generations—and four more after that. By the time I arrived on the scene, April 13, 1946, born at home and wrapped in swaddling clothes by my grandmother, my mama and daddy were well on their way to supplying a whole new crop of field hands for the Benton plantation. Five brothers and sisters had arrived before me—Walter, William, Mary, Odessa, and Robert—and four would follow—Margaret, Maxine, Larnelle, and Cluster. And behind all of us was a family history as colorful and confusing as any royal lineage.

It seems there was a wild acorn on the Greene family tree that would pop up every once in a while, and that goes a long way toward explaining how Al himself got to be the way he is. There was my great-great-great grandfather, for example, who never did take to sharecropping and made his way instead as a professional gambler, complete with a set of silver-handled revolvers that he'd fire off into the floor to get people dancing when he was drunk and wanted some entertainment.

I used to hear such stories from his son, my own great-great grandfather, Ira Sims, who himself had a great big smile and in his younger days was far and wide considered to be God's gift to women. He'd tell me all his stories and then I'd sneak off into the pantry and he'd come up behind me and catch me drinking his cans of condensed milk and chase me around the yard on his old bow legs. I think he loved that sweet Eagle brand milk as much as his father loved whiskey and rye.

But if you try and go too far down the Greene family line, you're likely to get all tangled up pretty quick. Nobody seems to remember, exactly, who was related to who and whose uncle's son was whose wife's father. It's not uncommon among the descendants of slaves to come up against a dead end when trying to trace your heritage, and the situation gets even more complicated with us when you consider that my daddy, Robert, and my mama, Cora Lee, were also distantly related—fourth or fifth cousins, once or twice removed—at the time they were married.

It was a big clan, sprawled out across Arkansas and Mississippi and Tennessee, and the Greenes who settled so long ago in the Forrest City area are just a small part of a family history that has long since gotten lost in the tucks and folds of time. I can't even tell you for sure what drew us to the tiny town of Jacknash, a place so out of the way it could get lost in the tall corn in late July. I'd been born just a few miles down the road, in another dot on the map called Dansby, but we'd made the move to Jacknash right around the time of my first birthday. Not that there was a whole lot of difference between one town and the next, or between one place and any other out there in rural Arkansas in the late forties. I remember a trip we took up the road to a town called Greasy Corner—check it on the map if you don't believe me—and thinking to myself, *My, my, this must be a busy place. They got a stop sign here!*

But as small as Jacknash might have been, there was room for two churches—Taylor's Chapel and the Church of the Living

God—and the Greenes went to both of them. Even if our family ties had gotten kind of loose and unraveled, the bonds of the church always remained strong and sure. Uncles and aunts, nephews and nieces . . . we all had a reunion every Sunday morning and it was in those times, crowding the pews with hymn books open, that we found a common trait that ran from father to son and mother to daughter in a straight and unbroken line.

We sang.

Every Greene, young and old, seemed to have the ability to make a joyful noise. My daddy sang and my mama sang and so did my grandparents on both sides. My brothers and sisters sang, and when it came to be my turn, I sang, too. Church was where we came together, an extended family, each one with a natural born gift for praising God. But singing was an everyday thing, too. It just seemed to flow out of the stream of our lives, making the chores and routines move by a little faster and giving the special occasions an extra measure of celebration. When one of my brothers would break out a guitar on the front stoop or sit down at the church piano before the service, we'd all gather around like flies to honey. But even without the musical instruments, plowing the fields or feeding the livestock, on our way home from school or over to the creek on a Saturday afternoon to catch catfish, we'd be trailing music behind us like the bright-colored tail on a kite.

Sometimes we'd be singing when we didn't even know it. I recall once, in shop class, while I was happily hammering away on a spice rack for my mama, the teacher came up behind me and put his hand on my shoulder.

"Do that again," he said.

"Do what?" I asked without the slightest idea what he was talking about.

"Sing that song you were singing," he said, then turned to the rest of the class. "Hey, everybody," he called over. "Listen to little Albert singing his heart out here."

I looked up at him, confused and a little bit frightened. "I don't know what you're talking about," I said. "I wasn't singing."

"Well," he replied, "I don't know what you call it, but it sure was pretty."

CHAPTER 2

My daddy only hit me one time that I can remember. We were at the dinner table and it must have been around harvesttime, which accounts for the piles of food heaped up and all of us all digging in like it was our last meal on earth. I guess I must have been getting a little carried away, stuffing biscuits in my mouth one after the other, because my daddy leaned over and said, "Slow down a little, son. You're gonna choke if you keep that up."

He was cool and calm and I was so busy eating that I didn't hear the note of warning in his voice. So he told me again, a little sharper this time, but right about then I noticed that there was only one more biscuit left on the platter, so I made a grab for it and stuffed that away, too.

Suddenly, even before I had a chance to swallow, he lashed out with the back of his hand and knocked me clean off my chair. I don't think my brothers or sisters even noticed. They were too busy picking the leftovers off my plate.

It's a story that, in the telling, says a lot about the kind of man my daddy was—slow to anger, even if he sometimes had cause; quick to act, even if sometimes he made the wrong move; not easy to read, even if sometimes all he wanted to say was that he loved you.

I never doubted that my daddy loved me . . . none of us did. He worked too hard to put food on the table and clothes on our backs for us ever to question his commitment to his family. But at the same time, I wonder if all that hard work didn't rob him of the simple satisfaction of being a father. He had no choice, of course, and he always wanted to do the right thing by us, but that's just another one of poverty's curses: A man will lay down his life, only to die a stranger to his own flesh and blood.

The poor will always be with us, Jesus said, and it's true that poor blacks in Arkansas are nothing new. But the time of my childhood was also a time of change—the Depression was over, the war was over, and people in this country, even the most hardscrabble 'cropper on the most played-out piece of land, were looking to a better life. My daddy was no different. He could sense the winds of change in the air, the sudden expectation that the way it had always been wasn't necessarily the way it was always going to be. Maybe four generations of Greenes tied down to the Benton farm was enough. Maybe it was time for a new beginning to get started.

But dreaming about a new life and making it happen are two different things entirely. What I remember most about my daddy in those Jacknash days was the sense of frustration he carried around with him like a sack of stones on his back. He *knew* there was something more to life than living and dying to plant and reap and plant again, but because he was uneducated, because he had no skills aside from farming, and because he had no money or means to provide something better for his family, he seemed to always be reaching for a goal just outside his grasp.

Living a life betwixt and between will eventually take its toll on any man. And like many another black man—and like his own son

Al, following in his footsteps—my daddy, Robert Greene, was torn between the comforts of the church and the lure of the roadhouse. He'd be a good Christian for weeks on end, serving the church and giving fully of his tithe, until that bitterness that was always bubbling under would get the better of him and he'd suddenly announce that he had to go to town for one thing or another. I'm sure my mama knew just what he was up to, but she also knew what her husband was bearing up under, so she'd just hold her tongue and let him go.

More often than not, us kids would clamor to ride along with him and, with no excuse not to, he'd pile us into the back of the truck and, grumbling and mumbling under this breath, drive us into town.

And after a while, we got to know just what to expect. He'd park on the main street, always in the same spot across from the general store and a little catty-corner from the tavern, as if he was kind of sneaking up on it unawares. Then he'd reach into his overall pocket and pull out a handful of change and hand it over to Walter or Bill and say, "Now, you all go on over to the store and get an ice cream sandwich for everyone. I got business to attend to. Take me about forty minutes."

And it did. You could almost set your watch by my dad's visits to the bar. The truth was, he was never much of a drinker. He'd have a shot of whiskey or a couple of glasses of beer, and that would set him up just fine. He come back across the street to fetch us with a little wobble in his step and, after warning us not to say anything about his business meeting to Mama, we'd lurch off down the road, grinding gears and frightening the livestock.

I always suspected that, as much as the booze, it was the music of those juke joints that drew my daddy in—the Chicago blues and Memphis R&B that kept the jukebox jumping and the walls rattling. And that always bothered me more than any liquor he might be throwing back in forty minutes' time, because, to my young mind, it was nothing less than hypocrisy, pure and simple.

My daddy always made a point of turning off the radio when we would tune in WDIA or WKEM in Memphis and he never missed the opportunity to deliver himself of a stern lecture on the evils of such devilish music and how it could turn us away from God and put us directly on to the broad road to perdition. *Well, if all that is true*, I told myself, *he'll be the one leading the parade right down the boulevard of lost souls.* The fact was, all his wailings and warnings just made me all the more curious about the sounds I was hearing outside the sacred walls of the sanctuary.

By the time I was ten years old, I not only knew the names and the musical styles of most of the R&B and rock & roll stars of the early fifties—I'd already picked my favorites. I could appreciate Elvis for that smooth-as-silk delivery and the way he could moan and croon and hiccup his way through a song until you couldn't help but laugh out loud in sheer delight. I liked Fats Domino for that rolling barrelhouse style that sounded like it was coming up out of the floorboards, and I always got a kick out of Little Richard, shrieking and wailing like he'd stuck his finger in a light socket. And naturally, I loved Otis Redding and Sam Cooke for the way they could wring longing and loneliness out of every last note. But the one who opened my ears to what real singing—not to mention style and showmanship—was all about was "Mr. Excitement, Mr. Delightment" himself, Jackie Wilson.

I'd never been to a circus in my life, but to me, the voice of Jackie Wilson was the closest thing I could imagine to an acrobat on a flying trapeze, flipping and twisting and somersaulting, soaring gracefully through space, and reaching out just in time to grab on to the verse, do a double back flip, and set himself spinning all over again. Church music was all about lifting up our voices to the heavenly realms, but to me, Jackie Wilson was already up there, flying through the air with the greatest of ease. I knew for sure that "Lonely Teardrops" wasn't about crying out to Jesus and "Reet Petite" wasn't speaking in tongues, but I didn't care. Jackie Wilson was showing off his own divine gift from God, no matter what my daddy said.

But I think what really got under his skin when he caught us listening to the devil's delicious music wasn't that we were putting our tender souls in peril. It was that we were jeopardizing his grand scheme to make it big on the gospel music circuit.

At a time when Jackie Wilson and others were just beginning to batter down the color barrier in popular music, the true superstars among black audiences were still the gospel quartets—legendary performers like the Swan Silvertones, the Dixie Hummingbirds, and the Soul Stirrers, where many a future soul vocal great would get his start. And despite the sanctified subject matter of their music, such groups had careers every bit as successful, sensational, and sometimes scandalous as their R&B counterparts. It's one more example of that razor-sharp line between sin and salvation that has always cut through black music. When Sam Cooke, the heartthrob front man of the Soul Stirrers, gave up his gospel career for pop stardom, you can sure bet that all those fine, upstanding ladies that followed him from concert to concert didn't give up trying to get his hotel room number for an after-hours visit.

It's easy to see what the appeal of a life on the gospel circuit must have been for my daddy. Even without all the willing young fans eager to offer comfort and solace, the freedom of the open road, the escape from backbreaking manual labor, and the promise of riches and renown for simply opening your mouth and doing what comes naturally—it all must have exerted a mighty pull on his restless spirit.

And he just naturally fit the part. A sharp-looking man, he

could fill even a cheap suit and make it look like a custom-tailored job and with whatever few dollars he could squeeze out of the family budget, he would sometimes treat himself to a nice shirt or a dapper pair of shoes. It was a trait I'm sure I must have inherited from him, and in my own early days as a singer, I'd spend a good part of my split on the latest fashions. As I said, there was a flamboyant streak that ran through the Greene clan, showing itself from time to time and generation to generation, and while I certainly never sported a set of silver-handled revolvers, in my day, I could hold my own with the flashiest showman on the scene.

But it takes more than a good wardrobe to make any man the main attraction and whatever singing talent my daddy may have been born with wasn't going to be enough to get his name up in lights. He needed an angle, a gimmick, and he soon enough found it in the crowd of kids that were taking up all the living space in that two-room shotgun shack we called home. Gathered on a Sunday at Taylor's Chapel or the Church of the Living God, we'd all be standing at attention in our Sunday best, lined up according to age and singing together in harmonies that came as easy as breathing. It was only a matter of time before the pastor or the choir director would say to my dad, "Brother Bob, why don't you and your boys come up here and sing us all a hymn?"

It was an invitation that started coming pretty regularly and it was only right that, if the Greene Brothers were providing the music for a service, well then, they ought to be entitled to a share of the offering. Calling his group the Greene Brothers wasn't quite truth in advertising, however. For one thing, not all the Greene brothers were part of the group—little Al was just too young and excitable, his voice too squeaky and his moves all out of step. For another, my daddy intended all along to be front and center and he wasn't about to give up the spotlight to any one of his sons.

But the Greene Brothers it was, and for a while it looked like my daddy's dreams of glory might actually come to pass. He and Bill would spend whatever time they could spare away from farm chores working up arrangements of old gospel chestnuts from "Working on a Building" to "Packin' Up" to "Every Time I Feel the Spirit." Somewhere or other, Daddy managed to scrape together enough cash to mail-order a Rickenbacker electric guitar for Walter to play. I'll never forget the day it arrived by parcel post and the whole family gathered around like an angel's harp had just arrived in our midst. Walter took to it right away, too, teaching himself to play by picking out the melodies to songs he heard on the radio.

I must admit that I wanted to be part of that family group in the worst way, especially after the Greene Brothers started getting invitations from other churches in the area to come and sing a service and, of course, receive a special offering taken up by the congregation for all of Daddy's time and trouble. Even at the age of six or seven, Jacknash's dusty streets and those endless horizons of fallow fields were starting to feel like a big, empty prison to me. Like my daddy in more ways than one, I also wanted to see what was over the hill and beyond the far rise, and when my brothers would come back with stories of the places they'd been—twenty, even thirty miles up the road!—I ached to go with them.

So I practiced. Instead of just walking along through the woods, singing whatever nonsense notes and words that popped into my head, I'd bear down on the songs I'd heard my brothers rehearsing. And sure enough, I improved. My technique got better, I could hold a note and stay in tune and remember all the words to all the verses. But looking back on that time, I get the feeling I was giving up something, too, trading the spontaneous joy of singing like the birds in the trees, just for the simple joy of it, and trying to fit myself into a structure that sometimes seemed lifeless and dreary in comparison.

Not that it mattered. I was going to be a singer, no matter what it took, and eventually I did earn an occasional spot in the Greene Brothers lineup, adding my tremulous, piping voice to renditions of "I Dreamed of a City" and "Down by the River." I even got to take a few trips on those special Sundays, sometimes clear over to the next county, and I can remember being a little disappointed that things didn't seem a whole lot different over there than they did back home.

Still in all, I was a singer and it was an identity I clung to and cherished, like other little boys dream of being cowboys or firemen. It was how young Al Greene defined himself—not as a poor kid or a sharecropper's son or an ignorant Arkansas Negro. No, I was a *singer.* There was dignity in that. There was pride. There was a future.

I remember clearly the day when all the possibilities of that future found their focus for me, and I grabbed hold with both hands, determined to never let go. I was back in school and it was "career day." A policemen and accountant came by as I remember, an army officer and even a shoe salesmen, all trying to get us kids interested in an upstanding line of work that might one day turn us into responsible citizens and regular taxpayers.

Afterward we sat around while the teacher asked us one by one what we thought we all might choose to be when we grew up. Of course, most of the boys wanted to be cops and firemen and most of the girls wanted to be nurses and teachers. Others weren't so sure. But I never had the slightest doubt.

"Albert?" The teacher nodded when I raised my hand.

"I want to be a singer," I said proudly and suddenly the whole class burst out laughing. I didn't know what was so funny, but I could hear the mocking echo in the laughter and my eyes brimmed with tears. "I'm *going* to be a singer," I said stubbornly.

The teacher quieted the class, then turned to me with an indulgent smile. "Now, Albert," she said. "You're going to have think about choosing another career."

"Why?" I asked, my lower lip still trembling as I brushed away the tears.

"Because the chances of a poor little boy like you making it as a singer are about a million to none," she replied. "Why don't you think about being a construction worker and building tall sky-scrapers. Or how about being a farmer, like your daddy, and help-ing put good food on folks' tables? There's so many things you could do, Albert, but you've got to be realistic."

"I don't want to be realistic," I answered, boldly looking her straight in the eye. "I want to be a singer."

CHAPTER 3

We've all had a dream at one time or another, plotting out the course of our lives, picking and choosing our options and setting out a plan that will carry us from the cradle to the grave. Not that it ever does much good. The Bible says that while we may announce that we're going here or there to do this or that, what we really should be asking is "What is Your will, Lord?"

I can't say that at eight years old I knew what God's will for my life was. But I had a pretty good notion that He didn't want me to be a construction worker. And if the good Lord didn't want Al Greene to sing for his supper, then He was sure going to have to make it crystal clear as to how come and why not. As far as I was concerned, the case was closed.

Now all I had to do was wait for the rest of the world to find out—and the rest of the world didn't seem to be in any particular hurry. Like it has a way of doing worldwide, life in Jacknash, Arkansas, took its own sweet time, one day folding into another without much to tell them apart. And when I wasn't daydreaming about being the next Jackie Wilson, I was taking my time, too, going about the steady job of being a growing boy.

Scrawny as I was, I rarely got picked to play in any of the

schoolyard games, which was just fine by me, considering I thought chasing balls around was a complete waste of time. And because I didn't go in for sports, I was cut off from one of the ways most kids make friends. Which also didn't bother me a lick. I'd always been something of a loner, the skinny kid in the back of the class who keeps to himself and doesn't much speak unless spoken to. The few friends I did have wouldn't have had any friends at all if it hadn't been for me.

There was Louis Ratchford, for instance, a neighbor kid whose sister would end up marrying my brother Bill. He and I would climb trees and eat persimmons and run each other around the yard. But our friendship didn't last all that long, thanks to an ornery pet deer Louis kept out behind the barn. The meanest animal I ever met, that deer would take a bite clean out of you if you were in range, and after it figured out just how afraid of those sharp teeth I was, the cotton-picking thing would chase me on the way to school every morning, snorting and chomping and pawing at the ground. It got so I'd have to take the long way around just to avoid that evil creature, which naturally didn't much—pardon the expression—"endear" young Louis to me.

Then there was James Talbot, who I started hanging with in the sixth grade and who was even more of an outcast and loner than I was. A childhood disease had left him crippled in his feet and he had a funny way of lurching along that got him teased unmercifully by the other kids. I guess I felt sorry for him, or maybe he felt sorry for Al Greene—the underdeveloped kid with those grandiose singing dreams—but whatever the case, we got close during a time in our young lives when no one else would have much to do with us. When we took walks together, James would often stumble and fall, so I'd pick him up and we'd just keep on moving, talking excitedly about our favorite singers and their latest hit discs.

See, James also fancied himself something of a vocalist, even though he only knew one song—Ben E. King's "Stand By Me." He would sing that same tune over and over again and while at first I thought it was a heartfelt tribute to our friendship, after a while I got so sick of it that as soon as he'd open his mouth, I'd shout, "God for glory, man, would you *please* give it a rest!" It wouldn't have been so bad, except that poor James couldn't carry a tune in a bucket and the way he mangled that song can still make me wince, just remembering his cracked wailing in a key I never heard before or since.

Whatever was left of my social life after school and my few friends was taken up with church. Along with music, all my earliest memories are wrapped up in praising and worshipping, preaching and prophesying. I can still feel the hot sun on my back and see the sunlight sifting through the tree on the riverbank when we all gathered for a baptismal service on a summer Sunday afternoon. And I remember thinking to myself, *Those people in their white robes getting dunked into that muddy water must really be trusting Jesus with all their heart and soul*. Because you couldn't have *paid* me to climb into that river with all those water moccasins and snapping turtles lurking around in the mud.

To say that church was the hub around which our lives revolved is to state a fact true for so many black people in America, country-born or city-bred. It's a tradition that dates back to slavery times, when church was the only place my people could gather together and be themselves, hidden from the eyes of the overseer. That sanctuary only grew in importance for blacks as time went on, and it was in church that our hopes were elevated, our community consolidated, and our spirits regenerated.

Given the importance of churchgoing to our sense of identity, it's not surprising that the two churches in Jacknash took different approaches to gathering God's children. Like the song says: "Different strokes for different folks." What was important was that you had someplace to go—someplace where you belonged and that suited your style. The Church of the Living God, for example, was more orderly and solemn, with a place for everything and everything in its place. They put a premium on dignity and decorum, even though, compared to some white churches I've been to, those folks were certainly capable of cutting up every once in a while.

Taylor's Chapel, on the other hand, was a certified, spirit-drenched twenty-four-hour-a-day Pentecostal salvation station. From the moment you stepped through those wide, white-painted doors and into those rough-hewn pine pews, the gifts of the spirit—casting out and calling down, prophesying and speaking in tongues, and laying on of hands and manifesting the Holy Ghost every which way—would be going on all around you in a dozen different little praise and worship services that seemed to feed off and bounce back on each other until you were sure the roof was going to lift off and the Heavenly Host descend to see what all the commotion was about.

I never did develop a preference for one church over the other. To me, shouting at the top of your lungs while hammering on a tambourine or whispering your prayers as the organ softly played were just two different ways of saying the same thing: *We're all down here, Lord, doing the best we can.*

The decision on which of the two churches we'd be attending on a particular Sunday was usually left up to my mama. The fact was, the life and love of the church was more deeply ingrained in her than it ever was in my daddy. For him, the churchgoing tradition was just that: a habit that black people had gotten into a long time ago and long since forgotten why, exactly, it was all so important. He used to say that if a body really loved the Lord, you could have church standing in a field or lying in your bed. For a man run up so hard against the limitations of his own life, going to church and praying for deliverance in the sweet by-and-by must have sometimes seemed worse than having no hope at all. It was better to accept things as they were and deal with the hand that God had dealt you than to go looking for some miraculous intervention on a weekly basis.

For Mama, on the other hand, it was in the faithfulness of their gathering together that God honored the prayers of His people. For her, church wasn't a means to an end, a way of getting what it was you wanted out of life by being good all year, like waiting for Santa Claus to bring you a shiny new bike. Church for her *was* life. It gave meaning and flavor and direction and fulfillment to the smallest details of her day, and no matter how hard and hopeless that day might have been, she always had a service to look forward to, friends to tell her troubles to, and a place to lay her burden down.

Church wasn't the only place folks would meet and make conversation. As in any farming community, there were chores where the whole town would pitch in, coming together for the common good. Well, I remember my mama and grandmother and all my aunts and the neighbor women getting together for a quilting bee, their needles flashing and their tongues clucking, starting at one end and working straight through to the other and then starting all over again. And I'm sure that feeling of being part of a whole—of lending a hand and making a difference—gave a sweet meaning to the lives of those ladies. But it was in the pews, fanning themselves with funeral parlor fans and lifting their hands in a hallelujah chorus that gave them a connection to something beyond themselves and the cramped limits of their lives in that little town.

My mama's people had been churchgoers for as far back as anyone could remember, and a few of them had even started chapels of their own at one time or another. I believe she drew assurance from that verse in Hebrews that talks about how we are compassed about with so great a cloud of witnesses, and from knowing that among that cloud were her own elders, who'd done the Lord's work and gone on to their reward and now were up there watching *her* and putting in a good word every time they saw her trudging down the road with a Bible in her hand and her brood trailing along, like chicks behind a mother hen.

But church was more than a place for us to meet God and petition His grace. It was also a combination country club, town meeting hall, and telephone switchboard where all the gossip and goings-on in our small town got traded back and forth. It's kind of surprising, in fact, that we ever had time for preaching and praying. The most eagerly awaited event on the church calendar wasn't the arrival of some circuit-riding minister or tent revival meeting: It was something we called "dinner on the ground," which was really nothing more than a box social where all the best cooks in the county gathered to show off their artistry with a skillet and a spatula.

Those Sunday afternoons are still vivid in my memory, with families sprawled out around picnic blankets on the front lawn of the church, with the little kids running and playing and the grown-ups talking about who was carrying on with who and who was in a family way and who was caught drinking on a Saturday night and only half-listening to the same old stories they'd heard time and again as the shadows crept across the grass and old folks dozed off in their straw hats and bright pink bonnets.

And then would come the time for the box dinner bidding, and all the ladies would bring up their fried chicken or meatloaf or barbecue with all the fixings and lay it out on a big table and stand behind their masterpieces as proud as you please, and everyone gathered around to eyeball their own particular favorite and give each other sidelong glances, trying to figure out who the highest bidders might be and which ones of those coveted meals would fetch the best price.

Mama would be up there, too, of course, standing tall behind her own justly famous specialty—roasted chicken with a diced egg dressing, cranberry sauce, and biscuits so light people would joke that she'd have to bake them with a stone to keep them from floating away. And she always got top dollar for her dinner, people shouting and stomping their feet as the price went higher and higher until some lucky neighbor made off with the goods and headed back to his picnic blanket to feast on Mrs. Greene's Famous Chicken and Dressing.

And, of course, we were all so proud of Mama as she handed over that bundle of bills to the deacon for the church fund, and no one more so than my daddy, who always beamed and smiled and admitted that, yes indeed he was the luckiest man in the county to have such a cook for a wife.

I laugh when I think about it now, how all of us kids looked at each other with our lips shut tight, as if one slip of the tongue and the truth would spill out and the family secret would be exposed, like a crazy aunt escaped from the attic. Because the *truth* was, Mama couldn't cook if her own life depended on it. Her chicken was always dry, her stuffing soggy, and her biscuits could sit solid in your stomach for three days running, as if they really *did* have a rock in them. The master chef in our house was, and always had been, my daddy. I don't know where he learned how, but he could cook circles around anybody else's dinner on the ground and he'd made up that diced egg dressing recipe right from scratch. I also don't know what he got out of Mama in exchange for letting her grab all the glory, but I'll bet you anything that great cloud of witnesses were looking the other way when she took her bows in broad daylight in front of all our admiring neighbors and friends.

But then, my daddy was a man full of contradictions, secrets, and sorrows, capable of great gestures of kindness and small acts of meanness. I may have deserved getting knocked off that chair for eating too much, for instance, but there was another incident from my childhood when I think my daddy actually enjoyed being purely mean.

Being a loner as I was, I naturally sought some sort of companionship as a boy, and I found it for a time in a little kid goat I named, appropriately enough, Billy. I had that goat out back behind the chicken coop, but he was a smart thing and he kept finding ways to get free and, whenever he did, he made straight for my mama's kitchen garden and helped himself to the beans and the purple peas and the tomatoes planted there. Well, Daddy didn't say anything the first couple of times that happened, just gave that kid goat the evil eye and told me to put him back where he belonged.

One day, not long after Billy had gotten out one more time, my daddy sent me off to a neighbor's down the road to fetch some farm tool or another and then over to another neighbor's to borrow some flour or lard or another such excuse to keep me out of the house for a few hours. In fact, I didn't get back until suppertime, and when I walked in the front door, I could smell the most delicious odor coming from the big cast-iron stewpot on the stove. We all sat down and said grace and Mama served us all with as much of that stew as we could eat, with little Al once again the front-runner.

After supper was over and the dishes cleared and washed, I headed out to feed Billy with some of the scraps, but when I got around the chicken coop to his pen, it was empty. I figured he was back in Mama's garden and I'd better hurry before Daddy found him out there and I was just about to hightail it across the yard when I turned and found myself staring eyeball to eyeball with Daddy.

"You enjoy your dinner, son?" he asked with a little smile playing at the corners of his mouth.

"Yes, sir," I said, edging my way around the coop and hoping he wouldn't notice that my goat was nowhere to be seen.

"Well, that's fine, son," he replied, "because I sure did enjoy cooking it for you." He busted out laughing then, long and loud, taking his time to savor the joke I wasn't getting, until a slow suspicion started to creep into my thick skull.

"Wait just a minute!" I cried. "Where's Billy?" It must have been the seasick look on my face as I realized that I'd just had my pet for dinner that set him to laughing all over again, and I could still hear him as I ran to the house, crying for Mama and cursing the day I'd ever been born to such a cruel man as my daddy.

I have to laugh myself now, thinking back on that billy goat stew, how good it tasted going down and how bad it tasted coming back up. But I learned something about my daddy from that experience. Even in the matter of a rambunctious kid goat, you could push him so far, and then no farther. It was like he had a switch inside of him and you could never quite be sure what was going to flick it, or how to turn it off again. I'm not sure he even knew himself, being the kind of man that, like so many of our day and age, really didn't know what his emotions were telling him until they were so strong they couldn't be ignored.

The way he handled life's ups and downs was the way he tried to teach us kids, too: Be patient, don't lose your cool, but when push comes to shove, push back and keep on shoving. That was the point he was trying to get across one day when a schoolyard bully we all called Shorty came looking for me in my own front yard. Now, don't get the wrong idea, he was short, all right, but so is a pit bull and you wouldn't have wanted to mess with Shorty, either. Anyway, he came around ready to stir up trouble, claiming he'd overheard me calling him some kind of name at recess and was there to settle the score.

I was never much of a fighter, being light and slight as I was, so I tried to talk my way around Shorty, denying that I'd ever said a word against him and, in fact, had always admired and looked up to him. He must have taken those words "looked up" the wrong way, because the next thing I knew, I actually *was* looking up at him—from down in the dirt through a black eye.

If talking didn't work, I could always try my second option— running. But almost as soon as that occurred to me, I realized I had no place to run. Shorty had come right into my front yard and, for all I knew, would follow me on up into the house if that's where I tried to hide.

As it turned out, it wouldn't have done any good, anyway. When I turned around, looking for an escape route, I saw my mama and all my brothers and sisters standing on the porch, just staring back at me, watching to see what I would do next. But it wasn't their eyes that caught my attention. It was Daddy's. I could see him at the door, his face half-covered in shade, which only made the light from his eyes burn that much brighter. And the message was loud and clear: *Al Greene, you had better get your skinny little butt off the ground and fight back.* No son of my daddy's would be allowed to stand there and let himself get whipped in his own front yard. He raised his arm and pointed his finger straight at me and I knew *exactly* what that meant: *If Shorty doesn't kill you your daddy will.*

So I fought back, gave as good as I got, and while it might have been a judge's call who won or lost in the end, at least I knew I wouldn't have to face Shorty *and* my daddy on the same afternoon.

But sometimes the very thing you thought would push that man right over the edge hardly seemed to give him pause. The best example I can think of was when he finally pulled together enough money to make the down payment on a new John Deere tractor. Getting that tractor was one of the proudest moments of his life, I think, and for the first couple of days, he didn't even drive it—just kept it parked where he could sit and look at it from the front porch. Finally he took it out for a test spin and it seemed like just knowing how much easier that John Deere was going to make his work day took ten years off his life and put a spring in his step.

Well, naturally, my oldest brother Bob wanted a shot at driving that shiny new machine himself, and after hemming and hawing, giving in and then changing his mind, my daddy finally handed over the keys and let Bob drive it straight down the road and straight back. After he passed that test, Daddy relaxed a little bit and the next morning told Bob to take the tractor out to a far field and pull up a stubborn tree stump that had been getting in the way of the spring plowing. Bob was out the door like a bullet and I was close behind, begging to ride along.

We got down to the field and Bob surveyed the situation like he was a general ordering an enemy outpost to be stormed at all costs. He hooked a chain around the stump, then attached the other end to the tractor's front end hitch, and, jumping back in the seat, revved the engine and started to slide it into gear.

The only problem was, instead of putting it into reverse, he slipped it into first. The John Deere lurched forward and went careening down the slope, smashing into that tree stump and breaking the front axle clean in two. Bob and I just stood there, watching, as the nose of the brand-new machine settled into the mud, and for a minute, neither one of us could say a word. I think I was the first one to find my voice and state the obvious. "You're gonna get it," I said. "You are *really* gonna get it."

We stayed in that field for the rest of the morning, turning over all kinds of ideas to save Bob's skin. Maybe we could say the tractor got hijacked by desperate criminals. Maybe we could say the transmission was suddenly possessed by the devil. Maybe Bob could run away and join the circus. Or enlist in the French Foreign Legion.

We were still trying to come up with a likely excuse for an unlikely situation when we saw Daddy making his way across the field toward us. "This is the most miserable day of my life," Bob said, burying his head in his hands. "You're gonna get it," I said again, trying to be helpful.

But then, something truly amazing happened as daddy came up over the rise and saw his precious new tractor sitting there like so much scrap metal. He stared at it for a long moment, then took off his hat and scratched his head and then looked at it some more. Finally he turned to Bob, who appeared to be afraid to breathe, and said in a calm, collected tone of voice, "This had to be an accident."

And that was it. He just turned around and walked back the way he came, never looking back, never calling after Bob for the whipping that seemed as sure as the rising of the sun. It was as if my daddy had kept his finger pushed down firmly on that switch inside—as if he realized there was nothing he could do about what was already done—and decided to save himself the trouble of getting mad at Bob or God or whoever else he might have thought to blame for the wreck of that glorious green John Deere tractor.

As I said, my daddy tended to keep his own counsel. It was a trait that might have counted against him as a father, with growing children who need to know that their mama and daddy love them. But even though I could never remember one time in my life when he actually said those words "I love you," I never had the slightest doubt that it was true. He had a way of letting you know how he felt and if you could read the little telltale signs, the message came through loud and clear. "Go on, boy," he'd say and reach over and give my head a rub. "Go on, boy." I knew just what that meant. It meant: *Al Greene's all right. He's a good boy and he makes his daddy proud.*

And that meant the world to me.

CHAPTER 4

By 1955, as I was reaching toward nine years old, whatever it was that had been keeping our family together was starting to come unraveled. The images of a prosperous, abundant America, beaming down on us from billboards along the road or on TV screens through an appliance store window, seemed to be mocking the poverty, the hunger, and the hopelessness that stalked our lives. Daddy knew there were better things out there for him and his family, but he had no idea how to get to the Promised Land.

The frustration that had been building in him year after year, as he rose every day with first light and went down every night too tired to even read his children a Bible story, was beginning to wear away at him, like a grinding wheel at the blade of an ax. That switch inside seemed to be on all the time now, with no way to turn it off, and we could all feel the tension settled in the house like an uninvited guest.

It was the cruel economics of sharecropping that ate away at him the most. Like those four generations before him, he was a victim of a system that the devil himself seemed to have devised, always keeping a man down but never quite dousing the forlorn hope that the next harvest was going to finally pull him and his family out of the hole. Of course, a harvest big enough to make us rich never came and, even if it did, the 'cropper was already so far in debt that the best he could hope to do was break even and start the whole soul-killing cycle all over again.

Sharecropping reminded me of the kind of tricky arithmetic I'd come across later in my career as a performer. I'd come into a town where I was billed to play a 10,000-seat arena for half the gate. Only the place really held 12,500. After the show, you might bring that to the promoter's attention, at which point he's going to whip out his calculator. Look out when you see that calculator. He starts adding up the comps and the radio giveaways and the record company freebies and before you know it, you're singing to 2,500 folks for free.

But it doesn't stop there. His fingers will be flying over those keys, pulling fees and taxes and special one-time-only charges right out of the air: security guards, newspaper advertising, union stagehands, and, of course, that backstage deli platter. That platter will get you every time. And when he's finally through with you, your half of the gate has disappeared on a long trail of adding machine tape and you're thinking you're lucky that you only owe this guy $5,000.

They call it show business. I call it indentured servitude, and it was the same shell game my daddy played and lost for all those years. He'd pick so many bales of cotton or so many bushels of corn for such-and-such a unit price, and by the time those field bosses finished subtracting for seed credit and rent and all the rest, that cotton and corn might as well have been picked by slaves in chains.

Which was really the whole idea of sharecropping to begin with. Back in the twenties and thirties, when my daddy's father and granddaddy were 'cropping for Mr. Benton, they were pure and simply slaves in everything but name. And that was about all they could reasonably expect. A man was tied to the land, and his life was timed to the rhythm of the seasons. He'd never think about a better way because, when it came right down to it, he was trapped in a life that reached back to those slave ships carrying his ancestors over from the motherland.

But if my daddy didn't feel like a slave, well, who could blame him? This wasn't 1935, in the depths of the Great Depression, when a man felt lucky enough to have a pot of okra to feed his family. This was 1955, when everywhere you looked they were telling you all about a shiny new future: with a bed for each kid instead of five to a mattress; with indoor plumbing instead of an outhouse with a blanket for a door; with a refrigerator instead of an icebox and a washing machine instead of a galvanized tub. But most of all, it was a time when a man finally had the right to expect some dignity and self-respect and an equal opportunity to make something of himself if he had the energy and the ambition it took.

My father had lots of energy—you can't raise ten kids and farm two hundred acres without it. And he had ambition—it was a Greene family trait he passed right along to me. The trouble was, he had no place to put it, no direction to point it, and, finally, no hope to keep it alive.

And so he drank. Those once-in-a-while visits to the local tavern started becoming more frequent, and the fact that he still couldn't hold his liquor was starting to work against him. It didn't take him much to get where he wanted to go, so he kept going back again, looking to ease the pain that always seemed to be right there, perched on the bed stand the next morning. Mama, who had started off trying to be tolerant of his occasional slips and slides into the saloon, was getting worried, and that worrying quickly turned to nagging and pleading, and it wasn't a big jump from there to fighting and cursing.

I mentioned that music was with me all the time as I was growing up. But it wasn't always the sweet song of the birds or the west wind in the pine branches. There was another kind of music, too, loud and discordant and full of evil intent. And it was the same old song, time after time. Daddy would come home, drunk and mean, and Mama would want to know where he had been. He would tell her to mind her own business, and that malevolent music would start to swell until the whole house was full of clashing cymbals and sounding gongs.

I'll tell you that, in those times, all I wanted to do was crawl under the floorboards, dig a deep hole in the dark earth, and die. I lived with the fear—all of us kids did—that one night the shouting and the pushing and the flailing fists would reach a new crescendo; that one of them would grab for a knife or pull out a gun; and that fear caused something to shrivel up inside me and made me shrink back from both of them. How could a little boy trust the two people he depended on the most if they were always threatening each other?

And that's exactly what they did, time and time again, as those days grew darker and more desperate. One or the other was forever talking about leaving, and if it wasn't leaving, it was calling the police. It was the same chorus of calamity over and over again until I told myself I didn't care what happened to them anymore.

But of course, I did. Every child does. They can't help it, no matter what their parents put them through. God made the family, and that's a bond that's strong exactly because it's been sanctified in God's law. And just because we don't keep God's law doesn't mean it's not written in our hearts, always there to remind us of what's right and to hold us accountable when we break His commandments. I hear a lot about guilt these days, how we all have got to wiggle free of bad feelings and thoughts that condemn us. But in my experience, a little guilt goes a long way. It's God's way of saying something's not right. You better look twice.

I'm not saying I felt the pain of my family's troubles more than anyone else, but maybe I did. In case you haven't gotten the picture so far, let me explain: I was what you call a "sensitive child." Any little boy or girl is going to curl up inside when they hear the grown-ups acting like wild animals. And I know that, more often than not, the child will blame himself, thinking he's done something to bring it all on. And I believed that, too, but when I recall those times, I can clearly see my sisters and brothers just turning off and turning away, like they were deaf and blind and numb inside. They just didn't seem to care anymore and were hunkered down inside themselves, waiting for the storm to blow over.

But I could never get to that place. Trying to separate myself from my mama and daddy—and the love I needed so badly from them—was just more than that young man could manage. I needed their nurturing, their protection, and their unconditional acceptance, and there was no way I could pretend I didn't. To me, such words were never just abstractions, things you said to explain what you can't describe. To me, love and happiness, like the song says, could make you do wrong or right. They were as real to me as water and air. And just as necessary.

And it seemed like I could never get enough. As a child, my idea of heaven—the absolute and final definition of "bliss"—was sitting on the lap of my mama, or my grandmother or my aunt, and getting hugged and stroked. There was a warmth and comfort and security there that I couldn't find anywhere else. Most all the women in my family tended toward the large size. They were big, with plenty of padding, and I loved nothing more than to just kind of sink into them like a soft feather pillow. I could sit for hours on my mama's lap without moving a muscle until I finally just fell asleep. And this isn't just the young Al Greene I'm talking about now. I'd seek out that comfort even as a teenager, and when I was out of the house and on my own, it sometimes seemed what I missed the most was a Greene woman who'd laugh in that throaty sort of way they had and say, "Come over here and sit on my lap and let me hug on you for a while."

My daddy, like most any father, was all about teaching his kids what they needed to know to make it out there in the cold, cruel world. But my mama was always a shelter from that world, a sanctuary and a warm place of refuge that I never felt quite ready to forsake entirely. Looking back on it now, I believe that's what Al, the soul-singing ladies' man, was looking for himself the whole time. All those willing women in all those lonely hotel rooms were a substitute for a mother's love when it got right down to it.

Please understand when I say that it wasn't that Mama didn't give enough of herself to me or to any of her children. There was no more loving woman on the face of this earth. It was just that I couldn't ever get ahold of enough. Like I said, I was a sensitive child . . . and I'm a sensitive man.

All of that's to say that when my mama and daddy took to fighting, it was like they were cutting me off from the one thing I needed the most—their love. How could I crawl into my mama's lap when she was screaming and shouting, promising to knock my daddy's drunken head off his shoulders? And how could I look to my dad for wisdom and guidance when he was spitting curses and throwing punches, aiming to break Mama's jaw? Who knows what would have happened to our family if things had kept up like that? Maybe one of them *would* have ended dead and the other in jail. Maybe we kids would have been farmed out to foster homes. Maybe this story would have had a whole different ending. Or maybe there wouldn't be a story at all. I think we all knew instinctively we were right on the edge of something terrible about to happen and that if something didn't change—and soon—we'd all go tumbling right off that edge.

Of course, things don't change just because you want them to.

Sometimes you've got to make it happen on your own. It's called initiative, and if I'm sure of one thing, it's that God will honor a man who shows a little get-up-and-go.

Which is exactly what my daddy did—got up and went. Regardless of the risk, regardless of the uncertainty, regardless of giving up everything you've ever known for something you've never had, Daddy made the decision that anything was better than watching himself and his family fall to pieces. So at long last he made his move, and God was right there to back him up.

The last straw came when he got his percentage cut of the harvest and the sum total of a year's work—not just his own work, mind you, but that of every other able-bodied soul in his family—came to nothing but $800. I don't know but that he wasn't doing the math in his head as we all sat there looking at the pitiful pile of bills on the kitchen table: 365 days minus 52 Sundays equals 313 days, divided by $800, comes out to about $2.50 a day, divided by all us full-time field hands, and . . . well, it's no wonder we saw a shudder run up his spine.

I think we all also sensed that switch inside of him flick on again, but for good this time, sending up jolts of resentment and rage against God and man for the fate he'd been consigned to. It was usually at moments like these that he'd get up, put on his patched denim jacket and his Burpee Seed cap, and head for the honky-tonk.

But not this time. This time he just sat there, staring at that money with all of us just looking at him and listening to the loud tick of the clock from across the room. I stole a glance at Mama, looking for clues to what might happen next, but she didn't seem to notice and never took her eyes from her husband's face.

It could have been a minute or it could have been an hour. I mean, how long can a roomful of people hold their breath? But however long it was, it seemed like an eternity before Daddy stirred, looking up from the money and around at all of us like he was noticing we were there for the first time. He stood up and, as the light fell across his face, I was surprised to find a look there that I'd never seen there before—a kind of a peace or a settledness or a made-up-my-mind finality that softened his craggy features and put a new light in his eyes.

"It ain't right," he said in a soft voice. "It just ain't right . . . work all year, hoeing corn and pickin' cotton, tryin' to live off purple peas and potatoes out of a kitchen garden. Kids got no shoes on their feet, woman wearin' the same dress to church every Sunday. Ain't got the time or money for a movie or a day at the county fair. Livin' to work and workin' to live . . . and all for eight hundred dollars."

He looked back down at those bills, gathered them up, and, walking over a dresser in one corner of the room, put them away in a drawer like they weren't so much as a bunch of old letters he was tired of reading and rereading.

And that was that. Daddy went out on the porch to take the night air and after a while Mama joined him and they sat without saying a word until it was time to put us kids down for the night. Mama gathered up the girls first, like she always did, and got them to bed in their room and then came in for us boys and herded us into the pantry that we'd turned into a bedroom with pallets on the floor. She kissed us each good night and then listened while we said our prayers, and even though we all had the weight of Daddy's burden bearing down on us, none of us wanted to say out loud what we felt so heavy inside, so we just thanked the Lord for a good day and our daily bread and to forgive us our trespasses as we forgive others and let it go at that.

All the drama of that evening must have worn me right out because I remember passing quickly into one of those deep sleeps like you're dead to the whole world and every trouble it contains.

And when I woke up again, it was one of those awakenings when you're not exactly sure where you are for a moment or what it is that woke you up.

My brothers were still laid out asleep beside me like peas in a pod and the moon was shining brightly through the little window over our heads. In that half-sleeping state, I could still sort of hear the echo of the sound that woke me up in my ears when suddenly there it was again . . . a scraping and a banging coming from my parents' bedroom. My first thought was that they were going at it again and that one of them had thrown something at the other, but then I heard a whole bunch of little noises I couldn't explain. Frightened, but more than anything just curious, I slipped out of the covers, clamored over my brothers, and went to investigate.

What I saw made my mouth drop open in sheer amazement. There was my daddy in the middle of the bedroom, with all the dresser drawers wide open and all their clothes spilled out on the bed and him stuffing them into a cardboard box just as fast as he could. I watched him for a moment, trying to figure what in the *world* he was doing, when he looked up and noticed me and a big broad grin broke out over his face.

"Al," he said, "go wake up your brothers and sisters. Tell them to get dressed and started packin'."

"Where we goin'?" was all I could say.

And all he would say was: "Outta here."

Just then my mother stepped in from the kitchen, carrying an armful of old chipped plates and cups. "What about all this?" she asked, and I could see the same wild look in her eyes that I saw in Daddy's, as if they had decided on the spur of the moment to do something crazy and didn't want to stop too long to think about it or they might change their minds. Which, of course, is exactly what they'd gone and done.

"Forget all that," my daddy said, chuckling to himself as the clothes went flying. "We'll get it all new when we get to where we're goin'?"

"But Daddy," I said again. "Where are we—?"

"—You ain't got those lazy kids up yet?" Daddy interrupted with mock severity. "You better hurry up, Al, or we'll leave you all behind!"

Then both of them laughed like that might not be such a bad idea, like maybe they'd get a whole new set of kids, too, when they got to wherever they were going, and I hurried back to the pantry bedroom to roust out my brothers and tell them the incredible news. We were getting out, once and for all, just like that and without looking back, lest we be changed in a twinkling to a pillar of salt like Lot's wife in the Bible.

By the time dawn broke over that shotgun sharecropper's shack that I'd called home for the entirety of my short life, Daddy had piled pretty much everything we owned into the bed of that old blue GM truck, strapping the mattress on last to keep it all from blowing away. I have to laugh thinking about it now, like something straight out of *The Beverly Hillbillies.* We all found a place up inside that pile while Mama ran back and forth from the house, trying to squeeze in a last few keepsakes.

"Good God, woman, *leave* it," Daddy shouted as he cranked the motor and I scooted over to make room for her in the cab. "We got to be on our way!" And he laughed again, a free and easy sound that echoed over those misty fields and caused me to shiver with delight, or maybe apprehension, or maybe something altogether more wonderful and mysterious than either of them.

As we were pulling out of the driveway, I caught sight of our milk cow, grazing in the pasture beside the barn. "Daddy!" I shouted, pointing. "What about the cow?"

"Got no room for a cow now," Daddy said and Mama laughed

at the rhyme he had made. "Got no room for a cow now," she repeated, like she was singing a duet with him.

The truck rumbled onto the road, creaking and groaning under its weight, and Daddy turned the wheel, pointing us due north. The last thing I recall was hearing that cow lowing forlornly as we headed out of sight, the sun breaking over the tops of the trees.

I never did find out what happened to that beast.

t's been said that when God sends you out on a journey, He will direct your path and light your way, even if it's only one step at a time. And from walking the mountains and valleys of my own life, I believe that to be true. When the Lord is with me, I can feel His presence and move out in confidence, and although I may not know my final destination, I have His assurance that I'm heading in the right direction.

If, on the other hand, I'm the one who's packed my own bags, bought my own ticket, and read my own map, then there's no telling where I might end up. Believe me, I've landed in some pretty shady places in my time, wondering just how I got there and just how I was going to get out again.

I can't say for sure whether my mama and daddy had that God-directed persuasion that they were on a road He had set before them on that morning we set out for parts unknown. I couldn't positively tell you, when Daddy steered to the left or the right, whether he was following a divine road map known only to him. And I'm not sure, when Mama turned around for a look at the state border sign that read YOU ARE NOW LEAVING ARKANSAS, THE RAZOR-BACK STATE—COME AGAIN SOON! whether or not she was wondering if we'd ever be coming back that way again, soon or late. What I can tell you is that as we cut through that pitch-black night, pushing though flat, empty farmland north into Missouri, it seemed that every pair of passing headlights were like the very eyes of God's angels, watching in silent witness to our pilgrimage as we passed across the face of His creation. Sitting snug between my parents in the front seat, I wasn't sure whether the Lord was for us or against us, or whether we had left Him behind altogether, up there at the altars of Taylor's Chapel and the Church of the Living God. As the excitement of our journey began to wear off, another feeling was making itself known—a terrible kind of loneliness, an insignificance in a world that had suddenly become so cold and wide and unfamiliar.

Of course, such fears were partly the magnifications of my own childish imagination, fears that only grew worse as the hours—and the miles—wore on. None of us kids had any idea where we were going or what we'd do when we got there and it must have given Daddy and Mama a good laugh to keep us all guessing, but as far as I was concerned, it was a cruel joke. They knew all along where that long, lonesome road was taking us, but in my young mind, we might just as well have been heading right over the edge of the earth.

As it turned out, many had traveled that same road before us, and many more would follow in our path. You can read about them in history books: how Southern black sharecroppers made their great migrations to the promised land of the industrial North, how they left behind the poverty of that played-out land and the shame of their slave heritage to make a new life in the mills and mines and factories up above the Mason–Dixon line. And you can read about the bitterness and broken dreams they found waiting for them in Harlem and the South Side of Chicago and the mean streets of Detroit—and all the other cold gray ghettos filled to over-flowing with poor folks looking for a way out.

What's much harder to find in a book is the *experience* of leaving behind everything you've ever known for something you've never seen. Pulling up stakes and striking out to chase the rumor of a better life can only be the desperate act of people who've got nothing left to lose. But as much as it might be a grim gamble, it also takes courage, determination . . . and faith. What else could give a man the boldness to become a pilgrim, to move his flock and family, as in the days of Abraham, to a strange land? I'm not saying that my daddy wasn't a desperate man—that, for him, anything was better than one more year chopping another man's cotton. But what I am saying is that his trust in God gave him the courage to act, to put purpose to his plans and a point on the compass to aim that old truck.

Our destination was Michigan and if young Al Greene had ever heard that name before or seen it on that multicolored map hanging from the classroom wall, it sure didn't stick in his mind. As far as I was concerned, Michigan might just as well have been the dark side of the moon . . . it sure was cold enough to be. I couldn't have imaged a place more distant and different from the warm nights and wide-open fields of my home or conceived a place where the wind and snow made it seem like the wrath of God was set against His very creation. Michigan . . . sometimes that name can still make me shudder.

But Daddy had hardly picked the place for its sunny days and sultry climate. It was work he was looking for; a good-paying job in one of the factories sprung up around the Motor City and Lansing, Kalamazoo, and Flint . . . a job and all the fine things that came along with it—benefits and overtime and paid vacations and a chance to move up the ladder to shop steward or foreman, or maybe even one day to be that man behind the desk, buying and selling and hiring and firing.

Why not? Like everyone else, he'd heard the stories: how black people up North were making decent money, buying cars and houses, and educating their children in a place where the color of your skin didn't matter quite so much. At least, that's how the stories went. And the fact was, while 1955 may not have marked the beginning of a great awakening for black people in America, they certainly were beginning to stir in their sleep. World War II had given so many young black men a chance to see a world beyond the South Forty, a world of opportunity where a man willing to work hard had the right to expect better for himself and his family. Of course, there was no use pretending that the odds wouldn't still be stacked against a man of color, no matter where he settled, but a feeling that maybe things could be—and *should* be—different was beginning to take hold and, along with it, that restless urge that made you want to get up and go find out for yourself.

It was my brother Walter who laid the way for us, the year before we pulled up stakes, when he'd gotten married and moved out with his bride to Grand Rapids, Michigan. And sure enough, he got a job right away, working on the assembly line in a refrigerator plant, with a salary that paid the rent on a little two-room apartment and a good time on a Saturday night down around Division Street and a TV and a vacuum cleaner and a washing machine out on the porch, all for no money down and easy monthly payments. He'd even been able to put a little extra aside and that summer sent for Mama and brought her up for the first vacation of her life. She'd come back with a new hat and hairdo, telling tales about a city full of black folks putting on airs and while Daddy sniffed and acted disapproving and said Walter was good for nothing and shouldn't have left, what with us so short of hands at harvesttime,

I guess somewhere deep inside a hook got planted, one that pulled and tugged until it finally reeled him in.

I got my first look at Grand Rapids that gray November morning as we rolled into town at dawn, and it seemed to me nothing like the stories Mama had told of a fine and fancy place. People, more people than I'd ever seen, were hurrying on to their jobs, bundled up against the bitter cold and dodging icy water splashed up by passing cars. Snow sprinkled with soot was piled up everywhere and the air was so thick with the smell of the city you could hardly breathe it in. The buildings were big, just like Mama said, but through the windows I got glimpses of tiny rooms and the cramped lives inside. The open fields of Jacknash, the endless sky, and the deep pine forests suddenly seemed more distant than ever, a fading memory on the far side of the world.

I looked up at Mama with tears in my eyes. "I want to go home," I said, and she turned to me with a wordless look that set me to crying even harder as Daddy turned the corner down a block of ramshackle row houses, looking for the address off the scrap of paper he clutched in his hand. "I want to go home," I said again before Mama shushed me and looked over to her husband like he might know how to tell a little boy that his home, for the moment, was right where he was sitting, inside a truck with Arkansas plates driving down Franklin Street, smack down the middle of Grand Rapids, Michigan.

Walter's wife had people in the area, and for the first few weeks, we somehow managed to squeeze in with them. I can't say I recall too much about those first days in Grand Rapids, aside from a confusing swirl of strange faces in a crowded apartment, the hustle and crush of the streets, and a cold that seemed to seep in through every crack and crevice right to your bones. I clung close to Mama day and night, wrapped in her arms for warmth and comfort, and I do remember a kind of fear mixed in with shame that always comes from having to depend on the kindness of strangers.

Daddy was gone most days, scouring the city for work and trying to find his family a more permanent place to live. He quickly discovered that the opportunities supposedly around every corner in Grand Rapids seemed instead to always be just out of reach. The first job he applied for was at a foundry; it was also the first job he was turned down for. The first of many. Seems like landing one of those good-paying spots on an assembly line depended less on a man's willingness to work hard than on who he knew and what kind of strings he could get pulled. The line formed at the rear, and there was a whole lot of other displaced dirt farmers with no prospects standing directly in front of Daddy.

Somehow, through a combination of odd jobs and a little help from Walter, we managed to rent an apartment across the hall from where we'd been staying and eventually moved farther down the block on Lafayette Street. The square footage wasn't a whole lot more than what we'd left behind, and after a few days, the walls felt to me like they were starting to close in. Back home, we had all the outdoors to roam free, and that was a liberty I'd come to take for granted. Now suddenly I'd lost my connection to God's creation and was too frightened to even open the front door and face those hard and hostile streets.

But of course, I couldn't stay cooped up in that tiny, two-room flat forever and, as those first fearful days turned to weeks, and the weeks to months, I slowly began to find my way around that strange landscape of sharp corners and concrete, through the constant rumble of traffic and across the frozen maze of city streets that stretched in every direction as far as I could see. And what I found was a whole lot of other folks in the same boat that we were in—black families from Mississippi and Georgia, Arkansas and

Alabama—all come to the promised land on a wing and a prayer and all wondering what happened to the pot of gold at the end of the rainbow. The few lucky ones, like Walter, who'd been able to get hold of a weekly paycheck, seemed to be making everyone else envious and uneasy, like he knew something they didn't. But it sure wasn't Walter's fault that his wife had family in Grand Rapids who'd been able to put in a good word for him. And it wasn't his fault that he couldn't turn around and help his own family up the ladder. In that struggle for survival, it was every man for himself.

For me, the struggle was in just trying to keep connected to the things that had made my young life worth living. Cut off from the glory of the natural world, lost in the shuffle of our uprooted family, feeling as forlorn and lonely as I could ever remember, I began to turn inward, losing some of the spontaneous joy that had always made the world seem bright in my eyes, and with it, that childlike innocence that trusted and believed the best in everyone.

It was my feelings about my brother Bob that most clearly marked the change that was taking place inside me. In our family, the kids pretty much tended to hang together in pairs, according to age. Walter and William were a team and so were Mary and Odessa. Among the younger kids, Margaret and Maxine took up together, followed by Larnelle and Cluster. My partner was Bob and, back home in Jacknash, we shared the same chores, swapped the same clothes, and played with the same toys. It was a connection that just came naturally, and the closeness I felt toward my brother was something I never thought twice about.

But in Grand Rapids, all that started to change. Like Walter being the only one with a good job, the rules of our new life seemed to come down to a single hard fact: You were on your own. As a family, our fates were still tied together, if only because you could never get away from each other in that cramped apartment. But the fact that we were all packed in together like sardines was actu-

ally beginning to drive us apart, each one trying to find some private space inside themselves to block out the clamor and confusion
that kept us all so nervous and on edge. So I guess it was only natural that the simple bonds of kinship that brought us together, in
pairs and as a family, would begin to tatter and fray. It wasn't long
before I found myself avoiding Bob altogether, leaving him to fend
for himself as I tried to stake out my own boundaries. Looking
back, it seems as if those days marked the beginning of the end of
my childhood, a time when I began to wonder who was on my side,
who I could trust, and who was looking out for me.

The only person I could be sure of anymore was the one who
looked back at me in the mirror. *I* was the only one I could really
depend on, I decided, and it was up to me to make sure that Al
Greene got what he needed to get by. It may seem like a sad state
of affairs when a nine-year-old boy comes to the conclusion that
he's only got himself to lean on, and the truth was that Mama and
Daddy were doing the best they could to keep the family together:
not only with food and shelter, but also with the everyday kindness
and love that are every bit as necessary for survival. We were all
adjusting as best we could to the new realities of city life, but the
sad fact was, some of us were just more adaptable than others. I
couldn't tell you, for instance, whether Bob ever had a second
thought about his new life, or the one he'd left behind. The fact is,
it was as if he just hunched up his shoulders, ducked his head, and
pushed his way through from one day to the next.

But for little Al, the change was almost too much to bear.
Where was the sound of singing birds? Where was the warm
caressing wind blowing up from the Gulf of Mexico? Where was
the tender, patient murmur of Mama's voice, singing about how
Jesus loved the little children as she rocked me to sleep?

Without those things as part of the regular rhythm of my life, I
began to dry up and harden deep down deep inside, and it wasn't

too long before that sadness started turning to anger. It made me want to strike out at all the cruel and uncaring circumstances that had cut away at my happiness, and for the first time, a mean and vindictive streak came to the surface like the marks of a pox.

After a few months, we kids were enrolled in school, and it was there, in the classroom and the playground, that I got my first brutal lessons in the law of the ghetto. At first, I did my best to keep off to myself, not bothering anybody and hoping that no one would bother me. But there's something about a loner that always seems to attract the wrong kind of attention, and I'll never forget that day after school when I was surrounded by a gang of hard-core street kids who wanted to see just what this raggedy country boy was made of. It wasn't the first time I'd had to face the taunts and torments of a bully, but these guys made Shorty back in Jacknash look like a choirboy. They started pushing me back and forth between them, knocking me around like a rag doll, and when they saw that I couldn't defend myself, the biggest and meanest one laid into me with a terrible vengeance. I remember being knocked down onto the frozen hard dirt of the school yard with him standing over me, kicking at my ribs, and a whole crowd gathering around, shouting and screaming like they wouldn't be satisfied until I was dead. Finally, I guess everyone just got bored with me laying there and taking those licks and I managed to crawl away, dragging myself back home, where my mama cleaned me up and held me in her arms, like old times, as I cried myself to sleep.

But the tears I shed weren't so much from the bodily pains I had suffered as from the humiliation and rage that was boiling up inside of me like a fever. And the comfort I found that night wasn't from resting my head on Mama's soft breast. It was from my newfound determination that no one was going to treat me like that again. I swore it to myself—a childish oath all the more terrible for the cold conviction in my heart.

The next day on my way to school, I ducked behind the alley of a corner grocery store where the owner piled up his empty soda bottles until the delivery truck came with a new shipment. I don't know if that heavy glass Coca-Cola bottle was the first thing I'd ever stolen, but I can sure tell you it wasn't the only sin I intended to commit that morning.

I arrived at the school yard early, lurking around the corner of the cafeteria until I saw that boy who'd gotten such pleasure with every punch and kick he'd landed on me. Moving quickly up behind him, I raised that Coke bottle and brought it crashing down on his head, sending him staggering up against he wall while his posse just sort of stood back, wide-eyed. I hit him again, right across the face, and I remember some part of me wondering why that bottle didn't break as I rained blows down on him until he dropped down to his knees, his face covered with blood pouring from his nose and from a nasty gash over one eye.

I let up then, stepping back, still holding that bottle and looking around for anyone else who might be foolish enough to cross me. While I'm not proud to say it, the fear and awe I saw in the eyes of those kids gave me a nasty feeling of satisfaction. In that moment, it was as if I'd unlearned everything I'd ever been taught in Sunday school or my mama's Bible lessons. God may love a humble and contrite heart and blessed he may be who turns the other cheek, but on a grammar school playground on a cold morning in Grand Rapids, Michigan, it was might that made right, and only the strongest and fiercest and most brutal would survive.

CHAPTER 6

In the months that followed the Coke bottle confrontation, my reputation as a badass dude spread through the school and the neighborhood. Although I never really cared a nickel for sports, I made a point of trying out for the football team. And I also made a point of getting kicked off the team a month later after repeated warnings for unnecessary roughness. It got to where I could hear kids whispering about me as I walked down the hallway and I felt proud of myself, a feeling that fed the dark certainty that I only had myself to depend on.

It would have been easy enough to guess where I was heading— a poor kid in the ghetto, trying to prove he's a man. That's a sure-fire formula for an incarcerated life. It was only a matter of time before my tough-guy attitude would take its course and I'd end up as another sad statistic of the urban black "crime problem."

Except that, even then, I could feel other impulses pushing against such an inevitable outcome. All my life, it seems that I've been struggling to discover who I really am: to find an identity that fits and a place within myself that feels familiar. I've been pushed and pulled in so many different directions, by so many different passions and persuasions, that it sometimes seems like my very soul had come undone. We all learn how to play roles just to get through life, and for me, each role I play reflects another facet of who I am; parts of a complex man—fractured and contradictory. Bringing all those discordant notes into harmony, building a whole person out of those ill-fitting bits and pieces, has taken me a lifetime . . . and I'm still not finished.

Back then, I might have fooled everyone else with my mean and menacing demeanor—everyone, that is, but myself. I'd taken care to hide the sensitive, vulnerable spirit that was so much a part of my childhood, but it was always there, just below the surface, crying for attention and seeking expression. And the best way—the *only* way—I could give voice to that deepest part of me was, as it always had been, through music.

Those first years in Grand Rapids was a time when music moved right into the center of my life, not simply as a way to entertain myself or others, or as part of long family tradition, or even as a way of letting out all the bottled-up feelings that simple words could not contain. For me, music was the way I kept from going crazy. Life in the city was so different from anything I'd ever experienced or expected, and the sounds of those streets, grinding and rattling twenty-four hours a day, was a harsh and high-pitched caterwauling that jangled my nerves and set my teeth on edge. Music was the only way I knew of reconnecting to the nurturing love of God that I had once drawn from the breezes in the trees and the water in the brook and the birds chirping for their breakfast on a bright spring morning.

I sought out every opportunity I could to sing, and if anyone thought it was strange that the toughest kid on the school yard also had the sweetest voice in the school choir, well, I guess they didn't dare say a thing about it. All in all, I wasn't much of a student and just couldn't ever seem to get my mind around history, geography, and math. It wasn't that I was stupid. In fact, most of my teachers were quick to tell me that I had what it took if I'd only *do* what it took. I just couldn't see the point of learning a lot of facts and figures that I couldn't ever imagine having another use for again.

And, of course, that was an attitude that quickly caught up with me. After my grades started scraping bottom, it was decided that I was a candidate for "special education" classes. In other words, the bonehead department. But before I was transferred, the principal of the school pulled me aside and laid a little wager on the table. "I'm betting that you're smarter than you're letting on, Albert," he told me. "And I'm going to put my money where my mouth is. I'm going to give you a brand-new hundred-dollar bill if you make straight A's in all your classes for the next two months. No B's. No B+'s. It's gotta be all A's or you don't get a dime."

I could hardly believe my ears. I'd never even seen that much money, much less been able to pull it in out of my own pocket. And you can be sure, from that very afternoon on, I was paying the very strictest attention to my lessons. I remember coming home after school, making myself a peanut butter sandwich, and heading back to my bedroom to study for the rest of the night. And sure enough, I was able to rack up two solid months of top grades to get that $100. And, sure enough, once I had it safe and sound, I was back to my same lazy ways, with all those A's turning back to C's and D's.

But through it all, I never got less than top marks in choir, all throughout my grammar school years, going from the soprano to the alto to the tenor sections as I grew and my voice continued to develop. For a long time, I was the youngest kid in the choir, thanks to my constant singing. It didn't really much matter where I was. I always seemed to be humming one tune or the other, and it wouldn't be long before I'd forget myself entirely and start giving it everything I had at the top of my voice. The school had a rule that you had to be a certain age to try out for the choir, but they overlooked the requirement in any case after I got caught singing alone in a classroom one day, waiting for the bell to ring and the lesson to start. I don't think I even realized what I was doing until I turned around and saw a whole crowd of people gathered in the doorway, looking at me in a way I'd never quite experienced before. I can't say I was comfortable with them staring at me, but I can't honestly say I was *un*comfortable, either. The truth is, I didn't mind the attention, even though I pretended to get mad and told them all to get on about their business.

But I guess word got around, because before I knew it, I got called up before the choir master, a sweet, gentle man named Mr. Nelson. He tried me out on a few tunes, accompanying me on his piano, and the next day I was told to report to choir practice. It seemed like a good way to get out of doing all that reading and writing, so I went along, even though I was more than a little worried about how it might affect my rough and rambunctious image. But by the end of that first morning, I had no thought to keeping up appearances. I'd found something I truly loved to do . . . and was truly good at.

I looked forward to nothing more than arriving early each morning for practice, the sunlight breaking through the dusty windows of the school auditorium with its high, echoing ceiling and listening to the sound of our young voices bouncing off the walls and coming back around until it seemed like the whole room was filled with an invisible chorus of cherubs and angels. I was proud of being singled out as a soloist for the Christmas program or spring pageant or those special evenings when all the grown-ups would gather to hear us perform our selections of popular and patriotic tunes, clapping and carrying on like it was a command performance at Carniege Hall and I was the star virtuoso, taking my curtain calls in the bright spotlight.

In those moments, I was worlds away from those dirty streets and dangerous playgrounds and crowded tenements. The music transported me, and the sound of my own singing was another kind of power, far different from the violent bullying that I used to keep the world at bay. Up on that stage, raising my voice to the rafters and feeling the notes fill me up from some abundant, radiant joy deep inside was a way of marking my place in the world, of standing firm and proclaiming loud and clear, "My name is Al Greene, and I am *somebody!*"

If it hadn't been for that school choir, I don't know but that I might have ended up locked in prison, brought down to the gutter, or buried deep in a pauper's grave. And I have to thank Mr. Nelson for giving me the first real opportunity I had in life to make something of my musical gift. Without his encouragement and the way he kept at me to improve my technical skills without ever letting me lose touch with the pure pleasure of singing, I don't know where I'd be today. You could say that music was an escape from the grim realities I faced every day, but it was more than that: Music *was* my reality.

And music was everywhere in those days. The late fifties was, of course, the Golden Age of American pop music, and so many of the sounds that would soon shake, rattle, and roll the world were just beginning to burst the bounds of the tired old Tin Pan Alley scene. It seemed like great tunes were pouring from every open window and every passing car, with most everyone's radio tuned to WCHB, blasting west across the state from Detroit. The fuse that would spark the Motown soul explosion had yet to be lit, but there was no doubt that something powerful and potent was in the air, getting ready to break out of the narrow bonds that had for so long defined "race music" and take its liberating message to a huge young audience, black and white. From Ivory Joe Hunter to Frankie Lymon;

Nat "King" Cole to Clyde McPhatter; Chuck Berry to Little Richard to Fats Domino and beyond . . . everything you heard in those days was like nothing you'd ever heard before.

As proud as I was to be front and center in our little school choir, I was prouder still of my family connection to the great R&B and blues that was the sound of the era. I had a distant cousin Herman on my daddy's side who used to live not far from us in West Memphis, Arkansas, and went by the name Little Junior Parker. I think my daddy, with his stern admonitions against worldly music, must have felt a little ashamed of his link to the down-and-dirty sound that was Little Junior Parker's stock in trade, but I also suspect that, if you'd asked him, he might have confessed to being at least a little pleased that one of our own had made the big time.

And there was no doubt cousin Herman was a genuine star in his own right. A singer with a distinctive, honey-smooth voice, Junior Parker had first come up in the thriving Memphis blues scene of the late forties, where he'd been a bandleader and song-writer. He could also play a mean harmonica and had learned the finer points of the instrument from the legendary Sonny Boy Williamson. He served a stint in Howlin' Wolf's band and then joined a Beale Street combo called the Beale Streeters that also included B. B. King, Bobby "Blue" Bland, and Johnny Ace. I remember hearing about his band the Blue Flames when I was still just a boy. His first big hit, "Feelin' Good," would come on the radio and my brother Walter would tell me that the man with the sweet voice that seemed to melt around the words he was singing was our kin. I could hardly believe it.

It wasn't too long after that when I heard another of my cousin's songs on the radio and this time nobody had to tell me who it was. "Mystery Train" sent shivers down my spine from the very first notes and that's the reaction I've had ever since. It's a tune that is so full of strange beauty and unspoken symbolism and, to me, it's always seemed to hark back to something real—something fundamental—in the history of our people. Like John the Conqueror, the Mojo Hand, and that hellhound on your trail, Junior's "Mystery Train" spoke to the myths and legends kept alive for centuries by the sons and daughters of African slaves.

Chances are, of course, the version most people are familiar with isn't my cousin's at all, but the one Elvis Presley laid down a few years later. Now, I've never subscribed to the notion that a white man can't sing a black man's music or the other way around, but I'm sure you'll understand when I say that I've always preferred my cousin's version to the Elvis cover.

By the time we moved up to Grand Rapids, cousin Herman had relocated from Memphis to Houston, where he recorded some even bigger hits for Duke Records including his signature tune, "Next Time You See Me," and classics like "In the Dark," and "Annie's Got Your Yo-Yo." I made a point of following his career in the pages of *Rhythm & Blues* and other music magazines and traced his itinerary across a map when he toured with his all-star revue, Blues Consolidated, sharing the stage with Bobby "Blue" Bland, Big Mama Thornton, and so many others. The road show would roll through Detroit and Chicago but never seemed to get even close to Grand Rapids, which isn't surprising, considering that the city wasn't exactly known for a hot and heavy music scene.

Not that it would have made much difference even if it had. Daddy wasn't about to let me loose to scorch my ears with the sound of hell's own house band. In the days since his secret— and not-so-secret—visits to the local honky-tonk, daddy had gotten steadily more strict and set in his ways. And to his way of thinking, there was God's music and the devil's music . . . nothing in between and no two ways about it. Maybe it was the fact of having moved his family from that simple, set-apart life on a farm to the bright lights and dark corners of the big city that made him all the more determined against exposing his children to the sinful influences of secular music. Maybe he wanted to atone for his own attraction to the backbeat bump-and-grind of raunchy blues at its best. Or maybe he believed that a sanctified soul must be saturated daily in praise and worship.

But I don't think so. I think Daddy discouraged us from tuning into the world beyond our four thin walls because he was still bound and determined to make a name for himself in gospel music and didn't want anything interfering with that goal. As soon as we'd gotten ourselves more or less situated in Grand Rapids, Daddy began blowing on the embers of his old dream, herding us kids into practice sessions in the front room and working us ragged with renditions of every gospel chestnut he could pull from a hymnbook.

And I must say, we weren't half-bad. My brothers and I were all a little older, and as we matured, our voices started to blend together with that smooth and polished four-part harmony that was essential to any self-respecting vocal group on the church circuit. I got a more prominent part in the lineup, doing background tenor parts and an occasional lead, and, like the day in class when I attracted all that attention, I didn't mind a bit when folks would hear me sing and set to stamping their feet and clapping their hands and shouting out praises to the Lord. It was only too easy to imagine that they were making all that fuss over *me*.

And just like in Arkansas, the Greene Brothers started working a regular circuit, doing our act and taking up offerings in little churches all around North Michigan, from Benton Harbor to Pontiac to Lansing, making the run every time Daddy could grab a few days off from work and hoping, always hoping, that a talent scout from one of the big gospel record companies—Peacock or Specialty or Gotham—might just happen to be in the neighborhood and catch wind of our undiscovered talent.

And our repertoire kept growing to keep pace with Daddy's ambition. We could deliver as stirring a version of "Precious Lord," "How I Got Over," "Mary, Don't You Weep," or "I Looked Down the Line and I Wondered" as anybody this side of the Swanee Quintet or the Sensational Nightingales and few could match our renditions of "Too Close to Heaven" and "Ain't Got Long Here." Daddy even tried his hand at a few original numbers, but when it came to that old-time religion, it was the tried and true standards that brought them out of the pews every time.

And for a while, it seemed like it was only a matter or time before we'd be getting that knock on the dressing room door and a dotted line would be just waiting to be signed. From North Michigan we started branching out, first west to Detroit, then over to Cleveland and Chicago, and eventually up into Canada and out as far as New York City.

Looking back, I can recognize what a rare opportunity it was for a young boy to see the width and breadth of this country. Those long nights on the road, sharing a sack of burgers, and harmonizing to the hum of the tires . . . those are some of the most precious memories I have with my family. The natural bond between brothers was strengthened on those long trips and cramped quarters, and whatever we had lost between us by trying to find our own way in a strange new land we almost made up for when we stood together, grouped at the altar of some church we'd never been to and would never see again, lifting up our voices high and proud. We were the Greene Brothers, and we were on our way.

Of course, it didn't quite work out like that in the end. The ties that bind a family together weren't strong enough to keep us from going, each off on his own way. My daddy's dream of gospel stardom would slowly but surely flicker and fade. And the sound of our voices, each one adding his harmony to the whole and all together celebrating the blood bond between us, would soon enough fall away into echoes and silence. But while it lasted, the Greene Brothers was the purest and sweetest and simplest way we each could find to say how much we loved each other.

CHAPTER 7

E ven if the Greene Brothers had never set foot outside the city limits of Grand Rapids, we would have had more than enough places to strut our stuff. The truth is, there are probably more temples, sanctuaries, and storefront churches per square block in that city than anywhere else I've ever been.

Within a block of our apartment, for example, we had no less than three full-time houses of worship, with packed-out congregations and anointed ministers of the Gospel. It was a real spiritual supermarket. Right around the corner, we had the Baptist church of Reverend Gants. And not too far up the street was the African Methodist assembly of Reverend Cecil. And right next door to our building was Mother Bates's House of Prayer, which was where the Greene family could be found on a Sunday morning.

Mother Bates was one of those folks with a connection to God so strong and pure it was like a light shining all around her. I'm not saying she had a halo exactly, but the simple goodness and selfless kindness that showed forth in her life provided a beacon for our whole neighborhood. Folks can debate religion all they want, deciding all those fine doctrinal distinctions and denominational differences and making sure every "i" is dotted and every "t" crossed. But when it's all said and done, the Christian life is lived out, day by day, by saints like Mother Bates, who take the Gospel at its word, preaching to the poor, caring for the orphans and widows, and loving their enemies as themselves.

For all the faithfulness of my own mother, who never missed a Sunday service and always had a Bible by her side, I think I learned more of what true faith is all about just by watching Mother Bates. There was no derelict drunkard so lost he didn't deserve a good meal; no ratty and worn-out streetwalker too forlorn to reach with a loving touch; no chip on the shoulder of a tough kid that wouldn't melt at her words of love or the promise of her prayers. It's no wonder that Mother Bates's storefront church was the hub around which the life of our neighborhood revolved. There was hardly another place along those dark and dingy streets where a searching soul might come for comfort and rest and a way back to the unconditional love of God.

Even to this day, when I meditate on what it really means to be a Christian, I'm taken back inside that empty store, with winter light leaking through the soaped-up windows onto the makeshift pulpit and rows of straight-back wooden chairs. Mother Bates, a big woman with a gap-toothed smile and head of gray frizzy hair, would be banging on a tambourine, her eyes rolled to heaven, her body heaving and shuddering with each wave of the Holy Spirit.

We hadn't been going to the church for more than a few months when Mother Bates picked me out of the congregation to sing in the choir, and it was there that I could really let go, without having to worry about hitting the right notes for the Greene Brothers harmonies or trying to sound just like Jackie or Sam or any other musical heroes I'd been drawn to on the radio. In those times, with two brothers behind me, banging out the rhythm on an old bass guitar and a snare drum, I was washed away in a flood of grace coming down from heaven, right through Mother Bates, and out across us all like a cleansing tide.

It wasn't too long before Mother Bates was taking me out with her on the revival circuit, stopping off at little churches and tent meetings all throughout the Midwest. I'd be up front singing gospel songs as the people filed in for the meetings, and afterward I'd sit beside Mother Bates as folks lined up to get her spiritual advice on their personal problems. She'd be praying and ministering for hours after each meeting, and before the night was up, she'd be sitting in a pool of golden light, shed from the scores and dozens of candles the people would light and leave behind as an offering to the Lord.

When I think back on it, the sense of freedom and serenity I felt in the presence of Mother Bates was all the more anointed, considering what was surrounding us on every side. I'm not talking about the crime and poverty, the broken lives and shattered hopes that are so much a part of life and death in the ghetto. It was Mother Bates's ministry to preach and heal and bring hope to the poor. But beyond the boundaries of the black neighborhood in Grand Rapids was a whole other kind of oppression—a religious spirit, bound by the law and as unforgiving as the dark heart of a Pharisee.

It's not my place to cast judgment. God reserves that right unto Himself. But I can say that the religion of the white folks who lived along the prosperous, tree-lined streets of that city was harsh and hard, light on mercy and heavy on condemnation. Almost from the time of its founding, Grand Rapids and the whole of that part of North Michigan had been a stronghold of Calvinist doctrine. It's a way of looking at God and His creation that leaves very little room for a man to repent, change his ways, and live a new life. According to the Gospel preached every Sunday from the lofty oaken pulpits of those churches, God had long ago foreordained who would be set aside for the glories of paradise and who would be cast down to the eternal fires of hell. It's a belief called predestination, and it claims that all of mankind is divided into the elect and the damned and there's nothing any of us, on either side of the fence, can do about it. God knew our names, each and every one, from the foundation of the world, and it was as if He put a gold star or a black X next to each one. No matter how much a man was to pray—for his own soul or the souls of family and friends—that mark remained, eternal and indelible. From the time we first popped out, bald and naked, from our mother's wombs, we were either children of God or spawn of the devil.

Now, it's not my intent to question the authority of the Almighty. He can do whatever He pleases in His good and perfect will. Like it says in the Bible, let God be true and every man a liar. If God has preordained me to heaven or to hell, then so be it. But it is just too hard for me to swallow the notion that all our fates are set and settled from the beginning and there's nothing we can do to change the course of our destiny. Too many times I've read in Scripture about God changing His mind, not the least of which was that long bargaining session with Abraham when He agreed not to destroy Sodom and Gomorrah for the sake of ten righteous men. Too bad for those sinful cities that old Abraham couldn't find those ten dudes.

But the point I'm trying to make is that the Lord changed His mind. The Bible says that "the prayers of a righteous man availeth much," and my life is a witness to that truth. Without the prayers of my mama and daddy; of the friends and relations that filled the pews back at Taylor's Chapel and the Church of the Living God in Jacknash; of Mother Bates herself and of all the other good people who have made it their business to lift me up and intercede for me—well, let's just say I wouldn't be writing this book today and you'd be reading the life story of some other lucky guy with God on his side.

I believe with all my heart and soul that at every important crossroads in my life I was faced with a choice: between right and wrong, between serving God and pleasing myself. I didn't always make the right choice. In fact, I stumbled down the wrong path more times than I marched down the right one. But God heard the earnest prayers of those who loved me and by His grace brought me to my knees. If you're one of those folks—if something in my story or my song stirred a prayer in your spirit for protection or provision or just plain mercy, then I want to take this opportunity to thank you. God heard your prayers . . . and He answered them. And to the good Calvinist brothers and sisters who might be reading these words, I've only got this to say: I'll be praying for you, too.

What with going to school, singing in church, and touring with the Greene Brothers, the last years of my childhood and the beginning of my teenage years passed by quickly and, with them, the cherished memories of my former life in the farms and fields of Arkansas. There came a time, right around when my voice began to change and I was starting to take a second look at the young ladies as they sashayed down the street, when I began to think of myself as a bona fide city boy: nobody's fool and only too wise to the ways of the world. I guess it happens to every kid, sooner or later. You get to thinking you've got it together, that your parents are too old and uncool to try and set you straight, and that it's time you took matters into your own hands. Finding out just how dumb you really are—that's what growing up is all about.

And like everyone else, I had a lot of friends around me who also thought the sun and moon revolved around their sorry behinds. Of course, I wouldn't entirely chalk that attitude up to the common foolishness of young folks. We were growing up in the ghetto, don't forget, where it was a matter of survival to mark out your territory and lay down a line as fast and firm as you could. Trying to be tough and ready to rumble was the only way we knew to warn off our rivals. Our reputations protected us, and it was important that we maintained them by stepping proud and talking trash.

Which wasn't exactly the best way to find out who your friends were. We were all so busy trying to prove ourselves to each other that we never really saw how much alike we were—scared kids, staring down poverty and despair and a generally hopeless future, all trying to act like we had the world on a string. Gangs weren't as much of a substitute family for poor kids the way they are today. Which isn't to say that in the black 'hood of Grand Rapids, there weren't more than enough turf wars to make life dangerous. But in the late fifties and early sixties, the terrible social pressures that would come to tear black family life apart—drugs and broken homes and children having children and all the other plagues we've come to witness over the past decades—hadn't yet arrived full-blown on the scene. Gangs were a way for kids to work out their aggressions, not a whole lot different from playing cowboys and Indians. Young folks still had mamas and daddys, a place to call home, and a reason to stay out of trouble. And as hard as those times might seem in my memory, I know they're nothing compared to the trouble kids face today.

Still, like young folk everywhere, we managed to break out of our roles, find each other, and form lasting friendships. And I guess it will come as no surprise when I say that I found my best friends through music. And it's probably equally obvious that the music that drew us together was hardly the hymns of praise or choruses I was singing for Mother Bates or the Greene Brothers. Like just about every other teenager in America—black or white, rich or poor—I was tuned in to the rock & roll wavelength that was keeping the whole country in motion from ocean to ocean.

The year was 1964, and the sounds sweeping the nation brought with them the first hints of liberation from those tired old pigeonholes of race and class and style. By then *Billboard*, the magazine known far and wide as the "bible" of the music business, was lumping everything—black *and* white musical hits—into a Hot 100 chart. But the real sign of the times was what was on that chart. It seemed like the British Invasion and the Motown Sound were racing neck and neck to make music history, and between the Supremes warbling "Where Did Our Love Go," "Baby Love," and "Come See About Me" and the Beatles chiming in with "I Want to Hold Your Hand," "She Loves You," "Can't Buy Me Love," "Love Me Do," "A Hard Day's Night," and "I Feel Fine," there wasn't much room for anyone else. But of course, great singers and great songs always make a space for themselves and there was no shortage of key cuts that would go on to define the era: Mary Wells's "My Guy" and the Dixie Cups' "Chapel of Love"; Dean Martin's "Everybody Loves Somebody" and the Four Seasons' "Rag Doll"; Roy Orbison's "Oh, Pretty Woman" (a song I'd be proud to cover myself years later) and even Louis Armstrong with his unforgettable version of "Hello, Dolly!"

I loved it all and, to my eighteen-year-old ears, it all seemed to be coming from the same single source of fresh new creative inspiration. The musical explosion of the sixties, fueled by drugs and free love and the emancipation of our minds *and* our behinds, was still a year or so from its full bloom, but change was in the air, even in the cold, damp, and sooty air of Grand Rapids.

The truth was, the music I was hearing on the radio, like those singles I'd save up my lunch money to buy down on Division Street, had become a whole lot more appealing than the rusty old repertoire I did over and over again with the Greene Brothers or down at Mother Bates's. Gospel music was lagging far behind pop, rock, and rhythm & blues and sometimes, standing up there singing to a lot of old folks in their stodgy Sunday best, I felt like I might go crazy if I heard them join in, flat and off-time, for one more chorus of "Savior, Pass Me Not" or "Standing in the Judgment."

And it wasn't just the music that was beginning to get up next to me. As I moved through those tumultuous teenage times, I was quickly losing patience with the messages I heard preached, Sunday in and Sunday out, in pulpits from Chicago to Cleveland, Brooklyn to Baltimore, anywhere and everywhere the Greene Brothers got a gig. Those preachers all seemed to be reading from the same playbook, telling us about how the meek shall inherit the earth and how God will exalt the humble and contrite of heart. "Be patient," they told us. "Wait on the Lord, and in due season, He will lift you up."

Meekness, humility, and long-suffering. That's the last thing any hot-blooded eighteen-year-old, with rock & roll echoing in his ears, wants to hear. All their sanctimonious Scripture spouting, their holier-than-thou attitudes and finger-wagging warnings about sin and damnation—church and churchgoing folk were starting to wear me out. I even took to avoiding Mother Bates, with those black shiny eyes that seemed to bore right through me like soul-scanning searchlights.

I took to spending more and more time away from home as well, where the crowded rooms and stifling smells of close-quartered living were pressing down on me like a suffocating wool blanket. Everywhere I turned—school, home, or church—the world was too small and too tired and just plain too *boring* to stand much longer. What solace I found, I found on the streets, which at that time seemed full of kids just like me, restless and rebellious and ready to break out—if only we could find a way.

And of course, the music was always there, spurring us on. My lifelong love of Jackie Wilson became a burning obsession around that time and, to my ears, he was working at the top of his form just about then. From the moment his smash hit "Baby Workout" topped the charts in early 1963, it was as if a tidal wave of pure, jubilant energy had crashed down on top of us. And he just kept topping the stakes—and himself—with each subsequent song: "Shake! Shake! Shake!," "Baby Get It," "Big Boss Line," "Squeeze Her—Tease Her." Every time a new hit from Jackie exploded out of the little red plastic RCA radio I kept close to my pillow—I felt like *I* was going to explode. Sure, I yearned to sing like my hero, to make the notes bend and sway at my command, to let my voice soar higher and higher, and then, just when it was getting ready to break through into outer space, give it that patented Jackie Wilson rocket-booster soul shout that would send it right into orbit. And sure, I longed to strut my stuff as suave and continental, cool and sharp-creased as the Man himself, in a sharkskin, single-button tux and cummerbund, with my hair conked and my fine Italian shoes spit-shined and gleaming.

But more than anything, I wanted to get a taste of the life he lived, full of excitement and glamour, bright lights and beautiful women. I wanted to be the center of attention, the main attraction, the star of the all-star cavalcade. And somewhere along the way, I actually convinced myself it could happen. All I needed was half a chance to prove myself.

CHAPTER 8

It's funny to think back on, but it was Jackie Wilson who gave me the chance to take charge of my life and try it on my own . . . at least in a roundabout kind of way.

The situation had been going from bad to worse for some time when the chickens finally came home to roost. I'd been missing a lot of school, flunking out of one class after the other, and my teachers and guidance counselor kept warning me that I wasn't going to graduate unless I buckled down and got myself together.

I couldn't have cared less. School was coming in a distant third to my musical dreams and my daily life on the street, where I was beginning to make quite a name in the neighborhood with the cool and collected way I carried myself. It was as if I was practicing for my role as a star, waiting around with complete confidence for the inevitable day when I would be discovered. It was an attitude that was easy to carry off as my boyhood awkwardness began to turn into smoldering teenage sex appeal. As I said before, there's no use trying to deny the obvious. There's something about me that women find very attractive. I've never had to try and catch the eye of the opposite sex. It just happens . . . for better or worse.

The funny thing is, as much as I strutted my stuff like the certified ladies' man, I was, more than anything, still a shy little boy
inside. The plain fact was, women scared me, and as my own sexual stirrings began to make themselves known, I started getting the
sensation of crossed wires and confused signals. For me, the female
form had always been a haven of comfort and safety. As a boy, I
knew I could always hide in the warm embrace of my mama, my
grandma, or any one of those aunts who treated me like their own
son. But when that boy began to become a man and those feelings
of security and protection began to get mixed up with the desire to
prove my masculinity, I wasn't sure which way to turn. Part of me
was aching to make my move, to relieve that intolerable itch
between my legs. The other part just wanted to lay my head
against a warm breast and have my head stroked until I drifted off
to sweet sleep.

Most of my first hesitant moves toward romance were spoiled
by that strange mix of motives. Girls would expect me to live up to
my billing, show them some smooth moves, and get down to serious business. What they got instead was a kid who wasn't quite
sure whether he wanted a girlfriend or a mama, who would follow
up a clumsy come-on with a bashful backstep, his tongue tied up
in knots and all that bravado melting away like late snow in early
spring.

I did my best to hide my inexperience and uncertainty, making
up for the lack with lots of big talk on the street corner. I guess
those girls were interested in keeping my secret, too. None of them
wanted to it to be known that they lacked the charm to win me
over, so in spite of my strictly amateur status as a lover, my standing in the neighborhood was safe. Out front of the candy store and
pool hall, I always managed to steer those bull sessions back to
topics I was more comfortable with.

Which was mostly music. And I found out quickly that there

were basically two types of music fans: those who had music as a backdrop for their lives and those who had music as a soundtrack for their lives. And I definitely fell into the second category. Everywhere I went and everything I did was with a musical accompaniment, almost as if I had a full orchestra following me in a truck with speakers sticking out the back. It got to where I'd put a theme song to my different daily routines: Little Stevie Wonder's "Fingertips—Part 2" was what I'd be humming when I brushed my teeth, combed my hair, and checked myself out in the mirror before going to school; "The Loco-Motion" by Little Eva was what got me percolating down the block to the school bus; "He's So Fine" by the Chiffons was my special melody for walking through the hallway and lunchroom; and the Supremes' "Come See About Me" was the music playing in my head after the bell rang and we all headed down Division Street, looking for a good time.

It didn't take me too long before I discovered other brothers who felt the same way about music that I did. I could almost swear I'd hear their own personal soundtracks playing as I passed them by and we had some kind of sixth sense that signaled whether we were hearing the same songs inside the jukebox of our minds.

And the one with a tune stack that matched mine almost exactly was a brother born and raised right there in Grand Rapids named Lee Virgis. Good-looking and street-smart, Lee was ambitious in the same way I was about making it in music and had created a loose-knit network of any neighborhood kids who displayed even the slightest talent for singing or playing. Among them were three guys who fancied themselves as the new Midnighters, on the lookout for their very own version of Hank Ballard. I'd seen Palmer James, Curtis Rogers, and Gene Mason at school; they were all within a year or so of my class, but I'd never really made a connection with them until Lee provided the introduction.

Of all of them, I'd have to say it was Palmer who'd thought the most about turning their shared flights of musical fancy into a here-and-now reality. He'd made it his business to search out the movers and shakers in whatever passed for a music scene in Grand Rapids and had struck up friendships with club owners and recording studio engineers all around the local area. He'd even been to Detroit a time or two, just to get a feel for the energy and excitement radiating out of the Motor City and maybe to figure out a way to bring some of it back to our sorry side of the state.

He never had much luck, though. Trying to spark a home-grown scene in Grand Rapids was like trying to light a match against that cold wet wind that blew down from Canada in November. The city just never seemed like much of a place for celebration, what with people scrambling to make a living and fighting each other for the jobs that started to get scarcer and scarcer the more those poor blacks from the Deep South kept showing up, just like we had not all that long before. When folks did think about having a good time, they'd mostly set themselves to getting drunk or picking up one of those sad streetwalkers that hung out in the shadows in their ratty fur wraps and fake leather miniskirts. Like I said, music was not much more than a backdrop to those kinds of activities.

Which was all the more reason that Lee and Palmer and the rest of us clung to each other like shipwreck survivors after we met. Along with Palmer, Curtis and Gene had been messing around with the idea of a vocal group for a few months before I arrived on the scene and, with Lee's strong encouragement, we decided to give it a shot. We set to rehearsing after school every day, taking over a small room out in the porch of the clapboard house where Lee lived with his family. Lee was older than the rest of us and had just gotten married and landed a foundry job, so it was only natural that he took on the leadership of our little group, picking songs from the hit parade to practice and giving out with all sorts of advice about who was doing what right and wrong—and why.

Trouble was, Lee couldn't back up his authority with much real musical skill. He started out singing tenor with us, but it wasn't too long before we all realized that he just didn't have what it took. I quickly moved into the spot and, I must say, Lee took it really well, moving into the background as our manager, coach, and all-round facilitator.

I think the excitement of actually making real music, harmonizing together and hearing our voices add up to more than just the sum of their parts, made us each want to give it our best.

But for me, that was beginning to pose a problem. If I'd had my way, I would have quit school, stopped going to church, and hung up my hat with the Greene Brothers, all to get that group where it was going. Unfortunately, my daddy wasn't quite ready to send me off with his blessings. In fact, he wasn't ready to send me off at all. Anything I was doing musically that wasn't directly connected with his goals for gospel greatness was more than just a waste of time—it was a direct threat. He even frowned on my Sunday morning stints in Mother Bates's choir, but knew better than to raise a fuss about that. It was when he caught me coming home late after a rehearsal and gave me the third degree, knowing I'd have to lie about where I'd been and listening to me do it anyway, that he laid down the law in no uncertain terms: "Your gift belongs to the family and it is completely up to me and only me when, where, and why you sing."

Of course, there's nothing unusual about a teenage boy and his father butting heads. That's all part of growing up and finding your own way. It's a rare young man that doesn't have to test himself against authority—whether it's his parents, the police, or the God of creation Himself. And rarer still is a teenager who doesn't balk at being told what to do. But when I fought those battles with my daddy, it felt like he was trying to rob me of my very life and soul. For me, music was what made every day worth living, what put a glow at the horizon of the future, where everywhere else I looked all I could see was folks held captive in an endless cycle of poverty, generation unto generation. Needless to say, I took my daddy's attitude very personally.

And it was an attitude I would have to confront time and again in the years that followed. I've said it before and I'll say it again— the battle between the secular and the sacred has brought down more great black musical artists than drugs or loose living or any other hazard of the trade. Most of us, one way or the other, hark back to the church as the cradle of our musical birth and of any ten soul stars you care to name, I'll guarantee that eight of them learned their licks in the choir loft. So when that siren song of worldly fame and fortune calls, it's not just temptation we have to wrestle with. It's that nagging voice in the back of our brains, telling us we've betrayed our calling and commission. Sam Cooke, Aretha Franklin, James Brown, Marvin Gaye . . . the list goes on and on, each one of them facing that dark night of the soul when they must make that choice between the things of God and the lures of the devil.

It's enough to drive you crazy and sometimes I think it actually does. A great artist and hitmaker like Little Richard has bounced between being a minister of God and a rockin' soul idol maybe a dozen times in his long career—and he probably still isn't quite sure which one he really is. For Al Green, it's a question that's dogged me for most of my life, until it was finally revealed to me that there is room to be both inside the spirit of a man who truly loves the Lord and seeks to do His will. It took me a long time, with a lot of pain and suffering, guilt and sorrow, to get to that point . . . but I guess I'm getting a little bit ahead of myself.

The point is, my daddy was forcing me to make a choice between singing gospel or pop music, and when I made that decision, it was as much about proving I was my own man as any true conviction I might have had. If I'd thought about it for a minute, I probably could have worked out the simple truth that, from my heart, I felt the same no matter what I was singing, that it was all about lifting up my voice and giving utterance to the sheer joy of being alive, a joy that can only come from the Holy Spirit, the single source from which all true happiness springs. But of course, at eighteen years old, I wasn't well practiced at thinking things through, or even knowing what I really wanted and standing up for it.

Things came to a head early one spring evening when I got home from a singing session with Palmer and the guys. We'd been working at our harmonies for a couple of months and the effort was really beginning to pay off. If I say so myself, we sounded good and I knew that we could sound even better if we kept at it.

I got back to my apartment just as the sun was going down, and it was one of those rare days in the city when the air was warm and sweet-smelling and the long shadows of twilight softened the hard streets of the neighborhood and the last light of the day cast a warm glow over the redbrick tenements. I headed up the stairs, feeling as pleased with myself as a boy could be. I was still humming the last song we'd practiced—it was Lee's arrangement of one of Jackie Wilson's big hits from a few years before, "A Woman, A Lover, A Friend"—and the tune just seemed to keep bubbling up inside me like a pot on a low boil, until I just about burst out laughing.

I bounded up the stairs two at time, never breaking stride with the rhythm running through my head, and didn't stop until I reached the front door. I slowed down then, trying to stifle my high spirits while I listened through the keyhole for the sound of

Daddy's voice. The last thing I wanted was to get caught in the mood I was in, with a line from a Jackie Wilson song about to burst out of my mouth. I waited a moment until I could sort out the sounds behind the apartment door: my mama cooking dinner, my sisters and brothers lazily fussing with one another, but not a trace of Daddy's deep baritone.

Reassured that the coast was clear, I walked into the apartment, hardly noticed among the crush of family all about their business and getting themselves ready for supper. I slipped through the front room and down the hall to where me and my brothers shared a cramped bedroom and, seeing it was empty, softly closed the door behind me. In the half-light leaking through that one window, looking out over the garbage cans and clothes lines out behind our building, I stood still and let out a long, slow breath, savoring the solitude that was only too rare in that cramped apartment. Somewhere outside the sound of a bluebird rose above the clamor of traffic, and it seemed, just then, that the whole world was balanced on the tender song of that creature. It felt good to hear the music of creation rising above all that man-fashioned noise and confusion, good to share the simple pleasure of music with that solitary bird—good to be alive.

Trying to hold on to that precious and special grace, I crossed the room on tiptoe as the bluebird finished its melody and the noise of the Division Street bus rattled the window as it passed by. I opened the closet and fished way in the back for my most prized possession—an old, battered 45 r.p.m. phonograph player that I'd traded off Palmer for a wristwatch I'd gotten for my birthday the year before. Along with it, I pulled out a handful of records I had begged, borrowed, and stolen from around the neighborhood. I shuffled through them, searching for that telltale sky-blue label color and bold script that spelled out Brunswick. Right then I wanted nothing more than to hear "Mr. Excitement, Mr. Delightment" himself singing the song that was brimming over in my brain: "A Woman, A Lover, A Friend."

I slipped the single onto that fat spindle and watched it drop onto the turntable. Turning the volume to just a hair above the "number one" notch on the dial, I leaned forward to listen as Jackie launched into that ode to undying love. Quickly shooting a glance at the door, I edged up the volume as far as I dared, even while his voice started resonating in my soul like an echo across a deep canyon.

When I saw that nobody was going to bother with me, I turned up the record player a little bit more, then a little more, and somewhere along the way I must have lost touch with where I was and what I was doing. Because the next thing I knew I had the music blasting out of that three-inch speaker and was singing along at the top of my lungs.

It was at that moment that the bedroom door flew open and I saw my daddy's silhouette in the light. The next thing I remember—and I've never forgotten it to this day—was the look on his face as he moved across the room toward me and yanked the phonograph arm off the record with a long, loud scratch.

I could see my brothers and sister crowded in the doorway and beyond, the vague shape of my mama, her face twisted in sorrow. She knew what was coming. So did I . . . and so did my daddy, for sure. The moment of truth was at hand.

CHAPTER 9

It took all of five minutes for me to land out on the street, right behind my broken record player and a pile of shattered 45s. Looking back, I can't say I really gave Daddy much choice. He had made it clear enough to me time and again that he wasn't going to tolerate the "devil's music" in his house and, since he *was* the one paying the rent, I guess I really didn't have much say in the matter.

Of course, another way of looking at it was that he didn't give *me* much of a choice, either. I know what he was all hot and bothered about—that I'd be turning my back on gospel and running a straight road to perdition, a road that was heading in the exact opposite direction of his own musical ambitions. And I also know that he was making a whole lot more of being down on "devil's music" than he actually believed himself. I never doubted that my daddy was a man of faith, but he also had his own independent streak. Anybody that would pack up his family one night and light out for parts unknown had to have the strength of his own convictions. But when it came to being smart about child-rearing, I think he could have taken a few lessons in the basics. If you tell a child he can't have something, then you can be sure that's the very thing he'll tend toward. But if you've got the patience to pretend that his bad habits and foolish desires don't matter much to you one way or the other, then you can bet he'll sooner or later lose interest and move on.

But whatever else he may have been, you couldn't call my daddy a patient man. And that night there was nothing holding him back from letting me know just how little patience he had with my contrary ways. With all the other kids gathered around gape-mouthed as he threw my clothes into a cardboard box, and my mama in the background crying into her apron but knowing better than to interfere, my daddy gave me my marching orders. The day I came to him to ask forgiveness for my wicked ways and submit to the authority God had given him as head of the household would be the day I'd be welcomed back, like the prodigal son, beneath his roof. But until that day, I would have to find out for myself the wages of my sin and the terrible price of my disobedience. He'd tried his best, my daddy told me as he marched me down the stairs, holding me out by the collar like yesterday's trash, but an ungrateful child is a reproach unto his family and he had no further use for me, except as a lesson to his other children that they might learn from my fate to honor their parents as the Sixth Commandment so clearly instructs.

Or—anyway—words to that effect. I can't say that I was really paying much attention. First of all, I was mad that he'd broken my phonograph and records, and second, I knew he was being just plain hypocritical. All his biblical pronouncements didn't amount to a hill of beans. I knew the reason he was tossing me out on my behind: because I had as good as broken up the Greene Brothers and, with it, all his grand schemes. To his way of thinking, as long as I was part of the group, I was earning my keep. But once I'd made the choice to go my own way, he couldn't see the point in keeping a roof over my sorry head. I can't count the times he made sure to let the whole family know that he was working himself ragged to provide for us, and the feeling we all had was that there would never be enough we could do to make up for his sacrifice.

The sad truth was, my daddy's dream of a better life hadn't ever become more than that—a dream. The good jobs on the auto line and at the foundries were beyond his reach and for a while, the only work he could find was at a Pontiac dealership over in Madison: washing, waxing, and detailing all the used cars that got traded in so they could be turned around and sold again. From there, he moved on to a car wash in downtown Grand Rapids where he and my brothers were on the Simonizing detail, running those heavy handheld polishing machines until their arms ached and the thick scent of car wax clung to their clothes and skin.

Daddy had more than once made his wishes clear that I would take my place with the rest of his boys at the car wash, which was one career path I had no intention of following. It all just came to a head that night, with that sweet soul music being the straw that broke the camel's back.

If he expects me to come crawling back, begging forgiveness, I told myself, *he is in for a surprise. And another thing—I'm going to sing any kind of music I please—God's or the devil's or whatever sounds good to me. And if he doesn't like it, well, he can kiss my—*

Or—anyway—words to that effect. I don't think my situation really sunk in until he slammed the front door of the building and left me standing at the front stoop, every worldly possession I had stuffed into a cardboard box with the shadows of night descending all around me. The first thing that came to mind was that I was missing a supper of Mama's black-eyed peas, my favorite. The next thing that I realized was that the warm spring day I'd been enjoying not an hour before had suddenly gotten a little chillier as a stiff breeze blew down the street, carrying scraps of paper and the smell of someone's dinner from an open window.

I stood there for a long moment, for all the world like a man at the crossroads of his life. Left or right—that was the choice I faced and down either direction an uncertain fate seemed to lurk. The sounds of the city rose up around me then in a noisy, confusing crescendo, mocking my plight, taunting my fading bravado.

I couldn't tell you exactly what prompted me to move, or even what direction I ended up taking. All I know is that I wandered around for a long time that night, holding my cardboard box and trying to make sense of what had happened to me. It seemed, just then, as if my whole life had been leading up to this point, as if every step I'd taken, from Arkansas to Michigan, had brought me down to these dark and dirty streets. Was I feeling sorry for myself? You bet I was. And if I'd had the choice, I think I would have walked clear back to Jacknash, along that country road to our shotgun shack on the Benton plantation where I could begin all over again, as a little boy, free and easy and wide open to the world.

I seem to recall spending a few hours in a Laundromat, watching the sad-eyed customers come and go, until the proprietor started giving me the evil eye. I headed back down Division Street, where the hookers and hustlers and all the others creatures of the night had started to congregate. I could hear loud laughter through the swinging doors of juke joints and saloons, and voices drowned out by music that, just then, did indeed sound like the devil's own.

I was beginning to think my daddy was right, that maybe if I came home, humble and contrite, he'd take me back, even slaughter the fatted calf to celebrate the return of his prodigal son. I was surely getting hungry enough to eat a fatted calf, but right about then I saw a familiar face coming down the street toward me.

It was Lee, heading back home from one of the clubs where he'd made himself a regular. It was easy to see, just by the way he was taking his ease and moving in time to some funky tune playing in his mind, that Lee was a well-known figure along these streets. Men hanging out in doorways with paper bags in their coat pockets would all offer him a taste and the ladies standing on the corner waving to the passing traffic all had a kiss and hug for him. Lee was the Man and I don't think I was ever happier to see his face.

And I also don't think he was ever more surprised to see mine. For all my streetwise attitude, I had lived a very protective life until that night, always faithful to be home when I should and staying there once the front door closed behind me. Other guys I knew, most of them my age or younger, were free to roam around all night long, with no mind to the worry and fret they might be causing their parents. I had too much respect for Mama and Daddy to ever treat them that way . . . or at least I used to. As of that evening, I was on my own and all bets were off.

"Little Al," Lee said as he came up next to me, "your mama gonna whip your ass she find you out this time of night."

"My mama's got nothing to do with it," I said with a lot more attitude than I was feeling. "I'm out of there. For good."

Lee's eyes widened for a moment and he stroked his chin and considered the situation. "So whatcha gonna do now?" he asked.

"Well, right now I'm looking for a place to stay" was my answer.

"Tell you what," Lee replied after a moment. "You come on back with me. I'll see if we can't put you up for the night. You had any supper?" I shook my head and Lee laughed. "Boy," he said, taking the box out of my arms and leading the way up the street, "you ain't off to a very good start."

I followed him over to Lafayette Street, down along a row of ramshackle houses and up a flight of wooden stairs to the Virgis residence, a little two-bedroom place where Lee, his wife, and his parents all lived. I wasn't all too sure about how they'd feel having to find room for another body in such close quarters, especially

considering that we'd already taken up the porch every afternoon
with our rehearsals, but Lee's family was nothing if not hospitable,
and while his mama sat me down to a warmed-up dinner of ham
steak and creamed corn, Lee's wife set about clearing out a space
for me to sleep in a little cubbyhole attic over the porch.

As I tried to settle down later that night in that musty-smelling
and overheated little closet, I tried to make sense of what had just
happened to my world. I'd spent my whole life as part of something bigger than just me, sharing the cares and concerns of my
family, most of the time thinking about "us" rather than just "me."

And now, all of a sudden, it *was* just me. And with that unac-
customed sensation of freedom came a frightening feeling of loneliness. There had never been a night, as long as I could remember,
when I wasn't sleeping up next to one of my brothers, hearing the
soft, familiar sounds of their breathing beside me. And now, here I
was, with only my own shallow breath to keep me company, laid
out in a room about the size of a coffin.

I somehow managed to drift off into a fitful sleep, waking with
a start just before dawn without knowing, in a moment of panic,
just where I was. When it came back to me, I sat bolt upright on
that cot, almost banging my head on the ceiling as my mind raced
to catch up with the events that had overtaken me. *What am I
going to do now?* Habit told me to get up, like I always did, and get
ready for another day of school. But with my newfound freedom, I
realized that today really *was* the first day of the rest of my life. I
could do what I pleased, with no place to be and no one to know if
I didn't show up. The problem was, now that I could go wherever I
wanted and do whatever I pleased, suddenly I had no place to go
and nothing to do. I sat there in the dim light for a long time,
weighing out my options and coming up short every time. Finally,
with nothing better to do, I rummaged around in that cardboard

box for my toothbrush and comb, put on a clean shirt, and turned up for choir practice like it was just another day.

I kept up my school routine for a few more weeks, living off the kindness of Lee and his family until it became clear that my welcome was just about worn out, unless I could at least find a way to provide for my own upkeep. There were moments, during those first uncertain days, when I wondered whether I could just show up back at home one afternoon and take my place at the dinner table like nothing had happened. But whether it was stubborn pride or some darker fear of rejection, I never acted on the impulse. It was up to me now to make something of Al Greene—or die trying.

And dying was becoming a real possibility as I faced the fact that whether or not I ate from one meal to the next was also entirely up to me. I guess as much as anything, the necessity of making a living pushed me into the decision to leave school. I might have stayed if that principal had been willing to bet another $100 on my academic future, but I had no such luck. I can't say there was a single soul sorry to see me drop out, except for Mr. Nelson, my choir teacher, who did his best to get me to stay, but in the end he couldn't find a way to make it work, either. My career as a student was over.

The funny thing was, trying to make a living was the very thing that brought me back in touch with my family again. I'd been over to the house a time or two since that night, always making sure beforehand that my daddy would be gone and grateful to Mama for fixing me a good meal and sending me off with an armful of groceries. But I was careful to avoid any suggestion that I wanted to come back for good and had taken to nursing my resentment. If my daddy was willing to throw me out in the cold and let me starve, well, I sure wasn't going to give him the satisfaction of watching me waste away.

Not that I was exactly destitute, mind you. Lee and his wife were willing enough to share what they had, even if I was more than a little ashamed to be taking it. But I knew that, sooner or later, I'd have to start making my own way and that meant doing the one thing I'd always fought whenever my daddy brought that sore subject up. I needed a job.

And that became the first lesson I learned from Daddy's point of view. Looking back, I think I had come to disrespect him in those first years after we moved from Arkansas. He had had such high hopes, hopes he'd shared with the family, giving us all the expectation of a better way of life. And while our standards did get raised and we never again faced the fear of going hungry, we were still a long way from holding our heads up high. I don't think it much mattered that most of the folks around us were as poor as we were, or that the good-paying jobs always seemed to go to whites on the other side of town. Deep inside, maybe deeper than I realized, I blamed my daddy for what we didn't have and what we couldn't get. A lack of education and opportunity, the fierce competition from thousands of other men in the same situation, and the racism that was built right into the American way of life—none of it was a good enough excuse for the failure that seemed to hang over him like a dark cloud.

That is, until I went up against the same system he did. As a minor, of course, I wasn't even eligible for those coveted jobs at the foundries and assembly lines. But I soon discovered that, even for the lowest job as a busboy or messenger, there were ten other guys in front of me: older, more experienced, and even more desperate.

I was stone broke. Lee and his wife were running out of goodwill and every job I tried out for was getting snatched up before I could blink. It was no wonder I was hanging my head and listening to my stomach rumble on that day when I unexpectedly ran into Daddy walking down Eastern Avenue.

"Hey there, boy," he said, and I must have jumped back a good foot from the surprise of seeing him. He smiled broadly and in that moment it was like it had always been. He was my father and I was his son and nothing could ever change that. "You look like you lost your best friend."

"Everything's fine," I replied warily.

"That so," Daddy said and nodded, stroking his chin like he always did. "Well, I'm glad to hear that. Your mama tells me you ain't going to school no more."

It was my turn to nod. "Too busy," I said and I'm sure any passerby would have heard that for the bald-faced lie that it was. "You know, what with the music and all." The fact was, our daily rehearsals on Lee's porch were about the only thing I had left on my schedule.

There was a moment of silence as Daddy looked me over. We were back to where we started: facing each other down, a stubborn boy and a world-weary man, trying to find a way around their pride.

"Well," he said after what seemed like a long time, "I wish you the best of luck with it."

I was turning to walk away when I felt his hand on my shoulder. Turning back at him, I saw a look in his eyes that matched all the mixed-up emotions I was feeling right then: love and anger, concern and that natural longing you get for a missing family member.

We stood like that for a good, long moment before he spoke again. "You getting along all right?" he finally asked.

" 'Bout as well as can be expected," I answered.

He smiled again, and I knew that he was only too well aware of my true situation and that he knew that I knew. But I wasn't about to admit that I needed anything from anyone—especially him— and I think he knew that, too.

"Well," he said, "you find yourself needing a job—you know, just to get you by—there's an opening just come up down at the car wash. Me and your brothers be happy to have you."

And with that, he turned and walked off, humming one of his old gospel tunes as the traffic roared by and my heart followed after him.

CHAPTER 10

That one night Lee offered to put me up turned to weeks and then to months as that little closet became my permanent home away from home. I took Daddy's suggestion, as much from not knowing what else to do than for any notion of keeping the family together. Seeing him and my brothers on a day-to-day basis was like a not-too-subtle reminder that my newfound independence was hanging by a thread, even though they seemed to be treating me with a whole new kind of respect. Daddy didn't feel at liberty to order me around like he used to: After all, we were both on the line now, both working for the same boss.

That boss was Mr. Kaminder, owner and operator of Kaminder's Car Wash on Eastern Avenue in downtown Grand Rapids. And there was no cutting corners or sliding by in his operation. The place was known for its hand-washing, wax rubdowns, and fine-detailed cleaning, and every car that came through had to meet the white-glove test of Kaminder's spot inspections, a demanding, exhausting, and monotonous job all around.

Daddy and my brothers worked as washers and polishers, but because I didn't have the build to handle those heavy buffers, they made me a detailer. Every day, five days a week, from seven in the morning until seven at night, I'd be jumping in and out of cars with a rag, a sponge, and a spray bottle, working dust and grime out of every crack and crevice until all my muscles ached and my fingers were rubbed raw. Now, some of the regulars at Kaminder's had beautiful automobiles—Cadillacs and Lincolns and big shiny Buicks—that were their pride and joy. They'd roll in the same time every week and order up the full treatment—and with cars like that, you'd sort of pick up on the pride of ownership yourself and polish that chrome until the gleam hurt your eyes. But some of those other customers would just make you groan when you saw them pulling up, their rattletrap old Fords and Chevys backfiring and belching smoke. They were always the ones who would do their own inspection after you'd finished all your buffing and polishing, walking eagle-eyed around their heaps, looking for telltale smudges and spots you might have missed. Most of the time, of course, you couldn't tell much difference between when the car came in and when it left, and if you work in a car wash long enough, you come to realize that no amount of elbow grease is going to take the rust off a bumper, the pits and chips out of a paint job, or the dent out of a fender. Not that you could ever tell that to the customer, of course. Because if you did, they were sure to get mad and forget to give you that ten-cent tip.

Hard work and low pay didn't exactly make Kaminder's a rung up on my career ladder, but looking back, I'd have to say that the daily routine of working and the weekly reward of a paycheck—small as it might be—put an order to my life that I needed about then. I'd get invited over to the house for Sunday dinner after church on a regular basis, and every once in a while Mama would slip me a few dollars, a pair of socks, or some clean underwear, but it didn't take me too long to learn that it was down to me to take care of myself from then on out. Maybe Al Greene had been gifted with a pleasing voice and a winning personality; maybe he could turn the ladies' heads as he strolled down the street and maybe even charm the birds right out of the trees. But the cold hard fact has always been that you can't eat charm and talent won't keep you warm. For the time being, whatever I earned to get me by would have to be by the sweat of my brow. That's one biblical principle I've never found a way around.

But life wasn't all hard work and dime tips. After I'd been living at Lee's for the better part of six months, I developed a groove that suited me just fine. Working from sunup to sundown, then back to Lee's for supper and an evening of rehearsal with the group. To my ears, we just kept getting better and better, and I was sure it was only a matter of time before we'd get our chance at the big time. Weeknights usually meant lights out early, but by the time Friday rolled around, I was ready to join the surging sea of humanity out looking for a good time. On more than one occasion, when I'd hear of some hot R&B show over in Detroit or up in Chicago—Otis Redding or Stevie Wonder or one of the great Motown vocal groups that were burning up the charts in 1965—I'd hop on a bus right from work and wouldn't get back until Monday morning, when I'd roll in, red-eyed and still dressed in my wrinkled party suit, to pick up my sponge and bucket.

It was at those legendary shows, packed out at the Grande Ballroom in Detroit or the Regal in Chicago, that I not only got an earful of music, but an eyeful of great style. After all, it was the sixties and everyone seemed to be dressing to make a loud and colorful statement. Seeing the Temps or the Four Tops, matched up in their three-button suits with those narrow lapels and french cuffs and pegged pants, was almost as thrilling as the music they were making, and not only did I want to sound like they did, but I wanted to dress like them, too.

It was then that I made myself a promise that, no matter what my station in life might be at any given time, I would always do my best to look my best. When I left home, I was carrying the full extent of my wardrobe in that cardboard box—a few pairs of jeans, a couple of shirts, and a worn-out old suit for church service. The only pair of shoes I had, blacktop sneakers with the soles about worn through, were already on my feet. So every Friday, just like clockwork, I'd stop off at Klein's men's store on the way home and treat myself to something nice—a bright-patterned shirt or a sharp pair of pants, or sometimes, if the money was low, maybe just a scarf or a belt or anything else that would make me feel good about myself.

I mark those days as the beginning of my own understanding that what you wear—and how you wear it—is an expression of your soul. In later years, when I could afford to buy anything I wanted, I made quite a name for myself with the colors and combinations I could create. But back then, when every dime had to count, I learned to make a lot out of a little, to express myself eloquently with a handkerchief in my pocket or a hat worn at just the right angle. I discovered that clothes are one of the very best ways we have to get to know each other, to describe who we are without using words.

And the sixties was a time when folks everywhere were wanting to express their free and fanciful sides. I'm so very thankful I came up in a time when a man was free to wear feathers and furs, paisley prints and pastels, to be as outrageous as a peacock and let the whole world know that he was special. I hope I'm not being boastful, but that's exactly how I feel when I put on a rabbit fur coat, wrap myself in a feather boa, climb onto the highest pair of platform shoes I can find, and drape myself with miles of gold chain. God only made one of me, just like He only made one of you, and that's a fact we should all be celebrating. They say that clothes make the man, but I say God made the man. He just left the decorating up to us.

Naturally, with the money I was pulling down at Kaminder's, I couldn't afford all the dazzling new fashions—those velvet bell-bottoms and embroidered vests I saw in the magazines, but that just made that promise to myself all the more real. One day the pictures they'd be taking would be of me, setting the latest fashion trends, and, sure enough, that day did come.

But I guess I'm getting ahead of myself again. To look at the scrawny kid in jeans and T-shirt vacuuming out the dust balls under your car seat, you'd wouldn't have given him a second glance. In fact, I was beginning to have a few doubts myself. A fancy wardrobe was one thing, but as I sat down to eat my sack lunch with the other wage slaves at Kaminder's, I could only too easily see myself as one of them—stuck on a dead-end track, working to live and living to work. The plain fact was, that for all our dreams and hard work, the only folks who had ever heard our group singing were Lee's next-door neighbors, and most of them would start banging on the walls before too long. As my first anniversary of leaving home passed unnoticed up alone in my room at Lee's, I began to wonder if maybe I hadn't made a mistake, after all. Maybe opportunity wasn't knocking because my door was just too hard to find.

It was then I decided that I needed to go back to school, to finish my education. I wasn't exactly sure what I'd do with a high school diploma, but I figured it was worth trying to find out. Already nineteen, I would have to face being the oldest kid in my class, but the prospect of being pointed out and laughed at like some kind of dummy didn't really bother me. I was determined to do whatever I could to back out of the corner I'd found myself in.

As it turned out, I really didn't have much trouble getting back into the swing of school. That's probably because, up to that point, I'd never really been *in* the swing before. School had always been something I *had* to do. When it became something I *wanted* to do,

it's amazing how I snapped to and started paying attention. Naturally, I signed up for choir again and there was Mr. Nelson, happy
as ever to see me, and as far as that goes, I was happy to see him,
too. Being in school again—timing my day to the ringing of bells—
gave me a sense of satisfaction and security I didn't realize I was
even missing until I got it back. I wasn't about to move home again
or pick up where I'd left off that night Daddy threw me out, but all
the same, it was as if I was getting a second chance to finish out my
childhood.

The only difference was, I was a child who had to fend for himself. Since I'd decided to get my diploma, I naturally couldn't be
spending my days cleaning cars at Kaminder's, so for that last year
of school, I kept myself together with all sorts of odd jobs, including stock boy at a shoe shore and a cook's helper at a fish fry stand.
I'd never been afraid of work and, the truth was, as long as earning
a living wasn't the only thing occupying my mind, I could tolerate
low pay and long hours as well as the next guy. I sometimes suspect
that maybe the real reason I decided to go back to school was to
give myself an excuse to quit spit-polishing bumpers, but I know
that there was another, more important reason. Daddy had never
been one to really encourage me to get an education, and I think it
was because he had been beaten down so long and robbed of his
own dreams and ambitions that he just stopped believing it could
happen for anyone else, either. Even his own kids. I think that,
deep in my heart, I wanted to prove something to him, to show him
that his way of looking at life, all bitter and bent, wasn't the only
way, that a young man with hope and determination and maybe a
little more luck than Daddy had been born with actually could
make something of himself. Anyway, that's what it felt like to me
and when I had occasion to let it slip to him that I'd enrolled again,
the look on his face told me I was right. It was as if one part of him

was hoping for the best in my life and the other part was wanting to warn me against setting my sights too high.

Maybe getting through high school doesn't seem like aiming for the moon, but in the Greene family, mine was the first generation that even had a chance of making it that far. College was still some kind of dream that only white folks could have, but it didn't matter because I didn't have the luxury of dreaming, anyway. Aside from choir, I concentrated on courses I thought might do me some good out in the real world. I got good at typing, banging out forty or so words a minute, and it felt good to have a new option in the back of my mind. If nothing else, I could maybe get a job in an office, even be in the civil service, get one of those good government salaries and retire on a pension.

Being out on my own for going on a year had done a lot to sober me up and bring me around to that kind of thinking. But even while I was busy putting together Plan B, I still had high expectations for Plan A. And there was good reason, too. After all that time getting our chops together, Palmer and me and the boys were really starting to develop our own vocal style. We still weren't doing original material—writing songs was a giant step we weren't quite ready to take. But we could cover just about anything Otis or Sam or Jackie were putting down and give it our special spin in the process. Slowly, over the course of trying out different combinations and setups, I started to take on the role of lead singer. There was never any kind of arm-twisting or buttonholing on my part. We just commonly recognized what sounded best, and what sounded best was the rest of them backing me up. I won't lie and say I didn't get pleasure from the recognition that I was the best singer among us, but on the other hand, who was I going to impress with my great talent? For all our work, we had still never played in front of a live audience. The time had finally come to get

off that cotton-picking porch and spring ourselves on an unsuspecting world.

The only question was, who were we? All the time we'd been
together, we'd never bothered to come up with a real name,
although there'd be many a time after rehearsal when we'd sit
around trying out all sorts of silly handles that never seemed to fit.

Then one night it came to me, and when it did, it was like they
always say . . . "right out of the blue." I was walking home from
my job at the fish stand, where I'd spent the afternoon tossing cod
into a deep fryer. I was hot and tired and I guess more than a little
discouraged. Spring was turning to summer, the second summer
I'd spent on my own, and the thought of coming back to that tiny
little closet, where the heat of the whole apartment seemed to rise
up and settle, made me feel homesick and heartsick, all at the same
time. My high school graduation was only a few days away, but
even that couldn't lift me up from the blues that had settled
around me. *Where am I going and what am I going to do when I
get there?* I had so many questions and, just then, I wanted more
than anything to rip back that curtain that hid the future and get a
glimpse of what was in store for me.

I was walking up Lafayette just as the streetlights came on and
could see them flicker and blink before they began to burn brightly
in the fading day. I was suddenly struck by how they looked to me
like the lights of a pathway, leading into the future that seemed so
dark and uncertain. As that image formed in my mind, I suddenly
felt a presence beside me, as real as if an old friend had come up
alongside to walk with me a spell.

It had been a long time since this particular friend had paid a
visit, but I recognized Him immediately. Even at that point in my
life, I knew by the tingling sense of awe that crept over me that the
Lord had come close, bringing with Him that grace and perfect
peace like a sweet savor.

I heard no voice in my head, saw no vision before my eyes. But I knew for sure, right there and then, that God, by His very presence, was comforting my troubled soul. It was as if He knew my every thought—my longings and fears and hopes for the future—and with infinite tenderness and love wanted me to know that everything was going to be all right. I was here for a reason, to fulfill a purpose He had established for me before the foundations of the world. And what He had established would come to pass. Of that I could be sure. All creation was in His hands and every creature had a place and part in His plan.

I somehow managed to dry my tears of joy before I got back to Lee's. The boys were out in the patio like always, ready for rehearsal. It was just as God had ordained . . . that moment was perfect, like all the others that had come before and all the others that would follow. We were all part of the big picture, each with a part to play.

"I think I got a name for the group." I announced without quite realizing what I was saying. The four of them turned to me. "The Creations," I told them and I could see them turning the word over in their heads. But my mind was made up. God had put us together to create beautiful music. Music to celebrate His creation. And that was enough for me.

CHAPTER 11

A
ctually, it wasn't quite enough. Now that we had a name, we needed a repertoire, someplace to perform, and an audience to hear us. And that's where Lee came in. For months he'd been letting it be known that he had a great new group under wraps, a group that was going to put Grand Rapids on the musical map . . . maybe even make it the new Motown. I don't know if anyone really believed him, but when he started putting up handbills announcing the debut performance of the Creations at a little club called the El Grotto up the road in Battle Creek, he was sure to get a good turnout of folks just curious to see what he'd been bragging about all this time.

Meanwhile, while we were rehearsing all our Jackie Wilson songs and James Brown moves, Lee and Palmer got busy writing up some original material for us to sing. It was as if coming up with that name had fired us all up and given us juice to jump to the next step. We were the Creations, one dynamite bundle of pure talent just waiting for the chance to prove it.

We got our chance one night in Battle Creek in the late fall of 1966, in that smoky dive on the outskirts of town, to a full house of folks who'd come out from the city to see us do our thing. I was twenty years old and, while I'd had plenty of experience singing in front of people at revivals and church meetings, it felt to me like I was stepping out onstage for the very first time. This was going to be the start of something big.

Actually, it was almost the *end* of something big. We arrived at the gig early, all keyed up for the show, when the club owner got a good look at me and demanded to see my proof of age. Still a few months shy of twenty-one, I had nothing to show him and he threatened to throw us all out on our ears until Lee calmed him down by promising to stash me in the car outside until showtime and then hustle me right out again after our last number.

Sitting out in the El Grotto parking lot, listening to the club's backing band run through their opening set, I was taken back in my mind to those days back in Arkansas when Daddy used to leave me in the car while he went into a roadhouse to drink and listen to the blues. Back then, the music leaking out those walls had seemed so strange and exotic, coming from a different, dark, and shadowy place like the songs themselves. Now I was about to enter that world, take up my place among the citizens of that night land, and, for one brief moment, I wasn't sure I was ready to make that step.

But then the music got a little louder and the backbeat a little more insistent and I felt myself being carried away all over again by the thrill and danger of the "devil's music." Whoever it was playing up on that bandstand sure enough knew their stuff, with a rhythm section right in the pocket and a sax player who took off like a rocket at the break. Suddenly I saw Palmer stick his head out the back door and motion to me. We were about to go on, and as I walked down the hallway toward the stage, I pulled him aside.

"Who are those cats?" I asked as the whistling and howling of the audience signaled the end of their set.

Palmer shrugged. "Never heard of them," he said. "I think they call themselves the All Stars . . . Jr. Walker or something." He grabbed my arm. "Come on," he urged. "We're on!"

As I joined the others on stage, I cast a quick look behind me. The band was still there, taking a break before backing us up on our set. I caught the eye of the sax player, obviously the front man of the group, and he lowered his shades to get a better look at me. I'd never seen anybody so cool, so sure of themselves and what they were doing, and I guess some of Jr. Walker's attitude must have rubbed off on me, because when I stepped up to the mike, all the nervous flutters in my stomach had disappeared. I knew who I was and I knew exactly what I was doing.

But I can't tell you what happened after those first few notes. All I can piece together are bright-colored lights shining in my eyes, the sound of the All Stars pounding away behind me, and, out front, the vague shapes of people moving around like ghosts in the dark. We might have been an instant hit. We might have been a laughingstock. I honestly don't recall. As much as anything, I felt like I was sitting at the front of a locomotive, spewing sparks down a long dark tunnel and heading fast and furious for the other side. I remember going in and I remember coming out, my voice hoarse and my body covered with sweat. What happened in between was a blur.

But there was no doubt that, whatever it was we did that night, we got over with the people . . . and then some. The owner of the El Grotto invited us back for a regular spot and within a month or so, word had gotten around to other nightspots all up and down North Michigan and we had all the bookings we could handle. For Lee, Palmer, and the others, it was as if we already had our name up in lights. As far as they were concerned, we weren't just on our way— we had arrived. And it was hard not to catch their excitement. After all, we'd spent so much time cooped up on that porch, it was as if we'd just been storing up all the energy and enthusiasm for music that had brought us together in the first place. Now we were getting the opportunity to let it all out, and we treated every show we did like it was the first, last, and only chance we'd have to prove ourselves. We gave it everything we had, because we hadn't ever learned to hold back.

And as much of a thrill as we were getting onstage, we were having as much fun just walking down the street. Whoever said that being a musician is a great way to get girls sure knew what they were talking about. Being in the Creations had turned us all into local heroes and we didn't waste any time capitalizing on our newfound status. We did our best to live up to the reputation that came with the territory. Of course none of us, with the exception of Lee, had much experience as ladies' men, but we were quick studies, you can be sure of that. Personally speaking, I adopted Jr. Walker as my role model, copying his moves, the way he dressed, and that certain, intoxicating air of cool that followed him around like the scent of expensive cologne.

The All Stars appeared with us pretty regularly at the El Grotto and did a lot to enhance the general quality of our music. The truth was, they were a lot better as a band than we were as a vocal group, which gave us a real incentive to improve. With Lee working the business end, it was Curtis Rogers who took up the songwriting slack with Palmer, and between the two of them a real musical chemistry started to develop. I'm not going to say they were the next Holland–Dozier–Holland or Gamble & Huff, but they managed to find a workable groove on a couple of their originals that suited us just fine.

But for me, the Creations didn't seem like all that big of a deal. I couldn't tell you exactly why I felt that way. It wasn't as if I had an attitude, like I was better than the rest of them or that my lead vocals were carrying the group. These brothers were my friends, we'd been working together for the better part of two years, and I can honestly say that I saw us as five equal parts of a whole—and that included Lee, who was working just as hard as the rest of us as our manager.

But the fact of the matter was something else entirely: I *was* better than the rest of them, and my lead vocals *were* carrying the group. That was just the reality, that and the fact that most of the songs we were performing, whether they were written by Palmer and Curtis or were covers of hits we heard on the radio, I could sing in my sleep. There really wasn't much of a challenge in shouting out those R&B standards, working the rhythm like a Southern preacher and getting everybody all hot and bothered by pretending to be the long-lost brother of Jackie Wilson and James Brown. I could make it look and sound easy because for me, it was.

As a result, after a few months of playing clubs, the thrill was definitely on the wane. I may have had a supernatural experience in finding a name for the Creations, but the inspiration had pretty much ended right there. It might seem strange or downright contrary to be having second thoughts just as my career was finally heading in the right direction, but I couldn't shake that nagging feeling that there had to be something more to my musical destiny than singing for the Creations.

I never said as much. I wouldn't have ever wanted those guys to know that I wasn't 100 percent behind what we were going for, but on the other hand, I guess my second thoughts must have been showing, especially after Lee came home one day with the big news that we'd been offered a recording contract.

Now, when I say "recording contract," I'm talking about how it used to be, back in the days before rock & roll stars could bid up the price of their talents and become multimillionaires before they even got in the studio. To get a record deal in Grand Rapids, Michigan, in 1966 was definitely an earn-while-you-learn, pay-as-you-go-type situation. Even in the glory days of Motown, nobody was exactly getting rich, except maybe Berry Gordy, and the deal we were offered wasn't even close to Motown.

The label was called Zodiac, a strictly local outfit who'd had some regional hits with bands and singers who'd made a name for themselves on the same nightclub and roadhouse circuit the Creations were playing. The business end was simple, easy enough for anyone to understand—Zodiac Records would cover the expenses for us to cut some sides in their studio: We'd cover the expense of Zodiac Records to sell our sides. Since no money was ever going to actually change hands, nobody had to worry about getting cheated or keeping an account of record sales and royalties. That was the way it was going to work—take it or leave it.

As far as Lee and the rest were concerned, there was no question about the answer to that particular proposition. Maybe Zodiac Records wasn't Motown or Chess, or even Brunswick or Imperial, but what could match the thrill of actually holding a round piece of plastic in your hands, with your actual name on the label and your actual song in the grooves? That's all that mattered right then and there, and no one was about to start scrutinizing the fine print.

Least of all me. If Lee said we were going to become the latest addition to the Zodiac Records stable of stars, then I'd be there to do the best I could. I owed him that much. But the honest truth was, I didn't care whether the Creations were on their way to the top or not. In my heart, I'd already decided this was going to be only the first stop on the road I was planning to travel.

I'd already taken the first steps down that road, even as the group got geared up for our big recording date. Without making too big a fuss out of it, I let Lee and Palmer know that, in between gigs with the Creations, I'd like to try my hand at doing a little different style of music. For some time, I'd been finding myself drawn to the sounds of an earlier time, particularly the great jazz vocal stylists like Nat "King" Cole, Joe Williams, and Billy Eckstine.

Using the reputation I was gaining as the Creations' mainstay, I made connections in some of the jazz dives along Division Avenue and started making solo appearances, backed by whatever house band the owner could pull together.

It was an experience altogether different from the Creations. As much as Jr. Walker and the All Stars could turn up the heat on R&B tunes, I always had the feeling I was fighting the band—and sometimes even my backing singers—just to be heard. In those jazz clubs, with only a small acoustic combo behind me, I could concentrate on the song: the meaning of the lyrics, and the soft shadings a melody can paint. Up there alone, with my eyes closed and the audience hushed as I gently coaxed the secret from a tune, I could sometimes feel as if I'd been transported, carried to another place entirely on a pure whisper of notes. I could get so carried away that, when the song faded out on a last, long refrain and I opened my eyes, I sometimes would be surprised to find myself back in a club with my feet on the ground.

Thinking back on those times now, it was as if I didn't want to let any part of my love for music to go by the wayside. I never would have thought of leaving the Creations because it was there that I was able to satisfy my soul and R&B side. As a solo jazz singer, I was answering to some other impulse entirely. And on more than one occasion, after a late Saturday night, I'd get the powerful urge to hear an old-fashioned gospel chorus again and make my way back to Mother Bates's for her midmorning service.

Eventually, however, something was going to have to give. With the Creations, I cut a few sides in some run-down studio on 28th Street in Grand Rapids. I wish I could remember more about those first recording sessions, but even the names of the songs escape me for the simple reason that my heart and my mind were already elsewhere. I was trying to be careful not to let my true feelings show, but earlier that day, I'd gotten an offer to sing some jazz shows up in Benton Harbor, and right about then, I was concentrating more on my repertoire for the evening than on the business at hand.

I do remember this much, though. My early experiences in the recording studio convinced me that I still had a lot to learn about being a professional singer. All my life I had sung in front of an audience. Large or small, it didn't matter, as long as there were some warm bodies out there to get some bounce-back from. In a studio, with only those machines out there listening, I found myself becoming stiff and self-conscious. It was hard to lose myself in the music, to enter into that place where the song and I became two expressions of the same thing, an act of love to be shared with anyone who was listening. But I needed to know that the audience was out there and that they were hearing what I was feeling. Otherwise, there was just no place for the love to go. It would be a long time before I found a way to make the music real in an empty room.

But the quality of my performance that day didn't seem to matter that much. I may have been somewhere else, but for everyone else, the music was right on the money. And in couple of weeks, just like the Zodiac people had promised, Lee got a box full of singles in the mail. I have to admit—it really *was* a magical moment as we all stood around, holding up handfuls of black platters spindled on our thumbs, laughing and carrying on as we listened to ourselves over and over again, reading the label and smelling the fresh vinyl. If we could have found a way to eat those records, we probably would have done that, too.

The Creations even got played a few times on the local radio stations and word got back to us that we were getting spins as far away as Chicago and Cincinnati. As a result of the exposure, we were invited to take a place in a big talent contest down in Cleveland, with the promise of a cash prize and lots of record company talent scouts in the audience. I'll never forget the day we arrived at the hall, up on Euclid Avenue, ready to walk away with the day.

What we walked away with instead was a whole new appreciation of what a big wide world it was out there, and how it was positively brimming with hopeful young singers, all of them absolutely sure they had exactly what it took and then some. There were probably a hundred vocal groups that had turned out that day, some from as far away as New York, Buffalo, and St. Louis. The place was so jammed we never did get a chance to even perform, and back in the hotel room that night, the reality of our actual chances among all that competition sort of took the edge off our enthusiasm.

At least it did for me. And the situation wasn't helped a whole lot when we got back to Grand Rapids and were greeted by the news that our El Grotto backing band, Jr. Walker and the All Stars, had just been signed to Motown Records after a stint at Harvey Records. Don't get me wrong, I was happy for the group and they certainly deserved the chance. I'd heard some early live versions of their song "Shotgun," which would go on to be a breakthrough hit for the group and Motown, and if anyone had the chops to make it all the way, that band surely did. But it was hard to get over the feeling that maybe God had a quota of bands He was going to allow to make it out of Grand Rapids and that number had just been reduced by one. In fact, my fears informed me, maybe Jr. Walker was going to be *it*, the first, last, and only musical success our town would ever be able to claim.

In desperation, I went to see my sax-playing role model just as he was getting ready to wrap up his stand at the El Grotto and head out to Detroit. I begged him to put in a good word for me with Mr. Gordy at Motown and he'd promised to try, even though, from that sly look he gave me over the top of his sunglasses, I wasn't quite sure he understood just how much it meant to me.

I waited around a week or two for that call summoning me to
Mr. Gordy's presence and, when it didn't come, I decided to take
matters into my own hands. All during that bus ride to Detroit, I
rehearsed my speech to the great man over and over in my mind.
Sure, I'd say, *you've probably heard a hundred different young
guys trying to convince you they were the next Marvin Gaye or
Smokey Robinson.* But I was different and I'd prove it to him, right
then and there, singing my heart out, standing on his desk.

But I never made it to his desk. In fact, I never saw Berry Gordy
at all. He'd left for vacation, his secretary told me, and wouldn't be
back for another week. But I'd come all the way from Grand
Rapids, I insisted. "Then next time," she gently suggested, "make
an appointment."

CHAPTER 12

Overage high school graduate. Sometime singer in a hometown soul band. Part-time jazz crooner. Former car wash employee and jack-of-all-trades. No car. No phone. No fixed address.

My résumé at the end of 1967 was hardly what you'd call promising. It seemed that I'd been knocking around out at the edge of things for as long as I could remember, and for all of my dreams and ambitions, I had precious little to show. Life was something that happened *to* me, not something I had anything in particular to do with. Sometimes I was able to tell myself that things weren't so bad, that other brothers were worse off than I was, in jail, in trouble, or dead, even. But other times, the lonely times, it felt like I was marked for failure before I even got close to success. I'd look around at the folks passing me by on the street and they all seemed so contented with their lots in life. A housewife, a factory worker, a man just standing on the corner, waiting for a bus. They'd never asked for anything more than what they had and they never got any more than what they asked for. I wanted to be like that, taking life as it came and not always reaching for something just outside my grasp.

But most of all, I just wanted someone to talk to. My family, the group, Lee and his wife . . . sometimes they seemed like strangers to me, people with familiar faces who wouldn't have been able to tell you anything more about Al Greene than the color of his eyes and the way he cut his hair.

The Bible tells us right up front that it is not good for a man to be alone, that the Lord meant for us to have a partner in life, and that without that soul companion we're forever walking around, looking for a missing part of ourselves. It's a truth you may not fully understand until you find that missing part and realize, for the first time, how you'd lived so long with that empty feeling. They say you don't know what you have until you lose it. But I say: You don't know what you're missing until you find it.

And when you do find it, you might not always recognize it right away. I sure didn't. When I thought about a woman to share my life, I always had some picture in my mind like a scene in a movie—one of those love-at-first-sight, across-a-crowded-room moments when you both realize you've found true love and then start running at each other in slow motion. Now, I'm not saying that doesn't happen once in a while. After all, God can arrange a chance meeting any way He wants. But let's get real. Most of the time you just bump into someone, back up a few steps, and go about your business until it suddenly hits you that there was something different about that particular person . . . something that stayed with you . . . something that took root and flowered in your spirit.

And it's my opinion that, most of the time, the person who God pairs us up with proves He's got a real sense of humor. You might be looking for someone tall, dark, and handsome and the man or woman of your dreams turns out to be short, pale, and homely. Not that it really matters. If that's the one for you, you're stuck.

When my moment of truth finally arrived, you could have

hauled out a stack of Bibles and I would have sworn on top of all of them that the woman *I* just met was somebody else's dream come true. And the moment when *our* eyes first met wasn't like a scene you'd ever catch in a Saturday matinee.

Her name was Juanita—at least that was the name she used on the street and, although I doubted it was the one she had been born with, I never pressed the question too far. But there was no question about her beauty. She was ten years older than me, with a high yellow complexion that set off her dark almond eyes and jet-black hair, straightened and swept up off her forehead as if she were a lady of true style and sophistication.

But Juanita, despite her regal air and aristocratic pose, was no high-born woman. She was a prostitute, working the streets of Grand Rapids for most of her life, giving herself to anyone who could pay the price and never thinking twice about it. And if she wasn't out on the street, she'd be back in her apartment on 28th Street, waiting on calls from the bellhops at the Tannen Hotel to come on over and entertain the visiting Shriners or the best friend of the county commissioner or just some lonely traveling salesman passing through town. Juanita was a working girl and she did what she had to do, just to survive.

In my mind, Juanita will always occupy a place in my life directly opposite from, but equally important to, Mother Bates. They are like two magnetic poles, forces that kept me in balance between them, the one calling me to the purity of the faith, the other to the pleasures of the flesh. I make no judgment, nor do I cast any condemnation. As Mother Bates was born to her work, so was Juanita, and if circumstances had been a little different for either one of them, they might have found themselves in switched places. Maybe God could have saved Juanita from a life of sin and degradation, or maybe she could have made the choice, somewhere down the line, just to give up the life. But He didn't and she didn't and it was never for me to ask why or try to change things around. I loved Juanita, as purely and simply as I ever loved Mother Bates, and I thank God for the day He brought her into my life.

It's a day I can remember as clearly as my breakfast this morning. I'd come back home to visit my family and go to church and, after services at Mother Bates's, I'd had a bite to eat and was taking in the air on the apartment building stoop. It was one of those warm and balmy Sunday afternoons with a slight breeze blowing away the car exhaust from the street and the neighbors passing the time of the day out the windows while lines of clean white laundry sparkled in the sun. I don't remember there being particularly much on my mind, except maybe an aimless tune or two, when around the corner came two ladies dressed up like they were just coming back from, or just about to go out to, a fancy night on the town. One was wearing a tight black dress, with long matching gloves and spiked heels, and her heavy makeup, in the broad light of day, made her look cheap and garish.

But it was the other one who captured my stare. As she came closer, I was vaguely aware that the chatter from the windows above me had quieted and that the whole neighborhood seemed to be watching with a disapproving air as the pair came down the street. While the one in the black dress was big and heavy-chested, the other one was slim and well proportioned, willowy in her red dress and fox fur stoll. As they got closer, I noticed that they seemed to be paying no attention to the sour stares out every window and were talking and laughing as gaily as a pair of schoolgirls on holiday.

Then the one in the red dress caught sight of me, sitting and staring on the stoop. She tilted her head toward her friend, said something in a whisper, and they both laughed again, not so innocent this time, but low down and deep back in their throats. They both stopped right in front of me and the shapely one put her foot up on the bumper of a car and proceeded to straighten the seam of her black fishnet stocking, giving me a long, slow look at her thigh as she pulled the tight dress up her leg.

I must have been staring bug-eyed, because she looked over at me and shook her head. "What are you looking at, young man?" she said in a scolding tone of voice that seemed, at the same time, to be mocking me.

I dropped my eyes and felt the blood rush hot to my face. When I looked up again, she was smiling, and if there was a moment when true love blossomed in my bosom for Juanita, that was it. Her smile was dazzling and bright and took up her whole face and made you want to laugh, tell jokes, stand on your head . . . anything just to bask in the warmth of her happiness.

"My," she said, "you certainly are a pretty young thing." And she laughed one more time, like the sound of tinkling bells echoing down that city street. "Isn't he pretty, Wanda?" she said, turning to her friend.

Wanda laughed, too, a husky, full-bodied chuckle. "Now, what you want to go robbing the cradle for, Juanita?" she asked. "That boy barely know what to do with it."

"Oh," replied Juanita, her eyes sparkling, "I believe he knows just what to do with it." She sashayed up to me. I could smell her perfume, a sweet fragrance gathered around her, and, up close, the glow of her skin seemed to soak up the sunshine and cast it over her in a halo. "You know what to do with it, boy?" she whispered.

"Yes, ma'am," I stuttered. "I mean . . . no, ma'am. I mean—"

Now they were both laughing and Juanita leaned in close until that perfume smell made my head swim. "What's your name, little boy?" she asked, and her false eyelashes fluttered like butterflies.

"Al" was all I could say.

"Well, Al," she said and reached out to touch me once— quickly—on the cheek. "I'm going to be looking for you again.

And when I find you, we're going to have some fun. That all right with you?"

"Yes, ma'am," I said. "I mean . . ." But by that time, she was already back with her friend and the two of them started back down the street, giggling and bumping shoulders until they got to the corner. There Juanita stopped, pulling a pack of cigarettes from a beaded purse and lighting one. Taking a deep drag, she turned and looked back down the street after me, waving and calling out something I didn't understand. I waved back as the last lingering trace of her perfume was carried away on the breeze.

True to her word, Juanita did come back, looking for me. When she did, I followed her home, packing up my belongings and moving out of Lee's attic room after a stay of almost two years. I shacked up with that beautiful hooker in her one-bedroom apartment on 28th Street and never looked back. Across the years that followed, our relationship took on every kind of variation you could imagine: from mother and son, to father and daughter, to pimp and whore. At any given time, I was her lover, her "pretty little boy," and her confessor. In the same way, she would play the role of the daughter, the breadwinner, or the hardworking mother who only wanted to have her feet rubbed at the end of a busy day. You could say our relationship was complicated, but to us, it was simple. We were everything to each other. She didn't introduce me to any of her people, at least not at first, and, of course, I never took her around to meet the family. She never volunteered any of her personal history—aside from the fact that she'd come from Grand Rapids and had been on the street since she was a teenager—and she never showed much curiosity about mine. All that ever seemed to matter, at least at first, was that we had found each other, that we trusted each other, and that the loneliness we had both lived with for so long was finally over.

There was something so natural, so right about the love Juanita and I shared, something that overcame every barrier, even as it broke all the rules. The difference in age hardly seemed to matter, or the fact that I was not much more than a babe in the woods, while she was an experienced woman of the night. Of course, I knew what she did to make a living . . . I wasn't *that* innocent, but at that same time, I understood that sex, for Juanita, didn't have a whole lot to do with love. Love was comfort and security and knowing there was someone there for you, no matter what. Of course, we made love, and when we did, she took care to show and tell me all the things that gave her pleasure. As far as what made *me* feel good . . . well, let's just say she had that all figured out a long time ago.

But even in the beginning, physical attraction wasn't what brought us or kept us together. At least, not in the way most people think of it. What we saw in each other was a kind of idealized beauty, and, to tell you the truth, sex was sort of a distraction from that enjoyment. We were content instead just to watch each other as we moved around the apartment, tending to small chores, or walking down the street, dressed up in our finest clothes. In fact, clothing was another of the common bonds we shared and we were constantly borrowing one accessory or another from each other—a scarf or a belt or a piece of jewelry—to finish off one of our more flamboyant costumes.

In that way, I guess you could say we were like children: a brother and sister playing house, but in another way, I served Juanita as a pimp and she was the whore who kept me in style. It wasn't that I ever actually procured men for her. She never had any trouble doing that all on her own. But what I did do was look out for her on the street. If I saw her pick someone up and head back to his hotel or the room she sometimes kept at the Tannen, I'd follow along behind and wait in the doorway until she came out. I was protective of her in that way, although it never occurred to me that what she might really need protection from was the life she had chosen.

But the truth was, she *had* chosen it of her own free will and I believe even to this day that there was a part of Juanita that liked being a prostitute. It was like a game to her, the way she could lure men on with the flicker of an eyelash, the way they looked at her as she got undressed for them, the naked need she saw in their eyes. It was her way of feeling wanted and, like every woman of the streets, even those out there alone this very night, it was a shame and tragedy, as well. But it was also just the way things were. I could either accept that reality or look for another one. Juanita had made her choice. It was up to me to make mine.

So I stayed, taking whatever odd job I could find to help make ends meet, but more often just hanging around in her place, with its beaded curtains hanging in the doorway and all the makeup and cold creams and beauty treatments shoved into the medicine cabinet and under the sink. There were movie magazines on the kitchen table, a nice big radio strong enough to pick up Chicago stations, and all kinds of stuffed animals spilling off the bed. There was no doubt that a lady lived there and I made sure not to make my own presence too conspicuous. Of all the pet names Juanita had for me, I liked "pretty little boy" best of all, and it gave me a pampered, lazy feeling to think of myself as her most prized stuffed animal, the one she wanted to hold as she drifted off to sleep in the gray light of morning after a long night.

I learned from Juanita that Grand Rapids wasn't quite the sleepy little backwater I'd once imagined it to be. She seemed to know about secret dives on every corner, places even Lee had never set foot into, and it was easy to understand why when you saw what went on there.

One of Juanita's favorite haunts was a basement club that didn't even have a name. It was dark, with a low ceiling and a stage that wasn't much more than a piece of plywood set up on some milk cartons. When Juanita took me there for the first time, the floor show featured some of the biggest and ugliest women I'd ever seen doing some kind of a bump and grind dirtier than I could ever have imagined. After the show, a couple of them came by to talk to Juanita. It was obvious they were old friends and when Juanita turned to introduce me, I thought my ears had deceived me when she called them Claude and Monroe or some such unmistakably masculine names.

They all got a good laugh from the look on my face when I realized that I was sitting with a pair of transvestites. It was the first time I'd ever seen men dressed up in women's clothes and the sight both fascinated and repelled me. The world was a stranger place behind the locked doors of Juanita's neighborhood.

C H A P T E R # 13

One of the most interesting parts of the New Testament, at least for me, is after Jesus is crucified and laid to rest in the tomb. According to Scripture, during those three days that followed, when the disciples and all his followers thought He was dead, Jesus actually descended into hell to proclaim His victory over Satan. I could always see that scene very clearly in my mind: the eternal flames and cries of torment, the writhing and twisting souls of the damned, and the wicked tortures inflicted by Satan and his host. Then suddenly a great white light breaks through the darkness and all the evil spirits shrink away, hissing and shrieking as Jesus Himself appears, the marks of His crucifixion—and of our salvation—still fresh on his body. What a glorious day that must have been!

But what lingers in my imagination is the thought of that descent into the netherworld: from light to darkness, from life to death. In my own history, it seems I've made that descent many times, into a dark and smoky chaos only to be raised up again, with proclamations of resurrection and eternal life pouring from my lips. I don't know that I've ever seen heaven, except maybe in a vision or a dream. But I can tell you for sure that I've seen hell and lingered there among the damned.

And the first descent I made into those realms was with Juanita, as her escort into the underworld of the city, where, night after night, the people of the darkness come out of hiding to gather together for their strange rituals. Like I said, it's hard to imagine that a place as everyday and average as Grand Rapids, Michigan, would have, right beneath the surface, a whole other way of life, with its own rules and its own code of justice, retribution, and recompense. But if I were a betting man, I'd lay a wager that right in your own hometown, no matter how small, no matter how wholesome, there's things going on that would shock and frighten you. We live in a fallen world—the Bible makes that very clear—and all you have to do sometimes is scrape off the top layer of polite society and good citizenship to see just how far mankind has really fallen.

When I made that journey into Juanita's world, I also made a clean break from my own world. My family, the church, and most of the time even the light of day became a memory as she and I prowled the streets after dark, working the clubs and dark alleys where Juanita plied her trade, then slinking back at dawn to sleep the day away. I managed to find myself some part-time work as a busboy at the Comet Club, one of the many dives that were part of our regular rounds, and it was there that I began to get my first lessons in the hustler's life.

As I said, I'm not a gambling man, but I could certainly tell you anything you might want to know about the gambler's trade. I could tell you how to run a profitable three-card monte scam or how to load a pair of dice so that no one would ever catch on. I could tell you how to play the spread on any sport you care to mention or when to fold them and to hold them in a poker game. I knew every bookie that paid on time and all the ones who didn't, and I could spot a numbers runner even if she happened to be somebody's grandma sitting in her parlor, darning socks.

I could tell you how to mix any kind of hard liquor you might have to make it go down smooth or how to brew up your own batch from a sack of potatoes. I could tell you the going price for a bag of weed just by smelling it or how your cocaine had been cut with a taste on the tip of my pinkie. I knew the best techniques for snorting, skin-popping, and mainlining, could show you how to raise a vein and keep your kit clean. And if you couldn't afford the good stuff, I knew every cheap high under the sun, from rug lacquer to airplane glue, nutmeg to cigarettes soaked in formaldehyde.

But that wasn't all I knew. I could tell you the sexual preference of each regular customer, which prosperous white businessman liked to dress up in women's underwear and which one liked to be tied up while Juanita talked sass and dropped cigarette ashes on his head. I could tell you who liked it straight and who liked it twisted, who liked it on top and who liked it on the bottom. And I wouldn't stop there, either . . . but I will. The simple truth was, in that first year with Juanita, I learned more about the dark and depraved side of the human animal than I care to pass along. Those are memories that have a left a scar on my soul, one I'd rather keep to myself.

A lot of what I learned I got direct from one of the most feared and respected citizens of that strange new world. His name was Leroy and he was the boyfriend of Carmen, Juanita's older sister and another longtime working girl. Leroy could talk the fur off a fox and usually had a half dozen scams, cons, and hustles running, all at the same time. He took it upon himself to take charge of my education and, while I ended up learning more than I ever wanted to know, Leroy also passed on some valuable survival tips.

Two of them I remember to this day, the first being about attitude. "Don't raise a whole lot of dust," Leroy used to tell me.

"Most things that are going to happen to you, there's nothing you can do about, anyway. Best to just lean back and let it roll on by. Sooner or later, things will change. You just got to wait out the changes."

Now, that was good advice. Up to that point, I'd always thought that being cool was about how other people saw you and what they thought about you. Jr. Walker was cool, for instance. It was an image that he presented to the world, a way of walking and talking that impressed everyone he met. But what Leroy taught me was that being cool was a way of *life*. It was how you made it out on the street, how you got through the ups and downs. It was all about balance, never going too far to one side or the other. When something bad happened, you didn't get too worked up. And when something good happened . . . same thing. That way, you could learn to depend on yourself. And that was a vital trick of the trade for life on the dark side.

The other lesson Leroy passed on was about moderation. "Keep everything cordial and casual," he would tell me. "If someone passes you a joint, you take it, then maybe take a toke or maybe not. Somebody offer you a snort, you accept or decline, depending on your mood. Don't let anybody hold the keys to your peace of mind, and whatever your pleasure may be, just make sure you can walk away from it when the time comes."

More good advice. It took me a while to understand completely, but what he was trying to tell me was to stay free, to let nothing rule you or run your life. In a scene where, whenever you turned, you saw folks enslaved to their vices, that was pure wisdom. And I took it to heart. I believe it was because of Leroy and the things he taught me that I never got seriously involved in drugs and alcohol. Getting high was all right while it lasted, but if I ever got to the point of craving the feeling, I'd make sure to back away, just like Leroy said, and let that feeling pass.

It was from Leroy's simple cautions that I was able to stay in touch with a deeper part of my spirit, a part that could watch what was going on around me, yet stay beyond it all. Maybe it was God or maybe it was just my own instinct for survival, but whatever it was, it kept me from falling headlong into the traps and snares that had been set for every unsuspecting soul since the world began. Yet, at the same time that I kept myself apart, I never found it in my heart to judge the folks around me. I couldn't have put it into words at the time, but I understand now what was behind all the sin that ruled their lives—it was the pain of living. And some people would do anything just to dull that pain.

Of course, we are told in God's word that the wages of sin are death. Only God can ease the suffering of the fallen human condition, and those who choose anything else must surely reap the harvest in due season.

That due season came for us one cold October morning at the tail end of 1967. I'd just finished the night shift at the Comet Club and was making my way home in that frosty half-light just before a winter's dawn when I saw a commotion up ahead, just out front of Juanita's apartment building. As I got closer, I realized what was going on. It was a bust and Juanita, along with Wanda and her sister Carmen, were being hauled off to jail in a paddy wagon.

It was not a scene unfamiliar to me. Juanita had probably been arrested by the vice squad half a dozen times in the first few months we'd been together. But she was always out within a day or two and back on the street like nothing had happened, with Leroy or one of her other friends always ready to go her bail until she could get pay them back. I had no reason to suspect that this time things would be any different.

But it was. The cops were acting like they always do—tired and bored and going through the motions one more time. But as the paddy wagon pulled off, with Juanita, looking pale and puffy-eyed, waving from the back window, I could see the old landlady standing on the stoop in her housecoat and giving me the evil eye.

"This ain't happenin' again," she scolded me, wagging her finger in my face. "I ain't gonna put up with these whores running their business here no more."

"Won't happen again," I mumbled, trying to make my way around her and up the stairs.

"Damn right it won't!" she shouted and blocked the door. "You two are bein' evicted as of this moment."

I just looked at her, tired and sad and wanting nothing more than to crawl up to Juanita's sweet-smelling boudoir and get some sleep. "Can we talk about this later?" I pleaded.

"Ain't nothin' to talk about," she snorted, folding her arms across her chest. "You can't stay here no more."

"But what about our stuff?" I insisted, my mind turning in tight little circles. All my fancy clothes were up there. Juanita's radio. Those beaded curtains with the sparkling colors.

"When you find a place to park your no-good selves, you give me the address and I'll send it over," she shot back and stuck out her hand. "Now give me the key before I call the police back here again and throw your sorry ass in jail along with your girlfriend."

I retreated down the steps, trying to get my fogged-up brain into gear. *Leroy*, I thought. *He'll know what to do* . . . I hurried over to Leroy's apartment and banged on the door for a good twenty minutes before a neighbor poked her head out the window and told me that he had gone to New York on business and she didn't know when he'd be back. By now, I was shivering with cold and got the desperate idea of going back to the Comet Club to get a few hours' sleep in a warm place before I tried to figure out my next move.

But the Comet was locked up tight and as I stood there, down below street level at the basement door, I could see above me the feet of everyday people as they headed off to their everyday jobs. In that moment, I wished with all my heart that I was one of them . . . a creature of the day, with a hot breakfast in my belly and someplace to go where they were expecting me.

But the only place I was expected was down at the precinct house, in time to pick up Juanita when she got of jail. Fortunately, she'd had enough money from the night's work to post her own bail, but poor Wanda and Carmen were stuck behind bars, at least until Leroy showed up again. I found Juanita sitting on the hard wooden bench of the waiting room when I arrived, her big almond eyes wet with tears, smudging her mascara like rings on a raccoon's face and streaking makeup down her cheeks.

"Oh, Al," she cried when she saw me and, throwing her arms around my neck, wept pitifully on my shoulder. "I'm so tired of all this . . ."

I felt like crying, too, but I just held her, patting her poor trembling shoulders and trying to soothe her soul as all around us cops went about their business, bringing in pimps and prostitutes, pickpockets and petty thieves in a never-ending parade.

After a while, Juanita's sobbing slowed and she straightened up. "I must look a fright," she said as she opened her purse and pulled out a mirror. I could see that she was coming back around, trying to patch up her dignity again, drawing on herself for the strength she needed to keep going. She dabbed at her makeup, then heaved a big sigh. "Let's just go home," she said. "I need a hot bath and back rub." She laid her hand gently on my cheek. "Will you give me a back rub, pretty little boy?"

"Juanita," I said slowly, "we can't go back home," and I proceeded to tell her all the dreadful details. Now, Juanita could put any sailor to shame when she was mad, and she began to swear a blue streak so raw in that police station that even those hardened cops looked embarrassed. It must have been five minutes before she wore herself out enough for me to bundle her up in my coat and head back out on the street.

The rest of that day passed in a bone-chilling dream. Between the two of us, we had about $1.37, and being broad daylight, it was impossible for Juanita to turn a trick and make any more. We spent our time sitting in one coffee shop and bar after another until the owner figured out we weren't going to buy anything and threw us out. By the afternoon, we'd found a temporary haven in the reading room of the public library, where Juanita managed to catch an hour or so of sleep, with an open book for a pillow and me standing guard, pretending to read a newspaper while I watched the guard watching us.

By five o'clock, the library closed and we were back out on the street again, just as the feeble winter sun was setting and a chill wind started blowing down those concrete corridors. I don't think I've ever felt more alone and lost in my life and, for a moment, I even considered going back home and throwing myself on the mercy of my family, like the prodigal son, returned from slopping hogs. But I knew I couldn't ever bring Juanita back with me—it would be like tearing a hole in the curtain that divided the two halves of my life. And there was no way I was going to desert her now.

We stood in the warm air of a steaming grate as the rush-hour traffic waned and the streetlights came on. Soon it would be night, and, with a little luck, Juanita could find one of her regulars and get enough to buy us a hotel room for the night. But as I looked over to her, stamping her feet to keep warm, even that seemed like a dicey proposition. The day's events had taken their toll on her, or maybe it was the events of a whole lifetime . . . those consequences of sin the Bible warns us about. She looked haggard and worn away, as if all those long nights had suddenly caught up with her and stripped away her beauty, leaving behind a poor and wretched creature.

She turned to look at me and it was as if she could read my mind through the windows of my eyes. "I just need a little rest," she said in a pleading way that tore at my heart. "And maybe something to eat. I'm so hungry, Al."

We ended up making our way across town to a deserted park, stopping to buy a package of hot dogs from a corner grocery. We sat on a picnic bench and ate those dogs cold, one after the other, trying to fill an empty place inside that no earthly food could satisfy.

CHAPTER **14**

God works in mysterious ways, His wonders to reveal. It's a wise old saying and, like most things that last, there's a truth in those words that give comfort and meaning, purpose and direction to people's lives. Our time on earth is so full of strange and unexpected occurrences, seeming coincidences and chance encounters and divine interventions, that you've either got to believe that none of it makes any sense at all or that God's got something in mind that's bigger than any of us can wrap our earthly thoughts around, and on that glorious day when His purpose is fully revealed, we'll all just take a step back, rub our eyes, and say, "So *that's* why it happened that way."

What Satan meant for evil, God meant for good. That's another old biblical truth that pulls back the curtain a bit on the perfect purpose and plan we were all born to fulfill. I believe that the Creator of this universe takes delight in turning the terrors and tragedies that come with living in this old, fallen domain of the devil and transforming them into something that strengthens our hope, tests our faith, and shows forth His glory. It might take us a long time to learn the simple lesson that every time God closes one door, He opens up another one, but just because we can't see the end from the beginning doesn't mean He can't.

The trouble and travail that Juanita and I endured on those cold streets, with nowhere to go and no one to turn to, were all an essential part of God's plan. I sure couldn't see it then, forlorn and forgotten in that bleak and freezing city park, and, to tell the truth, it would be years before I was able to fit the pieces together and see what the big picture looked like. But when I was finally able to make sense of those seemingly wasted years of my life, all that was left for me to do was turn to heaven and to the fact that with the Lord, and by His perfect will, there's no such thing as an accident.

Left up to me, I'm sure I would have stayed right where I was for as long as I could. There was comfort and security in the life I led with Juanita, although to look at it now, I'd have to say it was a strange and forlorn harbor where I came to seek safety from the storms of life. The fancy boudoir we called home—with its colored lights and satin sheets and beguiling baubles—was nothing more than a dream, a shadow world we had put together out of fantasies and fleshly desires, a dollhouse where we hid from the real world and its terrible responsibilities.

But then, like it always does, the real world crashed through, chasing away the mists of that dream with the harsh wind of poverty and nakedness and wretched need. We may have thought we loved each other—and it may have been true—but that love was a pathetic shelter against the hard facts of cold reality. She was a full-time whore and I was her part-time pimp and, between us, we had nothing to be proud of. Sooner or later, life on the ghetto streets catches up with everyone—I don't care who you are, what kind of car you drive, or how big a wad you flash—one day it all comes down to paying the price for a wasted life. I'm just grateful—profoundly and eternally grateful—that for Al Greene, the day came sooner than later.

It wasn't but a few days before Juanita and I were able to set ourselves back up in an apartment, fetch our clothes and furniture, and get down to business as usual. Except it wasn't ever going to be quite the same again for me. Something shook me deep inside when I found myself out on the street in the dead of winter, a fear that my life was going to stall for good right there in Grand Rapids and, with it, a determination that I wasn't going to let that happen, no matter what. Juanita could continue turning tricks and treading water, living between a hope and prayer and shaking off that feeling of despair each afternoon when she finally woke up from another late night and got a look at herself in the mirror with no makeup, her face puffy, her skin and hair losing its luster, and her eyes reflecting back the specter of doom that was wrapping around her like a shroud.

But for me, it was different and I struggled with a feeling that I couldn't shake—a feeling that it was now or never and that if I lingered too much longer in the smothering embrace of that world we had created, I would never again see the light of day.

And with that feeling came the conviction that there was only one direction I could turn to, one path for me to follow. I had to make the music matter, give it everything I had and anything it took to turn the corner on success.

But almost immediately I ran into problems with the rest of the group. It seemed like the only corner they were interested in turning was down to Division Street, where they could prance and preen and show off to all the pretty young things who were all too easily impressed by a guy who had his name on the label of a 45. Our Zodiac Records releases had done exactly nothing, no airplay and sales you could count on the fingers of one hand, but for Curtis and Gene and the others, those platters fulfilled all their expectations and then some—we were hometown heroes in all of a ten-block radius and anytime we wanted to make an impression, all we had to do was leave a lady's name on the guest list of the El Grotto and look her right in the eyes from up onstage. I had the sneaking suspicion that these guys had just about come up to the limits of their dreams. They were local boys who made good. The problem was, they'd only made good locally. But that was enough for them.

I knew that if we were going to get any further as a group, we were going to have to make some changes—and quickly. Since then, of course, experience has taught me the value of momentum. When you're in the business of entertaining people for a living, if you're not moving forward, you're moving backward. There's simply no such thing as standing still. Your whole life has got to be about staying on top, up front and out ahead, giving your audience what they want at the same time that you're keeping them guessing. Keep fresh, but stay familiar. Work hard, but make it look easy. And whatever you do, make sure the hits just keep on coming.

Of course, with the Creations, the hits didn't keep coming. They never even got going. I was beginning to think that whatever we had done up to that point was more of a liability than an asset. The Creations were old news. We didn't need a comeback. We needed a go-ahead.

That was my frame of mind that night in late 1967, just before Thanksgiving as I remember it, when we gathered as usual on Lee's porch for a rehearsal. We had a couple of gigs coming up on the weekend and had gotten an out-of-town booking up on the lake, but playing live, even for money, was getting to be strictly routine for us, and we hadn't added a new song to our repertoire since we'd played with Jr. Walker back in the spring.

We hadn't gotten too far through a Jackie Wilson medley that we could already sing in our sleep, when I suddenly just stopped singing, sat down on the old sprung sofa, and folded my arms across my chest like an angry man holding in a swearing spell. Lee, the one among us all who I felt shared my frustration, straddled a chair across from me while the rest stood around, waiting for the other shoe to drop.

"So what's got under your skin, Al?" Lee asked, even though I was pretty sure he knew what the problem was. "You got somethin' better to do tonight?"

"Yes, I do" was my reply. "And I got somethin' better to do tomorrow night, too. And the night after that. I got places I want to go that have got nothin' to do with this sorry old porch and the sad bunch of songs we keep singing night after night."

I could hear an uneasy muttering among Palmer, Curtis, and Gene, and I knew exactly what was passing between them. *Who does Al Greene think he is all of a sudden? And what exactly is he trying to say? That he is better than the rest of us? That he's too good to be up front, singing lead for the little ol' Creations anymore?*

"It's nothing on you fellas," I said quickly, trying to keep the peace and still get my point across. "It's just that we've been out on this porch for so long, I'm starting to wonder if we're ever going to get off and go someplace else. We've been having a good time and I don't know about the rest of you, but a good time just isn't enough for me anymore."

"Al's got a point," Lee piped in, and I was grateful to know that I had at least somebody on my side. "I mean, what *are* we doing this for, anyway?"

I knew the answer, of course, and so did everyone else on the porch that night. We were doing it to keep alive some faint hope that our lives wouldn't necessarily come down to working in a factory, getting married, and having a bunch of kids who'd take our place on the assembly line until they got married and had a bunch of kids and so on and so on, goodbye and amen. We were doing it because being an R&B star, like being a basketball player or a pimp with a classy stable, was a ticket out of the ghetto, a way to beat the odds and be someone besides who we were—which was five black guys on the short end of the American Dream.

We all knew it, but nobody said it . . . nobody dared say it, because by admitting the truth of our situation, we'd have to admit that our chance of grabbing that ticket was somewhere between the proverbial slim and the legendary none. In that moment, on that frosty evening with the streetlights shining through the barren trees and the sound of car passing high and lonesome through the slush outside, we all understood that we'd arrived at a moment of truth, a crossroads, a point of no return.

I jumped up from my seat and began pacing back and forth, trying to contain that uncomfortable mix of fear and excitement. I knew that if I didn't make my case, right then and there, there probably wouldn't even be a group left to pin my hopes on. I was the one who had brought it all out into the open—our future, our prospects, and, along with that, the unmistakable challenge to put it all to the test. Now it was up to me to press on and point the way.

"See here," I began, "we're good. There's no doubt about that. We can sing rings around most any other group out there. Talent ain't the problem."

"So what is the problem?" asked Palmer warily.

"The problem is we ain't got the ambition to go with the talent," I said and I could hear my own voice crack when it got to the word "ambition." Lee shot me a quick look. *Take it easy*, he seemed to be saying. *Give it to them gently.*

"Look," I said, calming myself. "We've all just got one foot in this thing. Most of the rest of the time, we're thinking about our jobs and our girlfriends and what we're gonna do on the weekend and all that other stuff that don't make any difference to"—and I stopped, searching for the word, the right word to let them know just how important this was—"to the *music*."

That was the best way I could describe it. I guess I could have said "the money," or "the women," or "the slick clothes and fast cars"—after all, those were the real measures of success, at least in the minds of my friends. But right at that moment, the word that forced its way out between my lips was the one that summed up what was real and meaningful and lasting to me and I'd have to say I was surprised as any of them. "Music." More than anything, it was singing that gave me satisfaction and the unmistakable feeling that I was doing something that mattered. It was about more than just entertaining people. It was about fulfilling a destiny for my life that pressed down like a weight until I answered the call and was set free to soar like a bird. Maybe that all sounds a bit too flowery and poetic, but when I try to explain my natural attraction to music, those are the only images that seem to fit.

I guess all the passion I was feeling came through in that single word, because as soon as it came out, everyone on the porch stopped right where they were and just stared at me. I knew I had a nerve, that I'd reminded them all of something forgotten somewhere back along the road we'd traveled together, an innocent enthusiasm that had brought us together in the first place, the sheer pleasure that comes from making a joyful noise, when your harmony fits right in place and the music lifts aloft like an angel taking wing.

There I go again. But the point I'm trying to make is simple. From that moment on, it was as if we all had a new commitment to making music and to making a success of our music. We reconnected with a common bond that we'd first discovered back in high school and it was like we'd all laid hold of the same high-voltage power line. That very night, we threw out all our old tired Jackie

Wilson and Otis Redding routines and started working on some new numbers. They may not have been originals, not yet anyway, but at least we were getting stretched in some different directions.

The enthusiasm continued on into the week and we started meeting every night to plot out our next moves. The first thing we decided was that, since we were getting a new start as a group, we needed a new name to commemorate the change. The Creations may have seemed like an inspired choice a few years before, but it was sounding pretty old and tired by then. We were looking for something that would grab people's attention, give them an idea of who we thought we could be and where we thought we were heading.

It was Palmer who came up with the Soul Mates during one of those brainstorming sessions and it seemed to suit the occasion perfectly. That's what we felt like, anyway . . . we *were* soul mates, one for all and all for one, five men on a mission with a musical message for the masses.

But something else had changed, too. Since that night when we rekindled our fire, the others had started to look to me as the natural leader of the group. Of course, it didn't hurt that I'd taken to singing most of the lead vocals, as well, but it wasn't as though I'd put myself forward as any different or more important than any of the rest of them. That was just the way they saw it. So when they decided that our newly reconditioned group should called themselves Al Greene and the Soul Mates, who was I to argue?

And as long as we were shaking things up, we had a unanimous vote and decided to take a walk from Zodiac Records. It seemed like a bold move at the time. After all, we were signed to a real record label, never mind that we hadn't seen a dime for our efforts or heard our songs on the radio. It felt as if we were taking an awful chance just throwing away that opportunity, but in the end, we made our move and asked to be let out of our contract.

As if turned out, it wasn't nearly the complicated legal maneuver we might have thought. We got up a good head of steam and all marched into the Zodiac offices, upstairs over a liquor store. It was only when we saw the FOR RENT sign on the frosted window of the door that we realized that the executives at Zodiac probably weren't going to put up much of a fuss, whether we stayed or whether we went. As far as they—and the rest of the whole world—were concerned, we were on our own. The next move was entirely up to us.

CHAPTER 15

Aside from me, it was a toss-up whether Palmer or Lee had more energy and enthusiasm for the newly minted Al Greene and the Soul Mates. Palmer had always seen himself as a creative force and was a lot more comfortable writing songs and producing sessions than he ever was singing up onstage. Lee, on the other hand, thought of himself as an inside operator, someone who could work all the angles and figure the odds, and there was no better way for him to give those abilities a workout than in the music business. For him, the new group was a way to prove himself, not with a bunch of high school kids who wanted to sing songs they heard on the radio, but with young men who'd gotten serious about doing what it took to get over.

Almost from the beginning, they were full of bold and brash notions to take us to the top. Palmer took to spending more and more time trying to come up with original material, and it wasn't long before he and Curtis formed a kind of loose-knit songwriting partnership, trading lyrics and hammering out melodies on an old piano in the parlor of Mrs. James's house. Some of their early efforts suffered from what you might call a lack of polish, but as the weeks went by, they began to steadily improve, and we tried out some of their new stuff in our stage show. I can't say it exactly brought the house down, but they didn't throw things at us, either. And that's always an encouraging sign.

Lee, meanwhile, was bubbling over with promotional and publicity ideas to get the Soul Mates noticed. We were still a pretty good draw in dives all up and down the North Michigan club circuit and had an open invitation to perform at the El Grotto anytime we pleased. But we could keep singing on to roadhouse crowds—seventy-five or a hundred at a time—until the bartender called out the final "last call" and it wouldn't have gotten us any richer or any more famous. What we needed was to get on the radio—and of course, that meant we needed something for the disc jockeys to play and a reason for them to play it.

None of us were quite sure how, but we all shared the same suspicion that Zodiac Records had shortchanged us from the get-go. Even back then, we had a pretty good idea that the deal we were handed wasn't exactly a ticket to the top of the charts. Whenever someone who wants you to sign something says, "Don't worry about a thing," well, that's exactly when I start poring over the fine print, and those gentlemen from Zodiac must have told us twenty times we had nothing to worry about as they pushed a fountain pen into our hands.

This time around we were going to do things differently. Zodiac had proven to be, literally, a fly-by-night outfit, and the next time we signed on the dotted line it was going to be with someone we trusted.

The problem was, there was no one around, trustworthy or otherwise, who was asking us to sign up. And with no record company interested, we didn't stand much of a change of getting a record made. That's just the way it was.

Except that Lee didn't quite see it that way. Looking back, I'd have to say that my old friend was way ahead of his time. It would be years before music stars would figure out that the best way to hang on to the money they were making from selling records was to start their own record companies. Back in the early months of 1968, most folks would have laughed at such an idea. Musicians made music. Records companies made records. Whoever was making the money depended on how good their lawyer was.

It took Lee to figure out that if we weren't getting any offers from established labels, it was time to make *ourselves* an offer. We'd start our own record company, press our platters, distribute and promote them, and when the time came to count up the cash . . . well, we'd do that, too.

But Lee didn't stop there. He knew from experience that making a record was only the beginning of the process. Once the music was etched into the grooves, you had to convince the radio programmers and the guys who stocked the jukeboxes and the folks who owned the record stores to give your product a shot. That was called promotion or, in some circles, payola. Now, we sure didn't have the kind of money it took to play the payola game. Which only left us the option of promotion. And most anyone in the business can tell you that a promotion campaign doesn't exactly come cheap, either.

But according to Lee, there was one form of promotion we *could* afford. It didn't cost a thing to have a newspaper reporter or a magazine columnist come out and see your show, listen to your record, and write up a rave review. Enough good press and it was only a matter of time before the offers started pouring in.

Naturally, Lee's plan was dependent on getting those writers and reviewers to give you some ink and inches in their stories, and that was no easy task in itself. Those guys were out chasing stories about stars everybody already knew most of the time, and the chances of getting them to champion an unknown commodity was about as good as getting your song played on the radio just because some DJ liked the way it sounded.

And that's where Lee came up with his particular stroke of marketing genius. If we couldn't get the local press to cover us, we'd just have to start our own magazine: give ourselves the cover, the lead story, and all the full-page ads. I'll be the first to admit that the whole scheme seemed just a little bit too complicated to really work. I was afraid that all Lee had really done was to outsmart himself, but since I was the one who had thrown down the challenge to make or break the group, I wasn't about to rain on his parade. If he wanted to start his own magazine, I wasn't about to stand in his way.

As things turned out, however, Lee's plan didn't get very far before fate intervened. He came up with a name for his publication—*Hot Line Music Journal*—and even did some sketches for a logo and some layouts for the very first cover, featuring, of course, Al Greene and the Soul Mates: "the explosive new vocal combination that's setting Grand Rapids on fire!" I wasn't sure we were setting anything on fire, but I have to admit I liked seeing my name and face on the cover of a magazine, even if nobody else was ever going to lay eyes on it.

And nobody else ever did. As Lee kept working on the grand premier issue of *Hot Line Music Journal*, the Soul Mates and I had gone back into the studio to record some more songs, including a new original written by Palmer and Curtis. They'd put together a slow soul groove with a nice change up at the bridge, and the whole thing chugged along nicely after we spent a few days rehearsing it and ironing out the rough spots. They called it "Back Up Train," and we tried our best to lay down an easy loping rhythm that would bring to mind the sway of a freight train moving down the tracks. The story behind the song was as simple as it needed to be—a lonely man pleads for the train he's riding to "back up" and return him to his baby's arms. It was R&B by the numbers, but, in spite of its obvious limitations, not a half-bad song with a hook that you could carry away with you.

We cut the track, along with a handful of other James–Rogers originals and even one of my early songwriting efforts, a ballad called "Stop and Check Myself," down at the same studio where we'd recorded the Zodiac singles, and after we'd gotten it on tape, I can't say I was overly impressed with the results. Even then, I'd started to develop a very critical ear, especially when it came to listening to myself, and this time around, my performance seemed a little hesitant, as if I were unsure of my voice or the songs or the interaction of the two. But as much as anything, it probably had to do with the studio jitters I still struggled with. I needed an audience, and when I didn't have one, all I could hear were the all the little faults and imperfections in my performance. I couldn't *lose* myself in the music, and that left me feeling vulnerable and exposed, like a kid at his first recital. I would have probably spent the next two weeks trying to get the song right, but Palmer and the rest of the group seemed happy enough with the results and wanted to move right on to the next number. Studio time, even in that funky place, didn't come cheap, which meant I didn't have the luxury of pleasing myself.

Lee, on the other hand, was more than pleased when he heard the results. "That's a stone-cold hit" was his verdict when he heard the tape of "Back Up Train," and I've got to say that his enthusiasm was infectious. My fellow Soul Mates were easy enough to convince and, even if I had my secret doubts, I wasn't about to spoil the party. If "Back Up Train' was going to carry us to the big time, then I was sure enough going to get my ticket punched for the ride.

The very next day, Lee went down to the plant to have a thousand copies of "Back Up Train" pressed. We'd chosen another track from those sessions, a song called "Don't Leave Me," for the

B-side. The only problem was, when it came time to put on a label, he had forgotten to come up with a name. He hemmed and hawed for a few minutes while the salesman looked at his watch and tapped his foot impatiently. "Oh," said Lee at last, "just call it Hot Line Music Journal Records."

Now, if you think about it, giving our record label the same name as our magazine, even though neither one of them was real, didn't make a whole lot of sense in Lee's grand strategy. I really wanted to ask him how folks reading the latest issue of *Hot Line Music Journal* weren't going to figure out that its latest discovery, Al Greene and the Soul Mates on Hot Line Music Journal *Records*, didn't have more than a little bit to do with each other, kind of like the right hand knowing exactly what the left hand is up to. But I never had the chance before we got caught up in a chain of events none of us, not even Lee in his wildest dreams, could have anticipated.

With an armful of fresh-pressed records under his arm, Lee began making the rounds of local radio stations and, with no crisp fifty-dollar bills to pass in a handshake to a DJ, none of us had much expectation that "Back Up Train" would ever leave the platform. But there was something about that song that caught and held, something that gave it that little extra push in the right direction . . . right onto the turntable.

Now, I'd been in the music business long enough to learn one important lesson that's stuck with me ever since: You just never know. You may have the best song ever written by the best songwriter money can buy; you may have the London Symphony Orchestra, the Vienna Boys Choir, and the Metropolitan Opera backing you up in a seventy-two-track studio with an army of engineers and high-priced producers. You may get the back page of *Billboard*, the front cover of *People*, and a one-hour special on *60 Minutes*; you may have enough promotion and publicity to run for president; you may have it all, and there's *still* no guarantee you're going to have yourself a hit.

On the other hand, you may cut that song your grandmother sings in the shower, back yourself on a ukulele and kazoo, record the whole thing over the telephone, and find yourself at the top of the charts with a cardboard box full of Grammys taking up space in your garage. In the world of pop music, the only sure thing is that's there's no sure thing, and anyone who tells you different should get down on their knees and repent for telling a lie.

"Back Up Train" is about the best example I can think of. In those few first months of 1968, the charts were exploding with all sorts of great new sounds from Otis's "Dock of the Bay" to Archie Bell getting everyone to "Tighten Up." The simple truth was that "Back Up Train" just wasn't in that league. I've done worse songs in my life, but I've also done a whole lot better songs, so believe me when I say I can tell the difference. There was just no logical reason for that that particular tune to take off like it did.

But it did. Maybe it just caught the passing fancy of the public for a short minute. Maybe they were looking for something at just that tempo, in just that octave, with just that inflection, to get them though that one hard part of the day or that one lonely hour of the night. Maybe it was because they were in the mood for something new . . . but not too new. Or something old . . . but not too old. Maybe they liked the chorus or the verse or the bridge. Maybe the moon was full when it started getting airplay, first right around Grand Rapids, then out toward Chicago and Detroit and Milwaukee.

Or maybe there was no moon at all. And maybe I could spent the rest of this book speculating on why some folks make it all the way and some never even get out of the gate. Talent's got nothing to do with it. You need to get lucky, but luck by itself isn't enough. When it gets right down to it, I guess I'd have to say that God is in control, even when it comes to what song makes the Top Ten on the national pop record sales and airplay charts.

By January of '68, "Back Up Train" was starting to break out all across the Great Lakes region, and no matter how many times we heard it on the radio—no matter how many times the DJ announced, "That's 'Back Up Train' by Al Greene and the Soul Mates," I don't think any of us quite believed that it was really happening. Gene and Curtis and Palmer were still working their day jobs; I was still shacking up with Juanita and hustling money whatever way I could; and Lee was still living with his wife and parents in their cramped apartment. The only difference was, we had a hit song on the radio.

Well, that wasn't *exactly* the only difference. It was getting so our gigs at the El Grotto were selling out on a regular basis, and we could feel this whole new kind of electric excitement every time we got up onstage. It wasn't like we had to prove ourselves anymore. They were there, primed and ready, to dig what we did. And of course, we picked up a whole new attitude off the neighborhood streets, where folks would stop what they were doing just to watch us walk by, and the prettiest girls would always find an excuse to come around and talk to us, making sure all along that we understood what was being said underneath all the idle chatter.

When I look back on those early days in the first flush of success, I get to feeling a little sad, a little sorry for those innocent young men with the world opening up at their feet. We were so sure we'd arrived, that we'd gotten past the hardest part and that all we had to do was reap our richly deserved rewards. We were already famous, at least on the streets of Grand Rapids, and if we weren't rich yet, well, that couldn't be too far behind.

But there was no way of knowing what lay ahead of us, no way to realize that, far from arriving, we hadn't even embarked. What seemed like the big payoff was really only a carrot dangling in front of us, just out of reach, spurring us on down a road where every twist and turn brought its own new beginning. If we could have somehow seen our way down along that highway, known the finish from the start, I wonder if we'd have been all so anxious to make the journey. I wonder if we would've been so ready to give up everything we'd known—friends and family and a simple life of simple expectations—and trade it all in for the slim chance of beating the odds and giving over our young lives to the whims and wiles of strangers who could only tell you want you wanted to hear, whether it was true or not.

I'm asking those questions now, but I think I know the answer as much today as I did back then. And that answer is *yes*. Because that's what temptation is all about. If any one of us, and I include myself as chief among the sinners, could have looked into the future and counted the cost of giving over our lives to the fickle affections of the public, to live from one hit record to the next, knowing all the while that this one could be your last; if we could have foreseen how lonely a man can be in the midst of an adoring crowd; if we could have weighed out family and friends against fame and fortune and seen the way the scales tip . . . even if we'd been able to know it all, all up front, I believe to this day that our answer would have been the same. *Sure. You got yourself a deal. Where do I sign up?*

Now, understand me when I say that living the life of a entertainer—whether you're a pop idol or a violin virtuoso, a movie star or a lion tamer—isn't a sinful thing in and of itself. The apostle Paul says that, with Jesus, "all things are lawful, but not all things are edifying." You can still be a star and sin not. But I speak from experience when I say that the temptations that beset a man of wealth and fame are all but overwhelming, except to the strongest and most resolute among us. Ask yourself: If you were able to get whatever you wanted—the finest meals, the fastest cars, the most beautiful women—whenever and wherever you wanted, what would hold you back, what would restrain you from losing yourself in the desires of the flesh in all their endless variations?

But naturally, we don't think much on such questions. We're too busy trying to get what we want, whenever and wherever we want it. And when we take the first step down that road, it's very hard indeed to turn back around. Even if you should find out—too late—what's waiting at the end.

CHAPTER 16

A little hit record on a couple of stations up in the tri-state area—not exactly the big time, is it? Well, I suspect that all depends on your perspective. And as February rolled around with its bone-chilling wind, the Canadian Express, howling down off Lake Michigan, our perspective just kept getting wider and wider.

"Back Up Train" went from being a local hit to a regional hit to an East Coast hit. From there, well, there wasn't anyplace left to go but all the way out West. In what seemed like less time than it took to wish upon a star, Al Greene and the Soul Mates were big, bad, and nationwide.

Not that we had a whole lot of time to enjoy our newfound status. The record began picking up more and more airplay, rising up the R&B charts, and reaching into the Top Ten before jumping over onto the pop listing, where it kept climbing up through the Hot 100. We could hardly keep up with the bookings that were pouring onto Lee's kitchen-table office. Any idea he might have had about putting out that first issue of *Hot Line Music Journal* was long forgotten. In fact, any thought of putting out another release on Hot Line Music Journal Records was a thing of the past, too. It hadn't been but about a week after "Back Up Train" first landed on the local charts, when Lee got a call from a man at Bell Records out in New York, asking him if he'd be interested in a distribution deal. I couldn't tell you for sure if Lee even knew what a distribution deal *was*, but that cat had always been a quick study, and after promising to get back to the man on the phone, he did a little asking around and when the time came, he cut us a contract with the label that at least kept a slice of the profit pie for the group. Now our billing became Hot Line Music Journal Records' Al Greene and the Soul Mates, distributed exclusively by Bell Records. And if you'll pardon the pun, that had a real nice ring to it.

Bell took care of getting the record to the radio stations and record stores. It was our job to show up and sing at every night-club, roadhouse, VFW Hall, high school auditorium, and fair-ground between Grand Rapids and any other direction on the compass where you'd care to point. It was as if word about the group was spreading in a concentric ring right around Grand Rapids and those circles just kept getting bigger and bigger.

Those of us who had day jobs quit them, and as my schedule began to fill up, I started seeing less and less of Juanita. I wasn't around much to cook her breakfast or rub her back after a long night working the streets. In fact, *I* was the one beginning to hope for a back rub and bowl of oatmeal when I'd return from five straight days of playing one-night stands. She always seemed to be leaving just as I was getting in, and at first we made the best of it, trying to accommodate each other and our unsettled schedules. I knew she was happy for me, that no one wanted me to succeed more than Juanita. But I also harbored a nagging doubt, way in the back of my mind: *Is there going to be room for Juanita where I'm heading?*

When Al Greene and the Soul Mates weren't out on the road, we were back in the studio, cutting more tracks. Bell Records let it

be known that, if we came up with a whole album's worth of material as strong as "Back Up Train," they'd be interested in putting it
out. That was as much incentive as we needed to pull some all-
nighters, rehearsing and recording some of the new songs that
Palmer and Curtis were coming up with. There's nothing like a
charting single to convince young songwriters they've got what it
takes, and the team of James–Rogers were no exception. In fact,
their songwriting chops—or, more exactly, their *lack* of songwriting chops—was the first real problem we had to overcome after the
success of "Back Up Train." The two of them would dash off two
or three songs in a night, and each one, according to them, was
another "Back Up Train."

Now, I've already said I wasn't *that* crazy about our hit song to
begin with, and the prospect of singing a whole album's worth of
their refried soul workouts didn't exactly set my heart fluttering. I
tried to gently suggest that maybe we should look somewhere else
for a follow-up song, but that just got the both of them to huffing
and puffing and claiming that, without the magic they'd worked
with lyrics and melody, why, we'd all be back on Lee's porch,
singing to the sparrows in the backyard elm tree. I knew enough to
let the issue lie, but, thinking back, I realize that was the first time
I began to seriously consider trying to write songs that came up to
my standards.

By the middle of February, "Back Up Train" had reached number 5 on the *Billboard* R&B chart and stalled out at number 41 on
the pop charts. We'd had a good run and, despite the fact that our
success was as much of a surprise to us as to anyone, we sure didn't
hesitate to take credit for it. After a few weeks, squeezing recording
sessions in between live shows, we felt we had almost enough
decent songs for the debut album Bell was asking after. We all felt
that we'd ridden the old "Back Up Train" just about as far as it
would go. But there was one more destination on the schedule, one

that really was like a dream you never dared hope for, coming true just when you least expected it.

We'd all gathered at my apartment to get ready for a gig over in Lansing that evening in mid-March, and we were waiting around for Lee to show up with the old Buick he'd bought to haul us around. It was one of those lazy late winter afternoons when you can just feel spring taking its own sweet time to get going, and we were feeling pretty lazy, too. The last six weeks had been a real whirlwind and I think we were all just trying to catch our breath. It was pleasant enough just to sit there with nothing much to do, at least for a few hours, just passing the time like in the old days, and though none of us had a whole lot to say, we also didn't have much reason not to say it.

All of a sudden we hear a pounding up the stairs and my first thought was *Oh, Lord, the police are back!* The door flew open and we all jumped up like we were ready to fly out the window.

It was Lee. He was shouting and waving his arms, and for a good couple of minutes, we couldn't make out a word he was saying. We finally had to set him down, give him a drink of water, and wait until he caught his breath before we found out what had gotten him so fired up.

"I just got a call," he said, still panting like he'd run all the way over from his place. "It was New York City on the line . . . the Apollo Theatre . . . they want us out there next week . . . for a show!"

There was a silence in the room. Outside we could hear traffic passing by and somewhere, far off, the sound of a siren. I remember looking around at the others and seeing them looking back at me, all of us struck dumb.

"The Apollo, you fools!" shouted Lee again, jumping up from his chair and commencing to wave his arms again. "We're going to the Apollo!"

At that point, general pandemonium broke out, with everyone yelling and whooping and doing Indian rain dances around the apartment. Everyone, that is, except me. I just stood there, as solid and unmovable as a statue in the park. I think one part of my brain was still trying to take in the news, while another part was racing at the speed of light, jumping into the bright future that had just that moment dawned.

The Apollo! For a black entertainer, there *was* no more legendary venue, and you can throw Carnegie Hall, the Royal Albert Hall, and any other hall you might care to name onto that list. It was Mecca, Jerusalem, and the Promised Land all rolled into one, for generations of great stars from the Golden Age of Jazz right down to today, when any hip-hopper or rapper on his way up has got to make a scheduled stop on that fabled stage.

And as much as the Apollo was a golden opportunity, it was also a baptism of fire. The theater's audiences were infamous for giving artists a quick and unqualified estimation of their talents. If they liked you, it could be hard to get off the stage. If not, they might drop that curtain down right on top of you.

But for us, five poor boys from the hard-knocks 'hood of Grand Rapids, Michigan, an engagement at the Apollo meant just one thing: We had arrived. This was the top of the ladder and if another good thing never happened, we could always sit our grandchildren on our knee and tell them about that glorious moment we stood under the spotlight on the greatest stage on earth.

Looking back, I've got to grin. I've headlined venues big enough to fit a dozen Apollos inside and sang my songs to kings and presidents. And of course, I've since played the Apollo itself more times than I can even remember. But the notion of having my name on that one particular marquee in the heart of Harlem still packs a powerful hold on my heart. It's the lure of legend, I guess, the luster that comes from being in the place where so many greats before you have been, like standing on holy ground. It never occurred to me that I should take off my shoes when I stepped onto the worn wooden boards of the Apollo, like Moses shedding his sandals in front of the burning bush, but the feeling was the same. It was a sanctifying moment.

All the way out to New York City, driving that battered Buick through those Midwestern farmlands just starting to stir from the cold grip of winter, we were unusually quiet, keeping our thoughts and emotions well to ourselves. And though none of us could find the words to express it, I believe we were all experiencing the same strange mix of feelings: excitement and dread, anticipation for the future and longing for the past, when all the risks and rewards had seemed so much simpler, easier to hang on to and easier still to let go of.

Hiding those mixed emotions was a lot easier than concealing how we felt when we got our first good look at Harlem in the gray light of a raw March morning as we rolled down 125th Street. Don't ask me what we expected—streets paved with gold, a brass band welcoming committee, or the town fathers with a red carpet and the keys to the city. The hard truth was that Harlem—the heart of black American culture and a magnet for our people since the first days of emancipation—didn't look a whole lot different from downtown Grand Rapids, the South Side of Chicago, or any other big-city ghetto where folks might live their whole lives waiting for something better and never seeing it come to pass. There's a hopelessness to tenement streets in a slum neighborhood, no matter how high the skyscrapers might rise in the distance, no matter how broad the boulevards that recall its past glory. And Harlem was no exception. It seemed, no matter where we went, black folks had all been shuffled into the same sad square footage, crowded with the same liquor stores and bars, scarred by the same boarded-up shop windows and junked cars, populated by the same citizens, crawling along the edge of survival. No matter where we went, we always ended up in the same place, and even Harlem proved to be no exception.

At first sight, the Apollo didn't exactly take our breath away, either. From the outside, the theater seemed small and cramped, sandwiched between two buildings with barely enough room to let its sign hang. Inside, the place looked even more forlorn as we trooped in to announce our arrival that first morning. With no spotlights or music, no shouting crowds or hard-selling MC, the theater seemed like a place haunted by the ghosts of great performers past. As Lee ran over the details of our performance that night with a bored-looking house manager, I stood behind the last row of seats, just staring at the stage. It was hard to imagine, in that dim and dismal light, the thrill of seeing Jackie or Sam or Otis strutting from wing to wing. In fact, the place hardly seemed big enough to hold the stars that had lived in my imagination: Jackie could have covered the width of that stage with a single backflip, Sam could have reached the balcony with a whisper, and Otis would have simply blown the house down with one of his patented soul shouts.

Looking back now, I guess it all goes to show how being a star is as much in the eye of the beholder as it might ever be in the personal power of any one man. People see and hear and believe exactly what they want to, what they *need* to, and from that need they'll construct heroes and idols to suit themselves. The Apollo Theatre of my mind was grander than the Taj Mahal, bigger than the Grand Canyon, and more splendid than Buckingham Palace because, in my imagination, I'd made the stars who headlined there bigger than life, too. It's a need common to all mankind—to lift up, to worship and adore. And of course, when it's only a human being that you bow down before, well, that's bound to be disappointing.

Naturally, if I'd known then what I've since learned the hard way, I might have just chuckled and shook my head at my own foolishness. But as it was, I stared into that cold and dingy auditorium, squinted hard, and tried to imagine how it might turn into a castle grand enough to suit my fancy.

And the funny thing was, within a few hours, that's exactly what happened. Lee took us over to a hotel around the corner and we had a good breakfast, a hot shower, and a solid couple of hours' sleep. Then it was back to the theater to practice "Back Up Train" with the famed Apollo house band Robin Phillips and his Orchestra. Returning to the theater that afternoon, the place had already taken on a different air. It was still drafty and dim and frayed around the edges, but the bustle of stagehands, musicians, and other artists getting ready for the evening's performance put an electric crackle in the air.

And by the time a crowd starting lining up on the sidewalk outside as the daylight faded and the street's first neon lights flickered to life, that crackle had turned to a jolting charge of sheer excitement and transformed the Apollo into a place more magical than any I could picture in my mind's bedazzled eye. Suddenly I wasn't noticing the tattered edge of the curtains, the grimy mirrors in the dressing room, or the disdainful looks of the horn players as they hung out, waiting for the gig to get started like workers on an assembly line. Suddenly the air seemed tinged with a silvery glow as, overhead, the spots came on, the house lights dimmed, and the rowdy crowd set up a roar that rattled the roof beams. It was showtime at the Apollo, and like a grand old lady getting dolled up for one more command performance, the place came to life—and all at once, there was no place else quite as close to heaven as that little corner of New York City.

For all the times I've been onstage—before and after—that night at the Apollo will stand as a milestone, a high point, and a personal best all rolled into one. Knowing how fickle that particular audience could be and how much they enjoyed letting you know just how they felt—good or bad— you would have thought that the rest of the guys and I would have been sweating puddles, waiting for our cue. But I honestly don't remember even the smallest tremor of stage fright or a single butterfly fluttering in my stomach. Of course, I'm not entirely clear about many of the details of that evening—I couldn't tell you, for instance, who we shared the bill with or whether we came on first, last, or somewhere in between.

But I do remember one thing—and it was as close to a feeling of floating on air as I've ever had. Suddenly a whole lifetime of musical dreams snapped into sharp focus and, as the MC gave us the usual rousing Apollo introduction and I leapt out of the wings and charged over to the microphone while the band cranked up the intro to our hit song—suddenly, when I opened my mouth and heard my own voice float out over the crowd like a benediction, I realized that, if nothing else was to ever happen in my life and career again, I could look back at that moment, standing on that stage in front of that audience, and say to myself, *Al Greene, you* are *somebody*.

pparently, I wasn't the only one who thought so. Al Greene and the Soul Mates made Apollo history that night by being called back no less than *nine* times to sing our song, in one encore after another. I think it must have been after about the third rendition that we all kind of slid into a wide-awake dream. Not only had we won over the notorious Apollo crowd, we had them eating out of our hands. I think even the jaded musicians in the orchestra were impressed, because every time the stomping, whistling, and shouting crowd would call us out for one more round of "Back Up Train," they'd put a little bit more soul and spirit into their playing. At least, it seemed that way to me.

We could have sung anything that night, I believe—"Mary Had a Little Lamb," "What a Friend We Have in Jesus," the National Anthem—it was just one of those once-in-a-lifetime connections between an audience and performer that makes everything that came before it—and whatever comes after it—seem worthwhile. Every time the MC would call us back and the band would break into those opening notes, I could feel a sharp, almost painful flush of heat shudder up the length of my body, explode in my head, and come pouring out of my mouth. Sweat drops glistened in the spotlight as I'd throw out my arms like I wanted to gather the audience, the theater, and the whole world outside the walls into that magic circle of light and sound and mutual love. This was where I belonged and I would have done anything—paid any price, traded any treasure, betrayed any trust—to stay there forever.

Yes, I can speak from experience when I tell you that nothing comes close to the love you feel coming at you on a stage. I've come to understand through all the stages of my life, the simple truth that, from cradle to grave, we're all looking to be loved. A baby at her mama's breast. An old man with a grandchild on his knee. It's all part of that same hunger to feel that someone, somewhere cares about you.

Now, take that feeling and multiply it by a hundred, a thousand, a million. Imagine a room full of people all focusing their love on you, showering you with their affection, pouring out approval and acclaim and unconditional acceptance like a mighty river washing over every fiber of your being. Then ask yourself, *Is this why everyone's always trying to become famous?* And you've already answered your question.

When the curtain finally came down that night at the Apollo, it drew a close to one part of my life, as surely as if I was reading lines in a three-act play. Act One: Young man yearns for fame and fortune. Act Two: Young man's dreams come true. Act Three . . . ?

Well, in 1968, Act Three was a long way from being written, but from my vantage point on the stage of the Apollo, standing behind the curtain and listening to the sound of pure adulation thundering from the other side, it felt like I'd reached the absolute peak of all my ambitions. There was no place left to go.

Except, of course, down. As the Soul Mates and I packed up for the trip back home, we were curiously quiet while we'd been heading out. I think each of us, in his own way, realized that whatever else might happen from here on, nothing was ever going to be quite the same again. Whatever we'd together decided was a good reason to keep on going—whether it was the thrill of hearing our song on the radio or seeing a crowd of familiar friendly faces turn out for one of our neighborhood gigs—well, from that point on, those reasons weren't going to make the difference. All that mattered now was getting back to where we'd just come from . . . or arriving someplace better.

In a funny way, the experience of playing at the Apollo made us each face up to our own selves, in our own way. We had to ask ourselves—did we have what it takes? And by that I mean not just talent and ability, but raw determination. Suddenly we were confronted with a whole new challenge. Before, our only desire had been to make it—to succeed as a group and get our music heard. Now all of a sudden, our job was to *stay* successful, to keep making hits and somehow—anyhow—remain in the center of all that attention. It was as if we'd been to the mountain and now that we were back down in the valley, we'd never be satisfied with the same old view again. Whether we knew it or not, we had to each make a decision—would we stop right here, call it quits, and walk away with a handful of golden memories? Or would we keep pushing, trying to climb back up the steep cliffs of that high peak?

I can't say for sure whether any of my other bandmates put the question to themselves that way, but for me, the direction I would take was never in doubt. I wanted to be back up onstage, under those lights, in front of those people, and nothing was going to stop me. It could have been right about then—heading back home somewhere out across the rolling hills of Pennsylvania, the sleeping cornfields of Ohio, or pulling away from the smokestacks of Akron, Ohio—that the thought first formed in the back of my brain, too small to notice and too bold to put into words, but lodged back there all the same, like a seed waiting for spring to take root. *I'm going to be a star.* Nothing was more important. Nothing could stop me. There was no turning back.

It was an ambition I secretly nursed throughout the weeks that followed our triumph at the Apollo, a goal set before me that put a whole new perspective on the life we returned to. Of course, once word about the show spread around Grand Rapids, we were even a bigger sensation than when "Back Up Train" first found its way onto the radio. Bookings came pouring in, Bell Records was pushing for a follow-up single, and we couldn't walk down the streets without turning heads and leaving a trail of admiring whispers.

But somehow it just didn't seem to measure up for me. I was looking at my little world through a whole new pair of eyes, ones that diminished instead of magnified, and I could feel the discontent welling up inside of me as every day passed and the memory of those golden moments on the stage of the Apollo began to take on a life of their own.

Lee had decided that our next single would be another Palmer–James original called "Don't Hurt Me No More." I liked that one about as much as "Back Up Train," but my power of veto was exactly one fifth of the total, so I sat back and kept my own counsel. The track was supposed to be a lead-up to the release of our first album and, for the cover, Bell Records had put a picture of me hanging out the window of a locomotive that looked to be running backward. By that time, I was heartily sick of the song and all the silly railroad symbolism that came with it. I had a lot of my own musical ideas, notions about a sound that would move things forward into a new decade of soul music and not backward toward that burnin', churnin' style that already seemed to me to be dated and dingy.

You always hear about "creative differences" breaking up a group, when usually it's nothing more than simple greed or selfish pride. But in the case of Al Greene and the Soul Mates, there really *was* a sharp division in the way Lee and the rest of the group wanted to go and the direction I was reaching for. By the very same token, black music itself had reached a crossroads by the late sixties, with most of the great innovators, including Sam and Otis, no longer on the scene and nobody yet come up to take their place. The era of the "soul shouter" seemed to be sputtering out and it was my positive conviction that the next wave in black music would bring along something altogether more smooth and sophisticated. Maybe it was just my long-standing love of jazz that put the notion in my head, but I was convinced that soul music was about to take on a whole new mood.

Not that I could have drawn a graph pointing out all the stops along the way or quoted chapter and verse to prove the point. I just had a feeling and as the spring of that year mellowed into summer, that feeling got stronger and, with it, my own discontent with the group and the music we were making.

I wouldn't say that I had the satisfaction of feeling vindicated when "Don't Hurt Me No More" didn't make a ripple on the music charts outside Grand Rapids and, even there, hardly made a dent. The same was true of our third single "A Lover's Hideaway." And I can't say that I felt justified when *Back Up Train*, the album, fell off the back of the truck like a sack of raw turnips. The last thing in the world I wanted was to have "one-hit wonder" tagged to my name, especially if the hit was as simple a ditty as ours. I *knew* we could do better, or, at least, I knew *I* could do better, and as the summer wore on and we found ourselves back playing the same old club circuit to the same old familiar faces, that certainty started eating away at me.

And if I did nothing to hide my discontent from the others, they did nothing to keep me from seeing how much they just didn't care. We'd been together for two long years—an eternity when you're young and impatient—and the dreams we'd shared together huddled out on Lee's porch had long since turned into the reality of three-set nights, midweek rehearsals, and twelve-hour road trips between gigs. The thrill of singing in front of a real live audience had become an exhausting routine and even hearing our song on the radio had worn thin after the twentieth time around. Now, with the failure of "Don't Hurt Me No More" and "Lover's Hideaway," along with the instant oblivion of our album, it was all too clear that we'd have to come up with a new set of dreams to keep us going.

And for Al Greene and the Soul Mates, that was one jump too many. For Lee, Palmer, Curtis, and Gene, it was time to wake up, grow up, and move on. We'd had a good run, no question about it, what with a national hit single and a show-stopping performance at the Apollo. They had clippings for a scrapbook and a surefire pickup line to use on a Saturday night: "Hey, honey. You ever heard of a little tune called 'Back Up Train'?" And that was all good and well. But life—real life—well, that was about working a real job for a paycheck you could depend on for a future you could build from the bottom up. It was time to get serious, start thinking about finding a wife, settling down, and raising a family.

Not that any of them said as much, at least not in those words. There was no final confrontation, no face-to-face farewell, no broken hearts or bitter might-have-beens. Instead, things just kind of slowly fell apart, with one guy, then another, then another missing a rehearsal or not showing up for a gig. We had a few fights; that was only natural. But the flying fur and pointed fingers only hid what we all knew was already a settled fact. It was over. And in the end, when the man from Bell Records finally made it official by telling us the label was no longer interested in a partnership with Hot Line Music Journal Records, Al Greene and the Soul Mates, or any parties thereof and unto, it all came as a kind of relief, like putting down a tired old plow horse. What was important was what remained—the memories and the friendships and the chance we'd had to make music together.

As I watched my former bandmates fold themselves back into everyday routines—finding steady jobs and picking up the pieces of their families and personal lives—it was only a matter of time before I would face down my own reflection in the mirror and have to ask myself the question: *So what about* you, *Al Greene? What's going to become of you?*

I was still living with Juanita, even though what we had was held together as much by force of habit as by any real link of love or affection. The life on the street was beginning to take its toll on her and as I watched the premature lines of hard living carve away at her beauty, I felt in myself the panic of time running short. After everything I'd been through in the past two years—throwing myself body and soul into a career in music—what did I have to show for it? I was back where I started, no better off than when I'd begun and still searching for the solution that would make sense of my life.

That feeling of being stalled spilled over into my family life, as well. My parents, along with all my brothers and sisters, were still caught in the vicious cycles, getting by on just enough from week to week and month to month. It wasn't as if I could have slipped back into that pattern, even if I'd wanted to. I'd set myself aside, in the choices I'd made and the chances I'd taken, and I could tell by the way they looked at me that I was somehow different now—on the outside, looking in.

But the truth is, I was exactly where I wanted to be. I wouldn't have gone back to the way things were if Juanita, my family, or the whole city of Grand Rapids, Michigan, had welcomed me with a brass band and the key to the city. My destiny had been laid out, as clear as a sign by the side of the road, from the moment I had stepped onto that stage of the Apollo. There was no turning back.

It wasn't but a few days after the man from Bell paid us his sorry farewell that I had completely put together the next step in my career. You wouldn't have needed a Ph.D. to figure out the logical step to take, but I was more than a little proud of myself for having come up with it, anyway. I was going solo!

Al Greene was always the focus of the Soul Mates, I told myself. *Without me, they wouldn't have amounted to much.* But without them, well, let's just say I was starting to feel most definitely *unencumbered.* I'd be calling the shots from now on, singing the music I wanted to sing, and walking away with the whole pie instead of just a slice. *I'm the boss now*, I told myself. *I'm going to do things* my *way!*

I've got to laugh when I think back on such foolishness. As if I could singlehandedly wish myself all the success and acclaim I knew I so richly deserved. But it was exactly that kind of attitude I needed to make a move as big and as bold and as risky as I was about to try. Maybe false confidence is better than no confidence at all, and maybe if you tell yourself something long enough and loud enough, you can make it come true. I wasn't sure, but I did know one thing—I had no place else to go, no one else to rely on, and nothing else to try.

Since I was about to throw caution to the wind, gamble everything, and pass the point of no return, I decided that I needed to make a statement—to myself and everyone else—that would announce my intentions in no uncertain terms. The old Al was dead and gone. The next Al was a whole new creation. And what better way to ring in the new than with a brand-new name? I would christen myself Al Green, dropping that final "e" that never seemed to belong there anyway, and give myself a fresh lease on life.

It may not seem like much, losing a single letter from your family name. People change their whole name all the time—and at the drop of a hat. But for me, Al Green was as different from Al Greene as day was from night. Trimmed down and straight to the point, it *suited* me. From that moment on, the whole history of Al Greene, that poor farm boy from Arkansas, belonged to someone else. Al Green was a singer. A star. A man on his way to somewhere.

CHAPTER **18**

hanging my name, even that little bit, felt like a daring thing to do, as if I'd thrown off everything that I was before and become someone else, brand-new and without the baggage of any personal history.

Of course, the truth was, if I'd *really* wanted to make a clean break, I'd have gone the whole way: become Al Red, Al Black, or Al Yellow, moved to a different city in a new state, and started singing country and western music. But while I might have been desperate back in the summer of 1968, ready to make a move that would change everything, I wasn't stupid. The last thing I was interested in was starting over, completely from scratch, building up a name and reputation for myself all over again, and wasting two more years in the process.

No, becoming Al Green was about as much of a transformation as I was willing to risk. It was enough to allow me to be my own man, do things my way, but still and all, hang on to the progress I'd made up to that point. And the truth was, without the name recognition that tied Al Green, no matter how you spelled it, to a song called "Back Up Train," I really would have had to start all over again. Lee, who had agreed to help get me a few bookings to start myself up, naturally brought up my one and only hit record to any promoter he talked to, and, whether I liked it or not, that was the connection that landed me my first gigs as a solo artist.

And that meant, of course, that I'd actually have to sing the dumb song, maybe two or three times a show, depending on the crowd and the mood they were in. In the beginning, I didn't mind so much. *After all,* I told myself, *the first rule of show business is to "give the people what they want."* But one night, I arrived at a gig to see my name written on the marquee as AL "BACK UP TRAIN" GREEN, and I could feel my heart drop into my shoes. That song was turning into a curse, one that I'd carry around with me forever, no matter *what* I called myself.

That first summer out on the road by myself was a revelation in more ways than one. I had imagined myself calling the shots, singing just what I wanted, how I wanted, and, after the show, collecting a fat check made out just to me. The reality I found myself in was a whole other sad state of affairs. Wherever I sang, I found myself at the mercy of a club band that, more often than not, didn't know the changes but to half a dozen songs. Rehearsals were, more often than not, spent in them telling me what *they* would play and not the other way around. And of course, none of them had a lot of sympathy or understanding for my subtle and sophisticated new musical approaches. If I couldn't belt it out by the numbers they were accustomed to, well, what was I doing onstage in the first place?

It was a question I often asked myself. Between the club owners demanding I do "Back Up Train" in every set and the audience screaming for that same sad tune even after I'd done it to death, I began to think maybe I would've been better off taking up a career in cowboy music. And as far as taking home an evening's proceeds all to myself, it seemed like there were more hands than ever reaching out for a piece of the action at the end of a show. I guess I

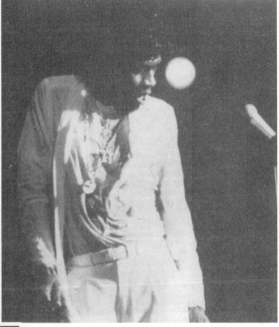

Can I get a witness? Both preaching and performing bring out the part of my personality that wants to reach out and make a one-on-one connection, whether it's a sold-out crowd or a standing-room-only congregation.

That's me and Willie picking up a gold record award for *Al Green Gets Next to You* from Phyllis Diller, but I couldn't tell you why.

Plaid all over. That's me with a lady friend, mugging for the camera with the king of Memphis R&B— Mr. Rufus "Walkin' the Dog" Thomas.

The front cover of my 1971 breakthrough album *Let's Stay Together*. I've always been partial to fine leather and suede.

Above and right: The Afro Years. When I look back on earlier versions of myself, like these pictures from around 1976, I'm always glad to see that I'm smiling. I've felt blessed in my success, and it's important that people know I'm grateful to God for everything He's given me.

This is a shot taken around 1977, the time of *The Belle Album*, when I was wrestling with God's will for me to be a minister.

For the good times: This picture was taken in the living room of my home in Memphis. It's a place where I've always been able to relax and unwind, even though in this very room a tragedy occurred that would change the direction of my life.

Below: Al Green, circa 1977. I can still see myself as a young child when I look at this picture. God was already about the business of softening my heart.

Above: This shot was taken at a photo session for *Al Green Explores Your Mind* in 1975, not long before my fateful encounter with the Spirit of God. If you look closely, you can see the light of Jesus dawning in my eyes.

This is me around the time I was recording *Full of Fire*, and that's exactly how I felt.

Clothes make the man: Stylin' and profilin' is as much a part of who I am as singing and preaching.

The Reverend Al Green, happy to be serving the risen Jesus.

During my recording session with Lyle Lovett when he cut "Funny How Time Slips Away." A very sweet man.

At work in the studio. No
matter where I am, I like to
look my best.

Performing in New Orleans in 1988. Don't let anyone tell you a preacher can't get down!

This one's for you. With all my love, Al Green.

hadn't really paid too much attention to the way Lee took care of business for me and the Soul Mates during our early days and, as a result, when it was my turn to handle the money, I could never quite get over the feeling that I didn't quite know what I was doing. And everybody knew. When some club manager started subtracting dressing room fees and costume storage charges and everything else he could think of, while the band leader hit me for double overtime for the third set and a beer-and-pretzel allowance for all his guys, there wasn't anything else for me to do but just keep shelling out the bills. I wanted to keep everybody happy, even if it meant, on more nights than I care to remember, going home with less cash in my pocket than I'd started out with.

And as the months rolled on, home just kept getting farther and farther away. Lee had finally turned me over to a booking agent friend of his, and this cat earned his 10 percent and then some, landing me gigs all up and down the Midwest and then moving me down into the Deep South for a string of one-night stands on the Chitlin Circuit. I'd bought Lee's old Buick and drove it into the ground, leaving it with a blown block by the side of a Mississippi highway one July afternoon, and after that took to riding the Greyhound from show to show. Everything I owned I carried with me in a ratty old cardboard suitcase, and when there was a day or two between shows, I'd sometimes even take on a dishwashing or floor-cleaning job just to get a hot meal and place to sleep.

There was no question but that those months marked the lowest point in my career and one of the saddest chapters in my life. There I was, going through the motions of making the music I loved, getting up onstage night after night for ten or fifteen or twenty people who maybe only came out because they just barely remembered a song about a train some time back that had sort of caught their fancy, and maybe I'd go ahead and sing it for them again if they screamed and shouted for it long and loud enough.

The truth was, I just didn't know what else to do. I couldn't go back and I couldn't move forward, and where I was from one day to the next was about as discouraging and humiliating as one man's life can be. All my high-flying schemes for solo success had come to sound like a cruel joke, and even those precious moments on the stage of the Apollo seemed like they had happened to someone else. I'd come to the tired end of a long and dreary road, run up against disappointment and disillusionment, too worn out to keep going but too proud to call it quits.

I had borrowed a couple of thousand dollars from Lee and a few of his friends back in Grand Rapids to buy some time in a recording studio for some demos and, while the sessions didn't turn out like I'd hoped, I still owed the money and was determined, one way or the other, to pay it back. The problem was, the longer I stayed out on the road, the poorer I got. It seemed like I was always making just enough to get me to the next gig and, if there was anything left over, well, you could be sure there would be a special surcharge or extra commission I had to pay to someone or other.

I'd pretty much hit rock bottom on a swing through Texas just before the holidays in late 1968. I'd been on the road solid for the better part of nine months and had less than nothing to show for all my efforts. I'd taken to sleeping in the bus station, usually wearing my stage clothes from the night before, and it had been a long time since I'd had the money to afford the fancy process do's that people expected to see on a soul singer. My hair was wild and nappy, I hadn't had a shower in a week, and when I rolled into Midland on the freezing January afternoon, I had about 35 cents to my brand-new name. I was hungry, tired, fed up, and disgusted, and the thought of getting up in front of a bunch of strangers and croaking out the chorus to "Back Up Train" was my idea of a night of eternal punishment. On the other hand, I didn't have much choice. I was literally in a position of having to sing for my supper, and I figured if I could just get enough cash together for a bus ride back home, I'd throw myself on the mercy of Lee and his friends and work off my debt the best way I could.

The Texas wind came howling down off the plains as I trudged from the bus station, heading in the direction a stranger had pointed out at the edge of town, to the roadhouse where I was scheduled to play that night. The cold had long since seeped though my lime green polyester suit and the mud off the side of the road had ruined my thin-soled imitation alligator loafers by the time I finally saw the sign along a forlorn stretch of highway just outside the city limits. Any pleasure I might have taken in seeing my name on the marquee had long since drained away and my thought right then was to get inside and out of reach of those merciless dusty gusts.

But as I walked a little closer, I noticed for the first time the name above mine, the act that was heading the show that night, and, despite the cold, I stopped in my tracks and wondered whether this, at long last, wasn't a sign from above.

The name I stared at for a good couple of minutes before the wind nearly blew me through the door was none other than Willie Mitchell. Now, you have to understand that almost everybody who grew up within the range of a Memphis, Tennessee, radio station was more than likely familiar with the name Willie Mitchell and the distinctive sound that went along with it. Memphis is—and always has been—a tight little music community that supports its own and, even growing up across the river in Arkansas, I felt a strong kinship with the city's music and its musicians. After all, Memphis was the place where any aspiring singer or songwriter from anywhere around that part of the country would have gone to make it. It's where *I* would have gone if my family hadn't moved up to Grand Rapids, and it was in Memphis that my cousin Little Junior Parker had first made a name for himself, singing about his

"Mystery Train." So when I saw the name of Willie Mitchell on that flickering signboard, it was almost as if I had been given a message from home, a reminder of a time and place when life was still beautiful and full of hope.

Anyway, that's the way I took it. Maybe I was just desperate for any scrap of good news, a signifier, no matter how unlikely, that I still had a place in this world. Mind you, I'd never laid eyes on Mr. Mitchell in my life and, if you want to know the truth, I'd always considered his music more than a little dated. But just about then, the thought of finding someone from Memphis out there in the middle of the flattest, most forsaken country I'd ever wandered through was like a blessing from above, and I picked up my steps and hurried across the gravel driveway of the roadhouse.

Inside, half a dozen men were lounging around the bar while a few others were setting up equipment on the bandstand with the slow and deliberate pace of the same task done a hundred times before. I peered through the dim light of the room until I made out a sharp, thin individual sitting by himself at a table, nursing a highball. His hair was shiny, conked back in a perfect wave, and even from that distance I could see diamonds and gold winking from the rings on several of his fingers. Cigarette smoke curled up around his mustache, drawn across his upper lip in a fine pencil line. As I moved closer, I could see the expensive cut of his clothes and glimpsed a pair of cuff links, with stones the size of walnuts, winking at his wrists. He had a faraway look in his eyes, distant and unattached, as if he were a million miles from this rundown dive in the middle of a freezing Texas night.

What I didn't know about Willie Mitchell then, I would learn soon enough. A solid son of the South, he hailed from Ashland, Mississippi, and, from nearly the cradle, had been into music in one form or another. While he was still in high school, Willie had played in a big band and, as a trumpet player, had been hired to play in some early sessions with B. B. King. He'd later become music director for the great bluesman's road band and worked the same job for another up-and-coming black artist by the name of Isaac Hayes. But that wasn't before he laid the groundwork for his own career with a music degree from Rust College.

In 1950, while I was still knocking around Jacknash in my diapers, Willie had been drafted into the Army and quickly landed himself a plush job as a DJ with the Special Services and from there, a gig backing Vic Damone in his eighteen-piece road band. Back home by the middle of the decade, Willie became one of the leading lights of the blossoming Memphis music scene, playing regularly at the swanky Plantation Inn with his own band that, at one time or another, featured just about everybody who was anybody on the city's jazz scene.

Willie was a man whose drive to make it was as grand as my own, but with one big difference. He had the experience—and the education—to do something about it. By the late fifties, he was known on the Memphis scene as an ace producer, cutting hit sides for the 5 Royales, Roy Brown, and others. But he'd always had his eye on a performing and recording career for himself, and in 1962 he cut his first charting single, "The Crawl," followed by "20-75" (the title was record number "2075"). He returned a few years later with the mellow instrumental "Sunrise Serenade," which was an even bigger hit, and on the strength of those two tunes, started touring the country.

But Willie was too far-seeing to simply be satisfied with one-night stands and a percentage of the door. When he wasn't on the road, promoting his own career as a band leader, he was back in Memphis, making business connections and putting together promising creative combinations out of the town's rich mix of blues, jazz, and rock & roll players. He produced sessions, wrote charts, and found new artists for almost every little start-up label in Memphis, including Sun, Stax, Chips, Goldwax, Home of the Blues, and a little outfit called Hi Records, which was owned by a pudgy, good-natured white guy by the name of Joe Cuoghi, with a real taste for blues and R&B. Willie cut his own sides at Hi and later became Joe's number-one A&R man and all-around talent scout.

Now all that's just so much ancient history, except for one important fact. Willie Mitchell was in a perfect position to bring together a lot of different musical styles into a harmonious whole. He was, by inclination, a jazzman, given to a smooth, uptown instrumental sound that made the most out of every note. By trade, however, he had become familiar with the stompin', shoutin', dance-floor-rattlin' style of cut-loose R&B. After all, the man had produced some of the very best tracks Bobby "Blue" Bland ever laid to wax, and there *is* simply no one better at breaking down a blues song than Bobby.

Memphis, of course, was not only the home of great jazz and R&B—it was also the crossroads where black and white musical styles mixed and matched. With the success of Elvis and others artists on Sam Phillips's Sun Records label, Willie sensed that the blend of black soul with white sensibilities was going to shape the sound of the future, and he was constantly on the lookout for artists who could cross that divide and bring the two sides together. Along the way, he developed a posse of truly amazing musicians—including an incredible drummer named Al Jackson, Jr., who would later anchor the sound of Booker T. and the MGs— that he kept in reserve for the time when he could bring all these different musical elements together and make his big move.

But Willie was never the kind of cat who was satisfied to let fate find his front door. Even while he experimented with a whole range of young singers, like Ann Peebles, Syl Johnson, Denise Lasalle, O. V. Wright, and Otis Clay, who he hoped could translate his musical vision into melody and lyrics, he was busy pursuing his own career. In 1968, just around the time we were still basking in the glow of our Apollo show, Willie recorded "Soul Serenade." The track had brought in some bookings on the West Coast and Willie put his big band together for a quick swing through California. On the way back, he agreed to play a pickup date in Midland, Texas, to help offset the cost of getting his boys back home, and the club owner had put together a package that included a young kid from up North who'd had a hit a while back and came cheap, real cheap.

Like I said, I was looking for a sign, something to let me know that someone up there still knew who I was and was still watching out for me. I was grasping at straws, and I guess my own desperation gave me the boldness to take a chance on a stranger who just happened to be from the same general area I'd once called home.

God works in mysterious ways. Don't let anyone tell you different.

CHAPTER 19

I can't tell you what I had in mind to say to Willie Mitchell as I moved toward him across the sawdust floor of that Midland, Texas, roadhouse in late 1968. Maybe I just wanted to hear the sound of a soft West Tennessee accent again. Or maybe I would've have poured out my whole life story in all its sorry details, drowning him in a bucket of my own self-pitying tears. To tell you the truth, my head was a complete blank when I walked up to him, focusing my eyes on the twinkling diamond of the ring on his pinkie finger. All I knew was that I had to talk to someone, make some kind of human connection, plead my case, and pour out my frustration. I didn't know what I was going to say, but, whatever it was, I knew that Willie Mitchell was the man I wanted to hear it.

I started to panic when, out of the corner of my eye, I saw a figure moving quickly across the room to intercept me. Tucking my head between my shoulders like a charging bull, I pushed on and picked up speed, but it was too late. I felt a hand on my arm, slowing me down and turning me around, just a few feet from my destination.

"Something I can help you with?" came a voice at my ear and I

turned to face a man who bore more than a passing resemblance to
Mr. Mitchell. I found out later that it was Willie's brother James,
but at that moment I didn't care who it was.

"I want to talk to Willie Mitchell," I said, trying to keep my
voice from trembling.

"And who might you be?" said the man, tightening his grip on
my arm just slightly.

"My name's Al Green," I said. When I saw the blank look on his
face, I added, "The singer . . . I'm opening tonight."

Willie and James traded a quick look before Willie nodded and
his brother let me go. With a regal gesture, Willie motioned me to
the chair beside him and I sat down. A long moment of silence
passed, marked only by the cigarette smoke curling up from the
ashtray. Willie looked at me, but it was more like he was looking
through me, trying to remember something.

"Didn't you . . . ?" He snapped his fingers, trying to bring that
recollection to the surface, "Didn't you have a song sometime
back . . . somethin' about a train?"

" 'Back Up Train,' " I said quickly. "Yes, sir, I did."

"Never liked that song," Willie responded, more like he was
talking to himself. "Like trying to make somethin' out of nothin'."

"Well," I answered, "it didn't have but three changes."

He was looking at me again, only now it was like he saw me for
the first time. He took a sip of his drink, a drag of his cigarette,
and, squinting one eye against the smoke, asked, "What've you
been doing since?"

"Well," I answered, swallowing hard, "I've been touring pretty
hard."

"I'd say you've been touring a little *too* hard," Willie said with
a chuckle as he took in my dirty clothes and uncombed hair.
Behind me I could hear his brother laugh and realized he'd been
standing there the whole time. I turned and gave him a dirty look.

"Jimmy," Willie said smoothly, "why don't you get the boys set up so we can rehearse the opening act?" He turned to me. "That all right with you, Al Green?"

I stood up. "That'll be fine," I said with all the dignity I could muster, and made my way to the little bandstand at the corner of the room. Up on that cramped stage, Willie's band had already set up and I could see them watching me, each with the same slight grin on his face, as if to say, *Now, who's* this *fool think he is?* The funny things was, not only did the grins all look the same, so did the faces. Just like Willie and his brother James, most of the cats in the band, I found out later, were related to each other. Leroy Hodges, called "Flick" because of the special way he plucked at the strings, had been Willie's bass player clear back before he'd recorded "Soul Serenade." Flick's brother Mabon was nicknamed "Teenie" on account of slight stature and had been specially trained by Willie to play guitar just the way he liked it: soft and spare. In fact, Willie had brought Teenie home to live with him a few years before just to make sure his musical education stayed on track. Charles, a piano player they used to call "Do Funny" because of the tricks he could play on the keys, rounded out the Hodges' lineup, which was augmented by another keyboardist, Archie Turner, Willie's brother James, who also played horn, and Al Jackson, Jr., on drums.

All these guys were more or less my age, and even though they looked sharp and had money to spend on cigarettes and aftershave, I sincerely doubted they could have matched me for raw road experience. I was sure I'd played in as many dives as any of them and I wondered just how many of these slick-looking sidemen could ever claim to have brought down the house at the Apollo. So I paid no attention to their smirking expressions as I turned to James and quickly ran through the chords to "Back Up Train."

But I have to admit, Willie's band had it together. No sooner had I called out the changes than they picked it up, played it, and were already starting to add their own little personal flourishes. I stepped to the microphone, closed my eyes, and waited to step into the verse. And while I was waiting, Willie's words kept going around in my head, about how he'd never liked my one and only hit song and about how it was trying to make something out of nothing.

Something out of nothing. That phrase just stuck in my head. I knew it was supposed to be a put-down, a way of saying there wasn't anything *behind* the song, no legs for it to stand on—and the funny thing was, I'd always felt the same way. "Back Up Train" had just been Curtis and Palmer's idea of what a soul hit should sound like, like they were trying to sell the *idea* of a song instead of the song itself. And I'd sung it that way, too, putting all kinds of huffing and puffing into my voice, as if I was trying to inflate the whole thing like a hot-air balloon. But the plain fact was, all "Back Up Train" had going for it was a simple little melody, some silly words, and a connect-the-dots arrangement. There was no use trying to turn it into something it wasn't. Better to just let it lie there, sing it plainly and from the heart, and let it rise or fall on its own merits.

All these thoughts ran through my head in less time than it took for the band to reach my intro, but by the time I opened my mouth and started to sing, I'd come up with a whole new way to deliver "Back Up Train." I started off soft, just barely making myself heard above the band, but then, instead of building up to some high, dramatic climax, I *kept* it soft and down low, pronouncing each word carefully, drawing out the suspense, teasing out the meaning. The band responded by playing softer, too, taking their time getting to the changes, trying to figure out what it was in that dumb little song that I'd found to savor so much.

I'd never sung "Back Up Train" like that in my life, and I never

would sing it like that again. In that moment, the music had
become a sweet meditation on making more out of less, putting the
feeling in the spaces instead of the notes, and pulling something
out of nothing. It's was Willie Mitchell's inspiration, pure and simple, and when the last quavering note died in my throat and I
opened my eyes again, I could see him still sitting there, unmoving,
without a hair out of place, the smoke still curling up over his head
like a halo. It was like that music slowed down everything, brought
it almost to a dead stop, and in the silence, for the first time, I
could really see this man for who he was.

I know it may sound strange to you who don't have a faith in
the supernatural world, but for me, right then, I knew that this one
individual human being and I had been brought to this Texas
roadhouse on this night of all nights for a very particular reason. I
couldn't have told you what that reason was—the vision I'd been
gifted with did not extend that far—but the certainty that Mr.
Willie Mitchell and I were meant to meet brought with it a great
peace and calm. For the first time in as long as I could remember—
maybe as far back as that night at the Apollo—I felt like I was back
on the right track again.

I turned back around and looked at the band. The smirks had
been replaced by nods of grudging admiration, and as I slipped
the microphone back onto the stand and stepped down off the
stage, I heard behind me the sound of strings being strummed.
Teenie had accidentally brushed up against his guitar, but as
quickly as the sound welled up, he muffled it with the flat of his
hand. It was as if nobody wanted to spoil the moment we'd just
created.

I walked back over to Willie and sat down again. With a wave
of his finger, he summoned the bartender, who brought over
another highball.

"No thank you," I said, barely above a whisper. "But if you

have a ham sandwich or some potato salad, I'd be greatly obliged."

"Where'd you learn to sing like that?" Willie said as we waited for the waiter to bring over my supper.

Where did I learn to sing like that? It was a good question. I thought back to the birds outside the farmhouse window, the radio tuned to Jackie Wilson way out across the Arkansas night, a moaning and groaning such as no human tongue can utter as the Holy Spirit swept in under Mother Bates's revival tent. *I never did learn it*, I wanted to tell him. *It just comes through me, like a breeze through the trees.*

But what I said instead was "Here and there. Round about."

"You from these parts?" he asked when my sandwich arrived. I tried not to appear too anxious as I bit into the first meal I'd had in two days.

"Arkansas," I said around a piece of ham. "Not far from Memphis."

"Do tell," he said, stroking his chin. I swear I could hear wheels turning inside his head. "I know just about everybody in Memphis. How come I never heard of you?"

So for the next few minutes, in between mouthfuls of sandwich and potato salad, I told him the story of my life—or at least the version I wanted to hear . . . which mostly concerned the talented young singer who had everything it took, except for that one lucky break to push him over the top. And Willie listened and nodded and in the end, while I was wiping up the last of the mayonnaise with a crust of bread, he threw back his highball, snuffed out his cigarette, and stood up, all in one fluid motion.

"Well, Al," he said to me, holding out his hand. "It was nice to meet you and I wish you all the luck in the world." He smiled. "You keep at it. I'm sure you'll make it one of these days."

And that was that. I'm not sure what I expected, except maybe that he'd be feeling the same tingling up his spine that I did, some acknowledgment that our encounter was fated to be, or at the very least that we should keep in touch, one professional musician to another. But I got nothing like that, and as the years went on and I got to know Willie like a brother, I realized that it was all part of the way he operated, in the studio or on the street. He was always circling around things, sizing them up, taking their measure. Sooner or later was always quick enough for him and if you had to hurry to get somewhere, well, then, it probably wasn't worth going to. He was the kind of person who waited for things to come to him, in life and in music, or at least he always wanted it to seem that way. And that's what mattered with Willie—the way things seemed. Appearances counted: how you dressed, how you held yourself, the impression you left behind. He was a master of understatement, the light touch, the nod and the wink. If you couldn't ever tell exactly where Willie was coming from, it's because that's just the way he wanted it.

And what Willie wanted that evening was to keep me guessing. We both knew I was good, that I had what it took to go all the way. I'd proved it—to him and to myself—when I took "Back Up Train" down to its fundamentals and built it back up into something it had never been before or would ever be again. I sung that song for an audience of one and won him over, but instead of trying to impress, indulge, or intimidate me, Willie was just going to let nature take its course. No matter how hard he worked to make it happen, in the end what mattered most was that I would be coming to him and not the other way around.

For the rest of the evening, whenever I caught his eye, he'd give me a friendly nod and a smile before going back to whatever it was he was doing. The place had filled up pretty nicely by showtime and I had worked out a quick opening set with his band, including a couple of Sam and Dave numbers, some Otis, and couple of Jackie Wilson ravers for good measure. I did my best to breathe life into those old chestnuts, and while there was nothing wrong with my version of a window-shaking soul shout, I got the feeling Willie was less than impressed with my efforts. I even tried the slowed-down version of "Back Up Train" again, but I lost the tempo somewhere along the way and had to struggle to get back with the band. That didn't even seem to bother him. It was as if he'd already heard what he'd come to hear.

After my set, I made my way back into the crowd to listen to the main attraction. Willie and his band were well oiled and polished, and they could work the crowd like the professionals they were, but to my ears, the music sounded stale and out of date. After all, Willie Mitchell had been hitting stages like this across the whole country before I was able to warble a single note. He'd played with the best and brightest stars of the Memphis jazz galaxy and had helped put great blues and R&B stars on the musical map. He didn't have to *prove* anything that night—not to a bunch of poor Midland, Texas, farmers, anyway—and if he was just going through the motions, well, they were pretty sophisticated motions, after all: a kind of smooth and easy blend of big-band jazz and the softer side of R&B with a little Basin Street blues tossed in for flavor.

But the plain fact was, Willie and his band sounded like they were on the downside of a road trip that had lasted a couple of stops too long. As I sat there and listened, watching as the couples cuddled on the floor for the slow numbers, I couldn't help thinking that behind Willie's debonair manners and cool exterior was a cat who was running out of moves to make. You couldn't exactly tell it to look at him, resplendent as he was in his custom-tailored suit and shiny brass trumpet, but I thought I could see in Willie a man who knew that times were passing him by. The music he'd been making since the fifties, the jazz and blues variations that his generation rode in on, had long since become musty and threadbare.

He could still cut a dapper figure out there on the bandstand, but there were others already waiting in the shadows, anxious for him to get off and give them a chance in the spotlight. Willie might not have been over the hill, but he was coming up on the last grade and, unless he could find a way to bring something new and exciting to his music, he'd have to look back to see his best days.

Willie Mitchell needs me, I suddenly realized, *as much as I need Willie Mitchell.*

CHAPTER 20

The joint didn't close down until two o'clock that morning, after we'd done two more sets and the last beer-soaked patron had wandered into the frigid night. I went back behind the bar where the proprietor had his office to collect my fee, and by then the trouble had already started.

It seems that that roadhouse owner was trying to weasel out of paying for the night's music, claiming that the take at the door, combined with the bar and food receipts, wasn't enough to pay his expenses for the night. As long as he had been in the business, he told me and James—who was back there trying to collect for Willie and the band—it had been his clear understanding that unless the entertainment could draw a crowd large enough to cover the basic operating expenses of the house, then the aforesaid house was under no obligation to honor its contractual obligations, regardless of all prior agreements between said parties.

Or some such double-talk. There was a lot of screaming and yelling, even a little pushing and shoving, but I knew the outcome had already been decided long before. If this guy wasn't going to pay us, there wasn't a whole lot we—a bunch of itinerant musicians just passing through this fine community—could do about it.

All this double-dealer had to do was put in a call to his close friend the sheriff or the chief of police, or even just a bunch of his friends from the local Kiwanis Club, and we'd be run out of town on a rail. Or worse, thrown into jail, where we'd sit around, missing our next four gigs where we really *might* get paid.

It was an old story, one that I'm sure I'd heard at least as often as Willie and the boys in his band. So, after another half hour or so of name-calling and fist-shaking, we gave it up and started clearing out. As you can imagine, everyone was fit to be tied by this time, tired and disgusted, with nothing to look forward to but another six-hour drive to the next show. But at least my partners in misery *had* somewhere else to go and the means to get there. Midland had been the last stop on my pathetic Texas tour, and without the payout I'd been counting on from that last show, I had no way to get back to Grand Rapids.

I stood around in the parking lot as James and the rest of the band threw the equipment into the back of a beat-up old Ford Econoline van that served as their tour bus and tried to keep my distance while I figured out what to do. I kept an eye out for Willie, but he was nowhere to be seen until Walter shoved his snare drum in the back and slammed the van doors. It was then, right on cue, that I saw Willie come out the door of another honky-tonk halfway up the block and, sauntering on down the deserted street, climb into the front seat. There was something sad about that small, slight figure silhouetted against the big empty Texas sky that even his dapper clothes and fancy jewelry couldn't hide. Willie Mitchell may have been an man of impeccable style, but out there by the side of the road in a strange and unfriendly town, he was just one more poor out-of-place soul.

James got behind the wheel and started the van. They pulled down the driveway beside the roadhouse leading out to the street and beyond, where the stoplight swayed overhead in the wind. As I watched the van disappear around the corner of the building, I knew I'd have to make my move now or never. I ran after it and was about to shout out, "Hold up, for pity's sake, don't leave me here to die," when I heard the sound of squealing brakes. I turned the corner of the building to see the driveway blocked by the road-house owner's big white Cadillac Coupe DeVille and James standing at the open door of the van, cursing heaven and earth with more imagination than a poet in love.

Willie and the others let him rave on for a few minutes before sending him off again to fetch the owner and, in the silence that followed, I made my way up to the door of the van and poked my head in.

"So where y'all headin'?" I asked as casually as I could manage.

Willie turned in the half-light from the dashboard, his eyes heavy-lidded and half-closed. "We got a few dates up around Memphis," he said. "Then we're goin' home."

"Lord, that sounds *good*," said a weary voice from the back of the van.

"Listen," I said, talking fast to keep my courage going, "this gig was gonna get me back to Grand Rapids. Now I got no way to get there. You suppose I might hitch a hide with you as far as Memphis? I'd be five hundred miles closer to home."

Willie looked at me and, in that uncertain light, there was no way I could read what was going on behind his eyes. A long moment passed and I made sure he could see me shudder as another gust of wind blew across the parking lot.

"Well," he said at last, "we ain't got much room in here." There was another long pause as he considered—or pretended to consider—the situation. "But if you don't mind sittin' on the floor. . ."

And with that, he opened the door and I hopped in, squeezing into place between him and James.

Looking back and recalling that scene just makes me smile. I think Willie knew all along he was going to give me a ride. He might have even known I was going to ask for one. He was always thinking three steps ahead of everyone else, but, as I said, he just had to make sure it worked out so, in the end, you came to him and not the other way around. In fact, if I had to venture a guess, I'd say Willie knew we were going to link up from the moment he heard me open my mouth up onstage and give a new twist to the old "Back Up Train." But he was a master of the smooth move, sly as a snake and patient as a possum, and he wanted to make sure I knew who was beholden to whom.

Yet even as we pulled out onto the interstate and James pointed the blunt nose of that van to the north and east, I couldn't help but feel what I'd felt earlier that evening, watching Willie do his tired old act one more time. There was a *reason* he was giving me a ride, showing a kindness, and taking an interest, and it wasn't solely from the goodness of his heart. He saw and heard something in me, something that could—sooner or later—do him some good.

For the rest of that long night and well into the dawn of the next day, while the boys in the band sawed logs in the back and James kept the van pointed straight and true toward home, Willie and I talked. We must have turned over most everything we could think of in those lonely hours, from the kind of music we liked to the styles of clothes that suited us. I rambled through my personal history in detail, embellishing or skipping over as the case demanded, and he did the same. We agreed and disagreed and sometimes we agreed to disagree and, as the miles rolled by, a friendship began to be forged like none that I had ever known before or since.

Willie was a good deal older than me, of course, and in that respect, part of what drew me to him was that he filled the role of a father, vacant since that day I had marched out of the apartment and turned my back on my daddy's plans for my life. Willie had experience and knowledge in the world of music, and those were things I sorely felt the lack of in myself. I knew enough to know that I needed someone to look out for me if I was ever going to make it in this business, which, come to think of it, was another reason I looked up to him, like a son to a father. Willie *had* made something of himself, taken his talents and abilities and turned them into a going concern, a kind of one-man corporation dedicated to the enrichment of Willie Mitchell, sole owner and primary stockholder. He was an entrepreneur, and the more he talked about the things he'd done— the musicians he worked with, the artists he discovered, the records he'd produced, the songs he'd written—the greater my admiration grew. Willie Mitchell was his *own* man, self-taught and totally independent, trusting his own ears and taking his own counsel.

But there was also another element to my growing friendship with Willie, sprung up almost from the moment I met him. Despite our difference in age and experience, we were, in another way, equals. In Scripture there are many parables about the potter and the clay, and when it comes to spiritual realms, the picture holds true: God molds us and shapes us according to His will. But here on earth, that relationship takes on a whole new meaning. The potter shapes the clay, just like Willie would shape me and my music in the years to come. But without the clay, the potter can't do his job. He's a man without purpose. Willie *needed* me—or someone like me—young, impressionable, and willing to learn. That mutual dependence was the most important part of our friendship from the very beginning, something we both recognized and respected. It was the basis from which everything else would grow.

Grow, that is, in time. Riding east that morning along the edge of a new day, heading across the Mississippi and over the familiar folds of Arkansas field and forest, it was still Willie calling the shots. Whatever was going to happen next was going to be up to him. He'd have to trust his own instincts when it came to taking a chance on me.

"So tell me," he said after the sun had been up an hour or so and the Texas cold was finally leached out of our bones by the warm throb of the engine. "Whatever got it into your head to want to be a singer in the first place?"

"I'm good," I shot back. "That's not bragging. It's just true."

Willie snorted. "Lot of folks good," he replied. "That don't mean they got what it takes."

"So what does it take?" I challenged him.

"Oh, you know," he laughed. "You got to stick to it."

It was my turn to laugh. "That all? I've been at this pretty near my whole life. I guess you could say I've been stickin' to it."

"So how come you ain't a star?" he asked, his voice low again under the hum of the tires on the road.

I looked up at him sharply. "I will be." I said. "That's for sure."

There was another one of those long silences when I could almost hear the gears meshing in his head. "I believe you will," he said at last. "I believe you will."

We both settled back, letting the words resonate. Beside me, I could sense James listening, taking in the whole conversation as he watched his brother make his moves. "Of course," I said, breaking the spell, "can't do it alone."

"No indeed," said Willie like an old sage.

"I'd need someone to kind of guide me along . . . point me in the right direction . . . you know, get behind me all the way."

"You got someone in mind?" Willie said, turning to face me for the first time.

I swallowed hard. "You think you could make me a star, Mr. Mitchell?" I asked.

He answered without a moment's hesitation. "I believe I could."

"And how long do you think that might take?"

Willie thought on it. I turned to look at James, who winked with one eye and kept the other on the road.

"I'd say about a year," Willie answered at last. "Maybe a year and a half."

My heart sank. *A year and a half!* I thought, *Why doesn't he just say it'll take an eternity!*

"I can't wait that long," I said with a little tremor in my voice.

Willie laughed. "Oh, so you got somethin' better to do with your time?"

"Mr. Mitchell," I replied, "please don't misunderstand. I want to be a singer more than anything. But I've been at this for so long, even if I started making money tomorrow, I'd have to work seven days a week just to pay myself back for all the time I've already put in. I got a hit record. I played the Apollo . . . nine encores, like I told you. I'm ready to be a star *now*!"

I stopped as much to catch my breath as to collect my thoughts. It's a funny thing when you're young and headstrong. You might know that life isn't fair, but you just don't want to believe it. I'd already worked so long and hard and I just couldn't get over the feeling that my dues had long since been paid up. It was time to collect. Now.

Willie just looked at me. "Al," he said. "You've come a long way, I'll give you that. But you still got a long way to go. You can give up now or keep going. That's up to you. But if you decide you want to put in the effort, then I'll be right there beside you. That's the very best I can do." He stuck out his hand and I shook it, even while I was shaking my head.

"I appreciate your offer, Mr. Mitchell," I said. "But a year and a half . . . I just don't know if I can wait that long."

Willie looked over to James and the two of them shared a glance, long-suffering and half-amused at the same time. It was then I noticed that we were pulling across the bridge from Arkansas into Tennessee with the skyline of Memphis laid out in front of us.

"Well," said Willie, lighting another cigarette. "You think about it. Give me an answer when you're good and ready."

"Where can we drop you, son?" said James, speaking for the first time since the trip had begun.

"Oh, just out the interstate, I guess," I answered as my mind churned. I couldn't quite believe that this portentous encounter was about to come to nothing. Something still needed to happen, some bargain or pact between me and Willie that would keep the connection alive. While I wasn't about to commit the next eighteen months to his plan for stardom, I wasn't quite ready to fall back on my own devices, either. Somehow I needed to keep him interested.

"Mr. Mitchell," I said. "I wonder if you might do me a favor."

"What's that?" said Willie with that same rueful smile he still shared with James.

"Well," I said, "I owe some people some money back in Grand Rapids. A couple of thousand dollars for some studio time. And I was wondering if you might see your way clear to . . . maybe advancing me a loan . . . until we hook up again."

On the other side of me, James did a double-take, and, I'll have to admit, it took some nerve. But since I couldn't think of anything I could leave Willie Mitchell with, I figured maybe I could take something from him that he'd remember.

"Let me get this straight," said Willie. "We just met last night and you want me to give you two thousand dollars. Just like that."

"It's a loan," I corrected him. "And all I really owe is eighteen hundred. I just figured I'd round it out and use the rest for some breakfast and a bus ticket home, plus a little spending cash." I flashed him my broadest smile. Whatever else he might remember about this night we'd spent together, I was pretty sure he'd never forget me now.

" 'Round it out,' " he repeated, stroking his chin as James pulled into the morning traffic of the Memphis commute. I waited, unsure whether he was getting ready to chuck me out onto the side of the road. Just then, we came alongside a gas station. "Pull over," Willie said to his brother and we both watched while he strolled over to a pay phone and made a call.

He was back a few minutes later and from the deadpan look on his face I couldn't have told you what he was thinking. He climbed back into the van, shot his cuffs, and straightened his conk with the flat of his hand.

"Take us on down to the bank, James," he said, as easy as if he were ordering a side of hash browns to go with his eggs and coffee. "We've got a withdrawal to make."

CHAPTER 21

Years later, I would find out that the call Willie placed that morning was to Joe Cuoghi, owner of Hi Records, asking for a $2,000 signing advance to bring a promising young kid to the label. I don't know where Willie got the kind of confidence to know that, one way or the other, we were going to be working together, but as things turned out, his instincts didn't let him down.

With Willie's—and Mr. Cuoghi's—money in my pocket, I made it back to Grand Rapids with as much style as I could muster, paid back Lee and his fellow session financiers.

Or maybe, in the back of my mind, I knew what it really was— a going-away present. Going away for good. On the bus from Memphis to Grand Rapids, I'd had plenty of time to turn over everything that had—and hadn't—happened to me in the past few years, and while I still wasn't quite ready to agree to Willie Mitchell's timetable for success, it was hard to deny that my own schedule hadn't brought me any closer to making my dreams come true.

From that train of thought, it didn't take long before I'd opened up my whole life to the prying eye of honest evaluation and began to see that, pretty much from that first night I'd been thrown out of the house to fend for myself, I'd been letting circumstances take charge of me, instead of the other way around. Sure, I had my ambitions and goals, but more often than not, I'd find myself falling into situations that would take me in one direction or the other. I was like a ship without a rudder, and as I rode along, staring out the window at the endless rolling landscape, I remembered a verse of Scripture that had always given me pause when I heard it quoted. "Without vision," the Bible says, "the people perish." I'd been going along to get along for so long now that I'd lost sight of the reward at the end of all my striving. Maybe Willie Mitchell was right. I had come a long way. But I still had a long way to go. And somewhere between starting out and finishing, I lost my way.

I looked back over the years I'd spent knocking around the streets of Grand Rapids, going to school, working in the car wash, hanging out on the corner, and making music with my friends. And suddenly, at the distance I found myself then, tired and defeated and worn down by the road, it all seemed like pictures from someone else's life and times. *The boy who lived that life*, I thought to myself, *never grew up. I just traded one family, my real one, for another, the hookers and hustlers who took me in and turned me out.* In a very real way, I hadn't grown a single day since I left home at age eighteen. I was still looking for whatever I was after when I slammed the door behind me and headed down the avenue with a cardboard box in my hands. Only now I was going on twenty-one and I didn't even have the cardboard box to show for my efforts.

It wasn't anybody's fault but my own, least of all Juanita's, who had only wanted someone around to share a little tenderness, even innocence, in the midst of all that was so cruel and degrading in her life. But that strange kind of man-and-woman, mother-and-child love affair that had kept us together these past few years had also kept me from finding my own independence. As much as I didn't want to look at it, the plain fact was, I was Juanita's little boy, the child she never had, nor ever could have.

I'm just like any other man when it comes right down to it, I guess: Women are a puzzlement to me. Half the time, I'm trying to figure out what they want, and the other half, trying to figure out how to get it for them. But I'm not like other men when it comes to the tender regard I feel for the female sex. I've always known that femininity is a godly virtue and that a mother's love is as close to God's unconditional acceptance as we can find in this world. I know that without the love of a woman, the world is a hard, dry, and unforgiving place. I know that our Creator fashioned the love between and man and a woman as a holy sacrament and, speaking personally, I could not live without it. I've never believed in the war between the sexes. I know that man makes war, wanting to conquer and dominate. But woman seeks peace, comfort, and to extend the sweet encompassing bower of her love.

It's beneath that bower that we find the true intent of God's purpose for joining together Adam and Eve, but there comes a time when a man—if he is to be a man—must step out from that protection and claim his own place in the world. That time had come for me. Juanita was as much a mother to me as she ever was a lover. But the time had come for me to let go of both sides of her.

The truth is, I told myself as I walked down the familiar blocks of Division Street toward our apartment in a pale midwinter afternoon, *that the time has come for her to let go as well.* The life of a street whore, no matter what clientele she might serve, isn't but ten or fifteen years on the outside. By then, you're almost certain to have pulled one too many wrong tricks, or gotten yourself a drug habit to ease the pain, or found yourself in jail for something your so-called friends got you mixed up in, or any one of a dozen other hazards of the occupation. Or if you don't turn up dead, you're sure to start losing your charms, looking ten years older than your time and losing customers to the young ones coming up hard behind you.

I'd seen it happen more than once in my time on the streets and I could already see it happening to Juanita. No matter how good she was with makeup and sexy clothes and the pure sass and attitude that had always attracted men to her, it was getting harder and harder for her to disguise that deep-down bone weariness that comes with the life and eats away at your looks until you're carrying around that gaunt, hollow-eyed stare that scares away the customers. If there was anything I was doing that was keeping Juanita from facing up to the consequences of her choices—even if it was just being there at the end of the day with a comforting touch and a kind word—well, let's just say that I didn't want to have to carry that burden of guilt. What I wanted for her, I wanted for myself. A clean break. A new beginning. A fresh start.

It was nearly dark by the time I made it back to our apartment, and as I opened the front door and walked into that crowded, overheated flat, I could smell her perfume from the night before hanging heavy in the stale air. All the blinds were closed, of course—Juanita wanted day to be dark as night when she was trying to sleep—and I could just barely make out her frail figure on the bed, huddled under a comforter and surrounded by her stuffed animals.

I sat down next to her as gently as I could and waited a few minutes, trying to put together the words I would say. I guess she must have felt my weight next to her because she stirred and turned and, for the first time, I could see that she had a black eye and an ugly bruise across her cheek.

I opened my mouth to ask her what happened, even though I already knew—another sadistic john, another alleyway brawl, another cop looking for his hush money—it was a too-sad story and before I could say a word, she reached up her hand to hush me, then reached around to hold on for dear life, crying on my shoulder like a little child.

I let her wear herself out like that, stroking her hair and rocking her back and forth until she drifted back into sleep, then gently laid her down and sat alone as the shadows of twilight drew up and the streetlights flickered on outside the windows. I must have sat like that for an hour, looking down at her face, peaceful and untroubled on her lacy pillow, her breath soft and easy, for all the world a little girl again. I thought about waking her up or writing a note, but when it came to choosing the words I might use, the thoughts just cinched up into a tight coil of sorrow and regret. The little room that we shared held just about everything we had to show for the life we'd lived together—some clothes with spangles and beads, a mismatched set of pots and dishes, a stack of movie magazines and record albums. It didn't seem like much, hardly enough to keep one person occupied, much less hold two people together. There were the good times, of course, or memories of them, anyway. But sitting there in the darkness, it was hard to bring them back to life, to remember those times when all we had was each other and that was all we needed. It was as if the whole time we'd been together had been leading up to this moment when we'd come apart, as if that very day we'd seen each other on the street outside Mother Bates's, a clock had started ticking, counting down the seconds to this very moment. And everything in between had just been marking time.

In the end, I just got up and walked away, leaving behind that sad bundle of flowers, already beginning to wilt in the stuffy air. Whatever I'd wanted to say, whatever words I imagined might ease the pain for both of us, just never came to mind. Maybe the saddest thing in life is what you never get to say. Or maybe it's that you don't how to say it. But I think the saddest of all is knowing that, no matter what you say, it won't do a living soul a bit of good.

I made my way down Division Street as the shop owners shuttered up their windows for the night and the bars switched on their neon signs. The old neighborhood felt small and shrunk, or maybe it was that I felt bigger, like a man who comes back to his boyhood haunts and is surprised to find how little everything has become. I guess the feeling I struggled with was of not belonging anymore, of outgrowing my own home and history but still with no other place to go. I could have been a ghost—or so it appeared to me—as the people on the street seemed to look right through me and the white puffs of cold air I breathed might as well have been my evaporating soul.

I found my way over to Lee's, wanting at least to settle accounts before I disappeared entirely and, while my old friend seemed happy enough to see me—inviting me to pull up a chair at the familiar kitchen table and share the supper his wife had just laid out—I felt as strange and unreal there as I had back out on the street.

Lee wanted to know everything I'd been up to since we'd folded the Soul Mates and, while I did my best to paint a rosy picture of my solo career, I think we both felt the weight of lost potential and wasted time pressing heavily on us. It was one of those uncomfortable reunions, where the bonds are frayed and you know you've passed on to different worlds, but you just keep talking anyway because you're afraid of the silence when there's nothing left to say.

But finally, the words just kind of washed away like water down a drain and we stared at our plates while the clock on the stove loudly marked the passing minutes. I dug into my pocket for the wad of bills Willie had left me with.

"Here," I said, passing it over. "I wanted to pay you back. You know, for that studio time a while back."

Lee took the roll and flipped it through his fingers. I could see he was thinking about something, trying to pull it down and put it into words. "You know, Al," he said finally, "we had some good times."

"We surely did," I agreed.

"You remember the Apollo?" he asked, his face lighting up.

I laughed. "I'll never forget it," I said, and we warmed our-selves in the glow of that memory until it faded away and left us where we were, back in the kitchen.

"Look," he said after a moment. "You're gonna make it, Al. I know you are. You got what it takes. What the rest of us only pre-tended we had." Lee reached over and handed me back the money. "I got a good job now. On the line over at Ford. I don't need this. You take it."

"I couldn't do that, Lee," I said.

"No. I mean it," he insisted. "I want you to know. I believe in you. I always have. Just call it . . . an investment."

I looked at the money in his hand, felt the walls of the kitchen pressing in on me with all the weight of the past we had shared. Just out that back door was the porch, where I'd spent so many restless nights, dreaming of Jackie Wilson. And out beyond, in the backyard, was the tree where I could hear the birds singing to greet the day each morning on my way to the car wash. I wanted to stop it all, slow it down and take a good look, one that would last me a lifetime, one I could fix in my mind forever. But even as I took back the bills, put them in my pocket, pushed back my chair, and got to my feet, I knew it was slipping away.

That fading feeling, like a spoonful of sugar dissolving in a glass of water, stayed with me as I headed across town to my next stop: the apartment my family had moved into a few years before. They were definitely moving up in the world—the place had enough bedrooms for the kids that were left and even a small back-yard where Mama could hang her washing and Daddy could cook up some of his famous barbecue on a Saturday afternoon. Even though I'd never lived in the place, all the old familiar smells and sounds were there to greet me as I walked in the front door, and I could always depend on my brothers and sisters, Mama, and even Daddy to greet me like the conquering hero whenever I managed to make it home. Maybe there I could find what I was looking for, that solid sense of belonging that settles deep down inside of you when you know you're where you belong.

And sure enough, everyone jumped up and gathered around me as soon as I walked through the door. From the look in their eyes, I might as well have just returned from a command performance for the crowned heads of Europe. I don't know whether they just didn't see my tattered clothes and dirty hair or whether they just chose to ignore it, but when my mama felt at my ribs, shook her head, and clucked her tongue, I was sure that at least she knew I wasn't exactly living high off the hog.

I think Daddy knew, too. Later that evening, after everyone had gone to bed and it was just him and me sitting up alone, he fixed me with one of his strong and penetrating looks, not saying a word until I started to squirm uncomfortably.

"What're are you fixin' to do now, Albert?" he asked me, but from the tone of his voice I could tell he wasn't coming at me as he might have years ago. He and I both knew that whatever he had for me—wisdom or warning—he'd handed out long ago. Something had changed in the old man since the days when he looked to me and my brothers to fulfill his dreams. It was like he'd come to terms with himself, all his shortcomings and failures, and had found a way to accept, once and for all, what was and what could never be. And now that his dreams had been put to rest, it was like he was interested, for the first time, in mine.

"Well, Daddy," I said as outside the window the lights of passing traffic moved by like solemn ghosts, "I met a man a while back said maybe he could help get me where I'm trying to go."

"Where's that, son?" he asked gently, as if he didn't want the question to ruffle the calm that had come between us.

I looked at him, his hard black eyes and the thrust of his jaw softer now and weakened with age. I remembered him coming in off the fields after a long day's work, the way he sat in the chair and looked at his hands while he waited for Mama to put out supper. I remembered the anger that flashed in those eyes when he counted out $800 cash for a whole year's work and the joy that had flooded forth when he made the decision to pack us all up and look for a better life. I remembered the unbending will that had sought to break me as he broke my Jackie Wilson and James Brown records, bending them double in his fist until they shattered. And I remembered the sorrowful weariness that he carried with him like a stone in his shoe after a day washing down other men's cars. I loved my daddy, just then, maybe more than I'd ever loved him before, and I had to ask myself, too, what I was seeking that couldn't be found here, under his roof.

"I used to know," I said, as much to myself as to him. "But now . . . well, I'm not so sure anymore."

CHAPTER 22

After I cleaned the road dust from between my toes and got a good night's sleep, I took the money that Lee had given back to me and bought a pretty decent ride—a '58 Ford Fairlane with good upholstery, an odometer that looked to be turned over only once, and an oil leak that didn't use up but a quart a day. I went down to Klein's, bought myself some new socks and underwear, a couple pair of trousers, and even a french-cut silk shirt I could use onstage should the occasion arise. Along with a few bags of groceries, a full tank of gas, and a road map, I was ready to roll.

Heading south, back along the highway I'd so recently returned on, I had plenty of time to lay out my game plan for when I got to Memphis. The last thing I wanted was to come off too anxious, like I didn't have any other options or opportunities, which, of course, I didn't. But Mr. Willie Mitchell was none the wiser that I was riding around with everything I owned in the back of an old '58 Ford, and I intended to keep it that way. My strategy was simple—to play it cool, keep him guessing, and make sure he knew he wasn't dealing with a fool who'd just dropped off the turnip truck.

The dreary overcast sky that had followed me all the way up

from Texas began to burn off by the time I made it to the Indiana border, and it turned into one of those rare and glorious late-winter afternoons when I pushed through to Kentucky, the sky as bright and clear as a clean window and the air so sharp with cold it felt like breathing crystals when I rolled down the window and let the wind whip away the cobwebs in my brain. The low swell of the hills unrolled beneath my wheels in a soothing, swaying rhythm and I began to feel, for the first time in a long time, a hope and optimism for what this day—and the next—might bring. God's grace gave me strength and from the infilling of my spirit, joy sprang forth and I began to sing—for the first time in as long as I could remember—for no one and no reason besides me and the moment.

I still had a few hundred dollars left over and treated myself to a Motel 6 that night, falling asleep as soon as my head hit the pillow. I woke up rested and fresh, that feeling of new freedom settling in my soul like a melody that carries you through the day. After a big breakfast, I was back on the highway, and as Kentucky took its time scrolling past the window, I began to rehearse just what I'd say to Willie Mitchell when we met. I really laid down the law that morning, insisting on all sorts of conditions and provisos to any partnership he might propose. If he was going to take charge of my career, well, then, I was definitely going to have some say in the direction we took and the way we got there. If my years at the bottom rung of show business had taught me anything, it was that no one should have a bigger percentage in your career than you do . . . unless you give it to them.

I had a pretty good idea what was behind my newfound mentor's offer to begin with. Ever since it got started back in the mid-fifties with a hit called "Smokie—Part 2" by the Bill Black Combo, Hi Records had pretty much been known as an instrumental label. They scored chart records with artists like Reggie Young, the gui-

tarist for Bill Black; the "yakety sax" of Ace Cannon; and of course, Willie Mitchell himself, who, as a trumpet player, weighed in with his own trademark instrumentals. Now, listening to someone play a horn, no matter how good they might be, only has a limited appeal. It's a man's voice that gives him his personal stamp to the public, and although Willie had worked with promising young singers, like O. V. Wright, who he produced for Don Robey's Backbeat label, he had yet to strike gold with a singer for Hi, even though the owner, Mr. Cuoghi, was trying to stay in the game with a roster of second-string rockabilly hiccupers.

At the same time, Memphis music itself was going through some major changes. Stax, the city's powerhouse label, wasn't racking up the big sales and radio hits that they'd had in their earlier heyday and the whole era of the blood-and-thunder soul shouter was fading away as audiences, black and white, started favoring a smoother, more sophisticated sound. Mind you, I was still very much in the Otis and Jackie mold myself, ready for any excuse to get loud and loose, but although I wasn't sure what the music of the new decade might sound like, I was sure *something* different was on its way. And I figured Willie Mitchell was as tuned in to any shifts in the musical wind as I was.

If he's willing to take a year and a half to shape and mold me into a singer he thinks could make it, well, then, I must be every bit as good as I already know I am! At least, that's what I told myself as I crossed over into Tennessee and followed the interstate signs straight to Memphis. But as I pulled closer into town and the sun began its long, slow drop off the other side of the Mississippi, I could feel my confidence begin to wane a little, as well. I guess I'd never bothered to ask myself, up until then, what exactly I might do if this long shot I'd bet everything on didn't work out. I'd pretty much already burned every bridge between me and Grand Rapids and, besides, even if I *could* go back, what would I be going back to? That life was over for me. The only one that remained was still laid out beyond my front tires, around the bend where only the unknown was waiting. *Maybe the best thing to do is throw myself on Mr. Mitchell's Italian loafers, beg for mercy, and be happy singing doo-wops for stars who've already proven they have what it takes.*

My mind went back and forth like that for a good long time as I drove through a neighborhood of modest brick houses and pocket parks, looking for the address that Willie Mitchell had given me. And even when I realized I wasn't but half a block away, I turned the first corner I could find and circled around a few times, just to get my nerve back up.

When I finally parked, I made sure it was well down the street, so he wouldn't be able to see the Ford's rusted fenders or my worldly possessions piled up in the backseat. I walked up to the gate and, before I had a chance to change my mind again, pushed it open and barged down the front walk.

As I got closer to the house, I noticed, from the construction tools and lumber on the front lawn, that some sort of remodeling was going on. *Mr. Willie Mitchell must be doing all right for himself,* I thought, not sure whether it was a good or a bad sign. I rang the front doorbell and waited, my breath held tight, for someone to answer.

A minute passed that seemed like five. Then another, which seemed like ten. I rang the bell again and waited, half-relieved. *Maybe he isn't home and I'll have to come back again . . . maybe.* Just then I heard a stirring in the house and a voice called out. "You can come on around the back!"

It sounded like the man I'd met, but I couldn't be sure and the only way to find out was to follow the path around the side of the house to the rear door, which had been left swinging wide open. I walked through and into the kitchen, which was obviously going through some kind of major upgrade, what with all the carpentry equipment and timber lying around. I stood there for a moment, trying to figure out what to do next, when I heard the voice again, coming from farther inside the house.

"I was thinking of a nice avocado green with a peach trim. Something to go with the new appliances."

"Sounds very charming," I said with a smile. I was obviously being mistaken for someone else.

" 'Charming' I don't care about," Willie Mitchell said as he came through the dining room door. "I want it cheap."

"I'll do it for eighteen hundred dollars," I said. "That'll bring us even."

He stopped when he saw me and matched my smile with one of his own. "Albert!" he said. "I thought you were the painter, son!" He laughed, long and loud, a liberating sound that did a lot to soothe my nerves. His warm greeting and real happiness in seeing me again were a little like a homecoming and, after clearing away old ceiling plaster and a drop cloth, he sat me down and poured me a cup of coffee.

"I was beginning to wonder if I was ever gonna see you again, Albert," he said. "You seemed so doubtful about whether I could help you out."

"I've still got my doubts," I said, looking him right in the eye but keeping my smiles turned on bright. "But I didn't want you to think I'd just run off with your money."

That brought about another gale of laughter. "Never gave it another thought," Willie said, then he winked. "I knew you and I had an understanding."

I stood up and walked to the kitchen window. Outside I could see Willie's next-door neighbor, hanging her family's laundry from a line. It was a quiet little neighborhood, nothing too grand, the kind of place where you might expect a shopkeeper or a civil service man to live. I liked what it said about Willie. Here was a man comfortable in his own skin, with nothing he needed to prove to anyone else. "So," I said, turning back to face him, "is this where you make the records?"

"Lord, no," said Willie. "I got a whole setup across town." He rose up from his chair. "C'mon. I'll take you over and show you around. I believe Teenie and the boys are out there now, laying down some tracks."

Willie's house may have been modest, but his ride was as flashy as you'd ever want to see, a big old Fleetwood with all the trimming, kept spotless in a garage behind the house. As we pulled out and drove down the street, I saw him cast a quick eye on my beat-up old Fairlane with its pile of worldly goods heaped up in back, but he never said a word about it, passing the time instead asking about my visit home and my trip down to Memphis. While we talked, the neighborhood passing by began to get a little more rough-and-tumble, the street broken with abandoned storefronts and the wrecks of cars, the curbs choked with weeds and crumbling onto the street. We pulled up to a building sitting on a corner lot in a block of small wooden houses on South Launderdale Avenue and Willie, with a grand gesture, announced, "Welcome to the Royal Recording Studios."

The place didn't look to me like a recording studio—although I really had no idea what a studio *should* look like. It just seemed out of place, sitting all alone on that lot, with some big double doors set in off the street at the back of a wide foyer. Willie escorted me in and the first thing I saw was a large open room where the front hallway should have been. At the back of the room, a plywood wall had been built and off to one side was what looked to all the world like an empty candy counter.

"Right this way," said Willie, as if he were showing me the penthouse suite at the Waldorf-Astoria Hotel, and I followed him back down a narrow corridor that had also been built up out of unpainted plywood. The whole place, in fact, looked like it had been thrown together the week before by a carpenter crew on their very first job.

"What kind of place is this?" I asked as the corridor opened up into a another big room with a floor that slanted down along one side and a glassed-in booth built up high along the opposite wall.

"Oh, it used to be a movie house," answered Willie. "The Royal Theater. In fact, that's where we took the name." Suddenly it all made sense. The big old lobby. The candy counter. And now this, a theater with the sloping floor, all the chairs ripped out and the screen taken down. I figured the sound booth must have been where the projectionist once sat.

Down at the far end of the room, the Hodges brothers and Al Jackson had set up their equipment and were running down some simple riffs, warming up for the evening's work. With them was another drummer I didn't recognize from the Texas show, a big, soft-spoken guy that Willie introduced to me as "Bulldog," because of the way he would hang on the rhythm of a song and never let go. His real name was Howard Grimes, and he had once played for Rufus Thomas and would sit in for Al Jr. when his time was taken up with the MGs. Everybody seemed laid-back and at their ease, like they were used to spending their daylight—and probably nighttime—hours tucked away in this windowless cave, with acoustic padding stapled up on the walls and that tilt to the floor that always kept you a little off balance. And if anybody had told me back then that I'd get used to it, too; that I'd come to consider it my second home, as familiar to me as anyplace I'd lived, well, I don't know whether I'd have laughed out loud or broke down crying.

I was only half-listening as Willie continued the tour, explaining to me how the slanted floor actually enhanced the sound of the recording sessions by making the music bigger as it traveled across that space. I didn't know quite what to expect and, given my attitude going in—that Willie would have to prove to me that he could do what he claimed— I was more than a little shaken up to see a place that looked more like someone's idea of a Halloween funhouse than a place to actually make music. Maybe Willie and his partners were faking it as much as I was. Maybe this was all a case of the blind leading the deaf, round and round in an old abandoned movie palace.

My misgivings weren't much relieved when I got a look at the recording booth. Two four-track tube-amplified Ampex recorders that looked like they'd been salvaged from a fire sale had been set up overlooking the theater studio, and while I didn't know much about the technical side of recording equipment, I knew that a four-track, even two of them, was hardly what you'd call state-of-the-art.

"Eight tracks," I said, trying to keep the skepticism out of my voice. "That enough to do what you need to do?"

"Oh sure," said Willie. "Most of the time I don't use but four, anyway. I got drums on one, bass on another, keyboards and guitar on one, and hold out one for the vocals. I think it works much better that way than having everything all separated out. The whole song sticks together better."

What with that four-track sticking it together, and the studio floor making it get bigger, I was wondering how Willie's music didn't keep from pulling itself apart, but I kept my peace. Willie was going on, singing the praises of his backing band and declaring how they could find each other's groove in a lightning storm in the dead of night, and I just stood there, nodding politely and wondering what exactly I'd gotten myself into.

"Well," said Willie after he ran out of things to brag on. "What do you think of our little setup here?"

I looked at him, then out the dusty glass window of the booth to where Al and Flick were thumping out the rhythm section of a song that sounded at the moment like a funeral dirge. I turned to Willie, whose grin never faltered, and said, as kindly and gently as I could, "I certainly appreciate you showing me around, Mr. Mitchell. And I'll be getting back to you. Real soon."

CHAPTER **23**

I spent the next three days hanging around Memphis, sleeping in my cars and passing the time sitting in the lobby of the Peabody Hotel, watching the fine folks promenading around in their evening wear, until the security guards escorted me out. One day I even took a ride over the bridge to Arkansas and paid a visit to Jacknash, the first time I'd been back to the cradle of my birth since we'd packed up and left back in '55.

In the fourteen years since I'd been gone, the place had changed more than I could have possibly imagined; the best way I can describe what had happened is to say that I drove up and down those country roads for over two hours looking for the town before I realized that it simply didn't exist anymore. Jacknash had just dried up and blown away like an old corn husk, and the same was true of Dansby, the town where I'd been born. All that was left of either of them was a wide spot by the side of the road, and even Taylor's Chapel and the House of the Living God had vanished, leaving only the faint traces of their foundations laid out on empty lots.

As I stood by the fallow fields halfway between where the two towns used to be and listened to crows talking loudly at each other down in the river brake, a strange and lonely feeling crept over me, like I was the last man on earth, paying a final visit to the place where he'd once known the warmth and comfort of human companionship. It wasn't true, of course. I'd lived a whole life since I last saw those wide-open fields and empty sky, but in that moment, it seemed to me that everything I could remember about my earliest days now existed only as fragments in my mind. And what would happen to those shards of memory once I was gone? It would be as if none of it had ever existed, as if the life I had lived was nothing more than a dream . . . even less than a dream, no more, really, than a shadow on a wall, here and then gone forever.

I think it was about then I decided that, whatever Willie Mitchell had to offer, I was ready to take him up on it. That slow-fading sensation, the haunting feeling that I was no more than the sum of what someone else might one day remember about me, sent a shiver up my spine that was more than I could bear. Whatever else might happen, one thing was for sure—I was going to leave something behind!

And that something was going to be music. As I climbed back in my Ford and pulled out along that deserted road, I realized that, even if the town where I was born no longer existed, what had been formed inside me from my youngest days still remained. Music was what held the memory of those times together in my mind and music was what would create the memories to come. The Bible says that all is vanity and that a man's life is nothing more than a twinkle of time in the eternity of God. It's what you do in that space of breath that counts and what lives is what you leave behind. At least, that's the way I saw it.

I showed up bright and early the next morning at Willie's house, just in time to see the painters start giving a coat of avocado green to his kitchen. That sly old fox acted like he'd been expecting me to come back the whole time, and, the fact is, maybe he had.

Like I said, Willie Mitchell was the kind of cat who waited for things to come to him. It's what gave him his power and authority and the air of respect that most everyone held for him. There was no use my pretending anymore that I had other fish to fry. Willie seemed to know that I was starting from scratch, and he also knew that I knew, without saying a word.

Instead, he took me across town to a ramshackle apartment building not too far from the Royal Studio on Haynes Street and handed over the keys to a one-bedroom flat up on the third floor. I found out later that Willie had a stashed half a dozen Hi artists in that building, including Ann Peebles and O. V. Wright, both of whom I'd get to know pretty well in the months to come. It was like a boarding school for hopeful singers, and we not only shared the same hopes and dreams, but sometimes the same plates and cups and cans of beans. It gave us a sense of solidarity and a feeling that we were all on the same team—the Hi Records team—which I'm sure was one of the reasons Willie put us all together in the first place.

Housing the young artists on his roster was a habit Willie had gotten into years before, when he'd first taken Teenie Hodges into his own home as a teenager to raise him up as a guitar player fit to his exact specifications. Willie was like that: He knew what he wanted, and if he couldn't find it, he kept looking until he found something close enough and then kept working and shaping and molding until it matched what he imagined in his mind.

In the same way, you could say Willie was an experimenter when it came to making music, but the kinds of experiments he conducted were more like putting together a jigsaw puzzle. He'd lay out all his pieces and then fool around with them, one at a time and in combination, until they started to fit together the way he wanted. It was like he was working backward, starting from a finished picture in his head and breaking it down into separate parts to see what made it work. Sometimes, if a piece didn't quite fit, he'd do a little shaving and sanding, and if it still stuck out, then he'd maybe throw it away. That didn't happen often, though. Willie Mitchell was an extraordinarily patient man.

And that was the way he worked with me, molding and shaping like a potter at the wheel, never demanding, but never ceasing to gently prod and push and caress and tease that special sound he seemed so certain was inside of me. From my point of view, it was actually a relief to have someone move in and take charge of my life and career. I'd been banging my head against the doors of success for so long I couldn't tell which way I was pointing, anymore. Willie's direction and guidance was a godsend, and it gave me a chance to relax a little bit and concentrate on the music.

Which isn't to say that I would just blindly follow the path my mentor was laying out for me. No, I was too stubborn for that and had been at the game of music for too long not to have formed some strong opinions of my own. I had been hung up for so long on being the next Otis or Jackie or Sam that I hadn't noticed the changes blowing in with the new decade and, to tell you the truth, I was a little apprehensive that the wind would sweep right past me and the change that was coming was going to leave me behind. So I just kept singing like I always had, loud and gritty and full of my mannish ways, hoping for the best.

Willie, on the other hand, had some different ideas. Mind you, he'd always been tuned in to a wider range of music than I had, and even though I knew my way around a classic jazz ballad from my days moonlighting between Creation gigs, I never considered the soft and mellow approach to be my strong suit. Of course, one reason for hanging on to what I knew best was sheer laziness. I had my soul chops down cold. To go back to the beginning, which is what Willie seemed to be suggesting every time he sat down to coach me, and develop a completely different approach was a little more than my pride could tolerate. It was like doing scales after singing grand opera.

Slowly but surely, however, I started to get the point of what Willie was driving at. "Slow it down," he'd tell me during those sessions around the piano, leaning uphill on that crazy tilted floor of the Royal Studios. "Soften it up. *Feel* what you're singing." Sometimes he'd have Teenie and Howard Grimes or Al Jackson come around and play behind me to give me an example of what he was talking about. "See," he'd say, "let *them* be gritty. You be smooth. Remember, Al. It's silky on top. Rough on the bottom."

Silky on top. Rough on the bottom. Jazz vocal style with those mellow chords and progressions laid lightly over a sandpaper-and-grits R&B rhythm section. It was a formula he had worked out to perfection—at least inside his own ears—and he was willing to wait around until I finally saw the wisdom of his ways.

Which, eventually, of course, I did. Singing softer, listening to myself, really understanding the words and feeling the melodic changes—these were all techniques that brought out the *real* soul in my music . . . and the real music in my soul. I'd spent so long fighting to be heard over the throb of a backing band cranked up to ten, or up on top of those Soul Mate harmonies when they were wailing away for all they were worth, I'd never really had a chance to hear what I actually sounded like . . . just my voice, simple and unadorned.

Well, that's not exactly true. When I was alone—in the shower, walking down Division Street, or driving along a lonesome stretch of highway from one gig to another—I'd have occasion to sing for the simple joy of it, a joy that was as old and familiar as those childhood days back in Jacknash. But without my realizing it at first, that was really what Willie was after in the first place . . . that pure pleasure that I seemed to come by naturally, issuing forth from the deepest parts of myself. It wasn't about showing off anymore, trying to hit those Jackie Wilson high notes or rattle the rafters with an Otis-brand soul growl. What Willie was trying to bring out in me was something more private and personal, something I was almost afraid to let another person hear. It was a soft, tender, vulnerable side of myself that could only express itself through singing, like a little boy crying out for his mama or a grown man weak for the love of a woman. To sing like that, you've got to let something inside of you loose, give up your pride and power, and let that surrendering feeling well up inside until it overwhelms you and uses your voice to cry out with a need that can't be filled. That's what Willie Mitchell wanted to bring me to.

And that's where we got, as those first days turned to weeks and those weeks to months. My life settled into a routine, altogether pleasant and satisfying to the Al Green who'd been trying for so long to prove himself a man in the world of men. Willie gave me the freedom to be a little boy again, to go back and relive a part of my life that had taken another direction when we'd pulled up stakes and moved to Grand Rapids, to exult again in every natural expression of God's grace and abundance and sing it from the heart. It was as if I'd been given a second chance and during those precious months I spent working with Willie and his band, I could feel some long-forgotten strength returning to my bones, like a man weakened by a long illness coming back into his own, growing stronger day by day. Willie, for his part, never let on that I was either living up to or letting down his expectations, careful not to put too much pressure on me, but simply letting the music rise up from deep inside, tapping that well of inspiration and letting the sweet oil issue forth.

Most days I'd wake up midmorning, feeling privileged and luxurious at not having any other job to report to than my music lessons. Willie always kept the cupboard of the apartment stocked with food, and while I never had more than a couple of dollars in my pocket, I never felt deprived. What did I need that I didn't have? What did I want that I couldn't ask for?

The truth was: nothing. Willie and Joe Cuoghi had worked out all the details of a recording contract with Hi and gave it to me to sign. I knew that, sooner or later, I'd have to make good on the deal, but until then I was well taken care of, like a pampered race horse in training for the Triple Crown.

After breakfast, I'd head down to the studio, where Willie seemed to have set up a permanent residence. He was always there, ready to run through one song or another he thought I might spark to, or sometimes just putting everything on hold to play the piano and run some impromptu jams with the band. I didn't realize it at the time, but those laid-back sessions were a part of my education, as well. Willie was teaching me that good music comes naturally, and when it does, you can't hurry it. The best thing to do is just to be relaxed and refreshed, ready to respond when inspiration opens up and looks for a way to express itself.

Most afternoons were spent in that aimless but instructive musical give-and-take, Willie trying out one thing or another and me working my own changes around it as the mood would strike me. By four or five o'clock, we'd all take a break, pile into Willie's Fleetwood, and head out to any one of half a dozen barbeque places on the outskirts of town or just over the border in Mississippi, where Willie was treated like visiting royalty and the meat was so tender it slipped right off the bone.

The day would generally be drawing to a close by the time we'd finished our late lunch, the sun drawing down in a misty red cloak over the river and the downtown skyline as we'd tool back to town, where Willie would drop me off at my place to get showered and dressed for the evening's festivities. We'd hit the Memphis hot spots almost every night, checking out the local talent or some star coming through on tour, most often from a front-row seat. Or sometimes, if the mood hit us, we'd take in a movie, passing a big tub of buttered popcorn back and forth and nudging each other when something on the screen pleased us. Then it was out for a late dinner, usually one of the catfish joints on the bluffs over the river, where we'd linger for hours over lemonade and corn bread, talking at length about nothing in particular.

I got to know the Hodges boys, Al Jackson, and the rest of the loose-knit family around Willie very well during those lazy days and nights, and while it was true that a bond grew up between us, as much like brothers as friends, it was also a fact that I was held in special regard by Willie's sidemen. They could all see how much time and energy Willie was investing in me and knew that, whether he told me so or not, he had some very high expectations when it came to our musical future. As a result, no matter how much they teased and taunted one another—and they could play pretty rough when they wanted to get under each other's skin—they always treated me with care, as if I were too fragile to join in their games. For my part, I just let them be. I confess I *enjoyed* feeling special and set apart. It was certainly a sensation I'd never had with my real family.

But as lackadaisical and easy-does-it as those early months in Memphis might have been, there was a slowly growing recognition that, sooner or later, we'd be getting down to business. I hadn't realized it at the time, but all during our practice sessions at the Royal Studios, Willie had been methodically putting together a list of songs he thought would be candidates for recording. That was one reason we tried out so many different styles of music—from Buck Owens and Willie Nelson country music to whatever might be climbing up the pop charts and even including Gershwin and show-tune standards—to see what I could best handle and what might lend itself to the arranging style Willie was perfecting even then. By the time we were ready to get down to some serious recording, he'd compiled a two-page collection of tunes that ran the musical gamut. I don't remember any opera on that list, but that doesn't mean he wouldn't have slipped some in if he thought we could take a run at it.

At the same time Willie was retooling my repertoire, he was also working on my appearance. Since arriving in Memphis, I'd let my hair grow out into a glorious Afro and had taken a fashion turn toward the funky, with super-wide bell-bottoms, chokers, chains, and sleeveless tie-dyed T-shirts. As long as we were we just warming up, Willie was tolerably well disposed to my hippie accessories, but as the time to take care of business got closer, he took me on a couple of shopping trips downtown and personally picked out some suits and sports coats that made me look and feel a good ten years older, even with the bright, wide ties that Willie picked out as a concession to late sixties fashion. Then one morning on the way to the studio, he took a detour and pulled up outside a barber shop.

"You want to be a star," he said, turning to me, "you got to look the part. You ready for that, Al?"

"As ready as I'll ever be," I answered, like it was nothing more than getting a haircut.

CHAPTER 24

Those first sessions got under way in the early months of 1969 and from the beginning, it was clear that all the time we'd taken warming up was well spent.

The band had been keeping their chops up with regular rehearsals since getting off the road, and it got to where they could read each other's moves in their sleep. Willie had been working out some string and horn arrangements and hiring some local guys who were every bit as polished as the Hi Rhythm Section. I never ceased to be amazed at the session players that he could pull out of his Rolodex—cats who could listen to a bar and a half of any song and play it cold in a single take.

As the date of our first session got closer, however, the question of what songs we were going to cut got to be something of a sore point between me and Willie. He presented me with a list of tunes he wanted to try—mostly stuff we'd been running through over the past several weeks and, for the most part, I was happy to oblige. But I couldn't help feeling that if this was going to be my record, my big debut as a solo artist, and my introduction to the public as Al *Green*, with no "e" at the end, that I should be singing some songs written by Al Green.

All during the time I'd been under Willie's guidance, I kept trying to remind him of the fact that I wanted to write and record my own songs. I'd bring him stuff that I'd written, and he was always patient and willing to give me an ear, along with as many pointers and suggestions as he thought I could tolerate. But when it came down to which songs we'd be cutting and which we wouldn't, he suddenly got very stubborn, and his gentle recommendations became adamant marching orders. Which, of course, made me dig in my heels just that much more. I knew what his approach to the album was—to get people used to a different kind of music by putting my newly polished voice and his smooth-as-silk arrangements to songs everyone was familiar with. It was as much of a marketing as a musical strategy and something in me reared up at being treated like a box of soap you'd buy off the shelf, just because it had a pretty package.

But Willie had too much invested in me to let it get away from him, and in the end, we reached a compromise. I could do a couple of my songs, as long as the bulk of the album followed his game plan. He even helped me to polish up one of my originals, a tune called "Tomorrow's Dream" that I'd written as a ballad and Willie turned up to midtempo and put some Otis horn changes to. I agreed to share songwriting credit on that one, but when it came to "Get Back Baby," I wanted all the glory for myself.

I probably shouldn't have bothered. "Get Back Baby," which had more than a passing resemblance to "Back Up Train," stood out from the rest of those sessions like a drunk guest at a tea party. Willie had carefully crafted the tune stack to showcase the vocal style he thought would mark me out from every other overheated soul strutter who was trying to keep the Stax/Volt legacy alive, and there I was, huffing and puffing through the changes of "Get Back Baby" like I really *was* trying to get back to the good old days. Needless to say, it was not my proudest moment on wax.

As for the rest of the album that would be released in the summer of '69 under the title *Green Is Blues*, as I listen back today, I have to admit we got off to a pretty good start. Willie knew what he was doing, sure enough, and right from the beginning it was like he was throwing down the gauntlet, drawing a line in the dust, and challenging the whole world to *"Check this out"* from the opening notes of the very first track. It was called "One Woman," a tune he'd had done especially for me by a couple of Hi Records staff writers and studio backing singers, Charlie Chalmers and Sandy Rhodes. The band steps lightly into the song, with Al laying down a simple metronome-steady beat and Teenie strumming softly along, setting down that patented less-is-more arranging style that set off the clear high note I came in on like a chiming bell floating over a fresh new morning. The words had a funny kind of sophisticated twist, picking up on the little details of a melancholy workaday world and the salvation of a good loving woman. Willie had laid over a solo flute that came up the long way on the chorus, where I let the feeling of the song swell up on a wave of horns and backing vocals. I guess what stands out to me hearing it now is how Willie gave me the space to express myself but never to wander too far out of the tight framework he built around my voice. As much as anything, "One Woman" sounds like a vocal exercise, with me running up and down scales, pulling off tight turns and fancy filigrees, and landing back on my mark in the exact nick of time. It was like Willie wanted everyone to know that the kid had chops.

The rest of *Green Is Blues* was a variation on that theme, with a couple of other Mitchell maneuvers thrown in for good measure. The idea of laying out the territory and giving notice of a new talent on the block was brought home from one track to the next by taking familiar songs and running them through Willie's clear, crisp arranging and recording. On "My Girl," I picked up where David Ruffin left off and took full advantage of all the room Willie and the band had built into the track. You can get the idea even from the distance of all those years—a song with lyrics and a melody familiar to everyone given a interpretative twist that spilt the difference between doing honor to a classic and taking it over for myself. I'd add a word or two here or there, a vocal inflection in a place the Temptations had moved right over, stepping back to let the horns come in with the refrain that had made the song a hit and then grabbing it all back again to turn it in another direction.

Or check out "The Letter," a big hit right around then for Memphis's own the Box Tops, that Willie slowed down, layered with some smoky horns and soulful backing vocals, and pushed me way out front to show off my very best pining and yearning style. We even managed to breathe some life into that old *Porgy and Bess* chestnut "Summertime," the hands-down, watch-me-do-my-stuff showboater of all time. Willie's jazz instincts served him well on that rendition, as did Leroy's rock-steady bass, mixed way up front and swinging low like a baby's cradle.

On the other hand, I can't say that, musically speaking, putting new wine in old wineskin was always the best idea. Doing a song like "The Letter" made sense because it was put together with soul ingredients to begin with. You could slow it, stretch it out, and the bones and gristle would still hang together. Willie had a notion that pop and soul sounds—that is to say, the music of blacks and whites—were going to come together sooner or later, and of course, he was right. Great innovators like Sly Stone and Jimi Hendrix proved that point beyond a doubt. But there were some round pegs that you couldn't fit into square holes, no matter how hard you hammered, as when Willie made me try to squeeze my voice around a Beatles song.

We recorded two for that session: "I Want to Hold Your Hand," which was released as the first single in April of that year, and "Get Back," which ended up on the album. Neither one of them had a

prayer of working from the beginning. The music was white rock
& roll, and British to boot, from the first note to the last, rushing
along full of words with barely a moment to take a breath and feel
what you were saying. It was music that rattled up there in some
upper register where I just didn't belong and you can hear it in the
results, with me trying to cram in little bits of emotion before hurrying off to the next verse before the band left me behind.

But Willie had his mind made up, partly because he was convinced that black artists could tap into the white rock & roll
bonanza, and partly because he had complete faith that, because
we had developed such a unique style together, we could lay it on
to any song we wanted. He wouldn't give up the notion until we
recorded my second album, when he insisted that I do a version of
the Doors' big hit "Light My Fire." The song sounded like I was
trying to catch my breath the whole time, talking through the
lyrics instead of singing them. I've got to laugh when I hear it
today.

I wasn't laughing when Hi Records released "I Want to Hold
Your Hand" and we all waited around for a week, then two, then
three, for it to make an appearance on the chart. I guess Willie's
vision of all the races united in music was still a little farther down
the road, because no one seemed quite ready for a black singer
doing a soul treatment of an British Invasion fave rave. Maybe it
was something Otis could get away with, but "I Can't Get No Satisfaction" was a song perfectly suited to his style, while "I Want to
Hold Your Hand" fit me about as well as a cheap suit.

I imagine that anyone who's been on the inside of the music
business will tell you the same thing: You can't buy a hit record,
but you sure can help one along the way. No DJ, music program-
mer, or anyone else that calls the shots at a radio station is going to
put your song in rotation, just because you slip them $50, a bag of
white powder, or the key to a hotel room and a hooker's first name.

They've got to have a *reason* to take your payola instead of someone else's, and that reason most times is because some other station
is already on the song. Like a lot of things in life, record promotion
is a real catch-22—they'll only play your song if it's already being
played. So in a strange kind of way, any one song can actually get
ahead on its own merits, because if it's going to be played, sooner
or later, it'll be because someone actually likes it.

Once that happens, then it's up to your manager, record company, or whoever else is taking a percentage of your gross to start
flashing cash to make sure your song *stays* on the playlists. That's
where payola makes the difference . . . the only difference. For
every number your song climbs up the charts, someone's got to be
greasing the wheels of the elevator and, the closer you get to the
top, the more expensive the ride gets. At least, that's the way it
worked when I was coming up, and if I was a betting man, I'd put
down even money that it hasn't changed since then.

Willie and Joe Cuoghi had invested a lot of Hi Records' time
and resources in my career up to the point where we finally
released "I Want to Hold Your Hand." After the record came out,
all they could do was step back, wait, and see. If the song caught
on in, let's say, the San Francisco Bay Area, then they'd send out a
promotion man with a suitcase full of cash to pay a visit to every
station within a hundred-mile radius. If he could hook in a few
more adds, he'd do the same thing in a circle around that station
and so on until he had a "West Coast hit." From there, maybe Mr.
Cuoghi would hire two more reps to take the song East, over the
Rockies, and down through the desert. Then of course, they'd go
out across the plains and surround the big radio markets like
Chicago or Detroit. The whole thing depended on keeping the
momentum, turning a local hit into regional hit, then into an East-
of-the-Mississippi hit, and then, if you got lucky and your cash

held out, a hit across the nation, coast to coast with the sound of renown.

But until you got that one, two, or half dozen DJs taking a chance on the tune because they actually remembered the melody, your name, or the color of the label . . . well, you had as much a shot as the next slab of black plastic.

There was nothing, it seemed, about "I Want to Hold Your Hand" that managed to stay stuck in the minds of the men that mattered, and the song just went down without a whimper.

For his part, Willie took the long view. If we didn't hit the first time, we'd come back at it again, and I must say I was relieved when he chose "One Woman" as the follow-up. At least it was more in the pocket with what I was actually about as a singer, instead of just showing off my abilities as a human jukebox. But to tell you the truth, if I'd had my way, we would have come back with "Get Back Baby," my one original tune and the closest thing to an old-fashioned soul song that we'd recorded. For all the work we'd done, and for all the faith Willie had put in me and his own vision of a new kind of pop-soul blend, I wasn't all that sure we were heading in the right direction. Maybe the world wasn't ready for this mellow, spare sound, arranged and orchestrated to within an inch of its life. Maybe what the world wanted was for its black singers to sound black, to get down and funky and stay there. Maybe Willie and I and all the rest of them were just being uppity.

When "One Woman" hardly caused a ripple, Willie and Joe turned right around and pressed "Gotta Find a New World," another song from the album, and by the time that one went down with a trace, we were already back in the studio, cutting new tracks. Whatever my doubts might have been, my partners made it plain they were in for the long haul, that they had faith in me and were going to put their money where their mouth was. And as much as anything, it was that attitude—that optimism—that kept me going.

But the truth was, the music that Willie was building around me, the way he was putting my voice right in the middle of a song and giving it room to stretch and breathe and feel its own power—all of that energy and focus that he was providing had already changed the way I was hearing myself . . . and my music. It was a change that was happening from the inside, deep down at the very source of my inspiration, and I knew that I'd been touched at my core when I woke up very early one morning with the simple notes of song echoing in my head . . . echoing so loud they wouldn't stop until I wrote them down.

I was on my way back from Detroit, where Willie had booked a date for me, just to keep me out in front of people and my live show from getting too rusty, and I had stopped off at a motel out in rural Michigan to get a few hours' sleep for the drive home. It must have been about six o'clock in the morning when I was awakened by the music in my mind. I tossed and turned for a bit, trying to get back into my dreams, but I already knew it was too late, so I switched on the nightstand light and climbed out of bed. The motel room was still and silent, with only the soft tick of the clock and the hum of the neon sign outside to disturb the peace. I found myself walking over to the window and looking out across the empty highway to the frozen fields on the other side.

As I watched while the sun slowly seeped into the dark sky, like milk being poured into a bowl, I felt myself standing in the middle of some great empty place, as if the universe and everything in it had been cleared away in a circle from all around me. It was a lonely, solitary sensation, but the strange thing was, I didn't feel the ache of a man left to himself. It was more a peaceful feeling, a kind of soothing sensation, as if I was far away from every human sorrow and strife.

I could see the trees and farmhouses start to take shape out of the shadows as the sky brightened and the stars faded at the horizon. Somewhere, far away, I heard a rooster crow and a dog bark in answer. I could still hear the melody of that dream song in my brain and, in that moment, like poets and songwriters through the ages, I tried to match words to my feelings.

It seemed to me, just then, that I might just stand there forever, in perfect peace, watching God's creation unfold in all its perfection. The morning was so pure, so beautiful that I wanted it never to end. But even as the thought came to me I realized that, with no one to share it, sooner or later I'd grow tired of being alone, tired of being on my own.

I caught my breath, turned, and sat down at the edge of the bed, searching through the nightstand drawer for a piece of paper and a pen, and wrote down the words just as they came to me, listening hard to make sure I got them all right. Half an hour later, it was finished and, after thinking on it for another moment, just as the sun rays rose up over the tops of the barren trees across the street and shined in through the window, I scratched out a title at the top of the page.

"Tired of Being Alone," it read, and underneath it, with a flourish I wrote, "by Al Green." Satisfied, I got back into bed and was asleep again before my head hit the pillow.

CHAPTER **25**

I t wasn't but a few months after we'd finished cutting *Green Is Blues* before we started work on a follow-up album, trying to avoid the mistakes and take advantage of the strengths that are always a part of the learning process in the recording studio.

Meanwhile, Willie and Mr. Cuoghi kept the embers of my career glowing by releasing another single, a song called "All Because I'm the Foolish One," recorded for the album but held back from the final tune stack. It was released right around Christmas, but it didn't seem to find too many folks in a holiday mood and it went the way of the four other ones that had already come out.

Green Is Blues was a warm-up album, there is no doubt about that. When I listen back on it, the one thing that strikes me is how short and to the point each track was. We'd set up the mood, telegraph the hook, and head for the fade almost before you knew what was happening, and even though the album didn't have but eleven tracks and timed out at just a hair over half an hour, it sounded like we were out to cover as many styles and sounds as we could fit on one album.

The next effort was going to be different. My disappointment with not getting a hit single off my debut showed itself with fresh determination to include more material I was comfortable with, songs that expressed where *I* was coming from and not some committee of Willie and Mr. Cuoghi with me as the junior partner.

Not surprisingly, Willie wasn't exactly ready to hand over the reins, and he wasn't at all convinced that doing renditions of well-known songs wasn't the best way to grab people's attention. We butted heads at more than one session over the choice of tracks, but I have to say that, in the end, Willie showed me a lot of respect, even when he was sure he knew what was best for me. I was the artist, after all, and while Willie may have been a lot of things—producer, arranger, A&R man, and record company executive—he was, first and foremost, an artist, too. He knew that if I wasn't happy with a song, it was going to come out—one way or the other—in the performance.

Which is not to say that he just rolled over and let me have my way. But as the song selection of my next album, *Al Green Gets Next to You*, shows, we were becoming experts in the art of compromise. That album pretty equally balanced covers and original songs and the result, while it didn't exactly hang together as a whole, definitely had its moments.

Some of Willie's choices were natural—"Driving Wheel," written and originally recorded by the king of barrelhouse piano players, Roosevelt Sykes, was a midtempo cooker that was perfectly suited to the percolating style that we were developing, with lots of opportunity for me to give the song the sass and strutting style that meshed so well with Willie's butter-smooth horn arrangements. The song had also been a big hit for my cousin, Junior Parker, and I was happy to keep it in the family.

By this time, the Hi Horn Section was pretty much in place, and the lineup would remain the same through most of the rest of my time at the label: Wayne Jackson played trumpet with James

Mitchell on baritone sax, Andrew Love and Ed Logan on tenor sax, and Jack Hale on trombone. They were every bit the equal of and, in my opinion, better than any of the other framed horn lineups playing in Memphis at the time.

We kept up the cooking groove of "Driving Wheel" on "Are You Lonely for Me," which had first been a hit for Freddie Scott back in 1967. Our version made good use of a trio of backing singers that would become as important to the Al Green–Willie Mitchell sound as anyone playing in the band. Willie's arranging assistant Charlie Chalmers and Sandy Rhodes, who'd written my first hit single, "One Woman," were joined by Sandy's sister Donna, and I think it never ceased to amaze people dropping in on our sessions that three white kids could create such a soulful sound between them. They would later go on to record on their own as Rhodes, Chalmers & Rhodes.

Aside from being a singer and arranger, Charlie was a fine saxophone player, whose work you can hear on a number of Hi Records releases from back in the early sixties, including some of Willie's own records. Sandra and Donna came from a musical family of high pedigree that included their uncle, Slim Rhodes, who formed the famous band the Rhodes Show back in the thirties. I remember seeing the group on television, where they hosted a local variety program broadcast out of Memphis for almost thirty years. The sister's father, Dusty, was a champion bluegrass fiddler who sometimes used the girls in his act and another uncle, Speck, had a country comedy act and made a name for himself opening shows for Dolly Parton and Porter Wagoner. It was always a great satisfaction to me that Rhodes, Chalmers & Rhodes would go on from working with me to make a name for themselves as a backing trio, singing sessions with Paul Anka, Mac Davis, and a whole lot of other people right up to this day.

Al Green Gets Next to You had a few surprises as well, some of them good, some . . . well, let's just say Willie got a little carried away with his own musical notion of remaking the hits when he insisted that I cut that version of "Light My Fire." On the other hand, "God Is Standing By" remains, to me, one of the best performances of my early career at Hi. Written by Johnny Taylor, who'd replaced Sam Cooke in the Soul Stirrers, it was one of those unmistakably great gospel progressions that took me right back to Mother Bates's revival tent and pulled out a truly heartfelt performance: natural, unforced, and brimming with feelings from a well of deep abundance.

Folks wonder, in light of everything that has happened before and since, how I felt at that point in my life and career about singing pop music in hopes of worldly success instead of giving my voice to God for His sanctifying work. The truth is, I can't say I thought too much about it at the time. I've known artists who were torn apart by the contradictions of secular and sacred music, and I would come to that crucible of conscience myself, but in that moment, I thought nothing of singing "Light My Fire" one moment and "God Is Standing By" the next. The fact was, I preferred the gospel sides I was allowed to cut, even though I knew they stood no chance of being on any hit parade chart. It was just that I never had to strain or struggle to find the heart of those tunes. It was right there, in each note and every word, and if I had drifted a long ways from the protective embrace of the church in those years, I still had a unbreakable link to the music of worship and revelation. "God Is Standing By" and other out-and-out songs of witness that I sang during those days was a way I had of giving back, a remembrance of the glory of my former days and a tithing in song to the Lord. And for the time being, that was enough.

Sometimes, however, the two conflicting sides of my music would get mixed in together, combining spiritual and sensual longing in a way that even I didn't recognize at the time. I can't think of a better example than a song on my second album called "I'm a

Ram," one of the first collaborations between me and Teenie Hodges, a partnership that would have a lot to do with my success in years to come.

At first listen, the lyrics to "I'm a Ram" are downright weird, with me strutting my astrological attributes as an Aries, a sexy ram with an urgent need, then turning around and talking about the Old Testament imagery of the ram with his horns caught in the bushes to provide Abraham a substitute sacrifice for his son Isaac. I'm couldn't tell you for sure what I was getting at exactly, other then to say that, in my mind as in my music, the anointing of God was spread abroad in the land through the actions and intent of His appointed messenger. And if the shoe fits well, you better put it on, and lace it up tight.

And speaking of fashion statements, I decided to make another declaration of independence before we went into the studio to begin work. Not only was I going to sing the songs I wanted, but I made it clear that I was going to dress the way I wanted, too. Willie had toned me down so much I sometimes felt like I was back in church, and to make sure I got my point across, I showed up at Royal one day with a fine new processed pompadour and a fringed suede jacket and matching pants, along with the highest pair of platform heels that I could find. Willie, God bless his soul, didn't say a word and I think from that day on we had an understanding that our partnership was on an equal footing.

Still in all, Willie's suggestions and directions, not to mention the professional support he was providing on a daily basis, were keeping my career afloat and I knew I couldn't afford to test the limits too far. So when he suggested that we include a particular cover song for the album, I went along with him, even though I had my doubts and good reasons for them.

The tune he had in mind was "Can't Get Next to You," a Whitfield and Strong hit for the Temptations less than a year before we went into the studio with it. I couldn't much see the point in redo-ing something that was so fresh in the public's mind, but the song had a good, strong melody and I knew I could take the lyrics some-place real. Willie had worked up a very appealing arrangement as well, slowing down the tempo and accentuating the frustration and anger that simmered just below the surface of the Temps' version. Willie encouraged me to vamp on the lyrics, move around freely inside the changes, and generally give the track everything I had, which helped win me over to his way of thinking.

At the same time, Willie was moving closer and closer to per-fecting his own production style. You can hear it from the opening notes, the way all the instruments are separate and distinct yet work together in perfect synchronization, like a machine that did its job with the fewest possible moving parts. Al's drums held the center, Teenie's guitar fills were as effective for what they left out as for what they put in, and the horn section punctuated the changes like a boxer with a lethal left hook. And floating above it all, you can hear me working my falsetto, growling and moaning, but never losing my grip on the meaning and momentum. For months, Willie had been nudging me toward this style of singing, where control counted for as much as cutting loose and a single note could be as convincing as a symphony orchestra sawing away. On "Can't Get Next to You," which opened the album, we took a giant step in bringing it all together.

The first single from *Al Green Gets Next to You*, a funky wah-wah pedal workout called "All Because," written by me and Tee-nie, was released in May of 1970 and we all waited, holding our breath, to see what would happen. The song was far from the strongest track on the album and I have to take responsibility for insisting that we put it out, just because I wanted to hear some-thing I'd written played on the radio. I made sure to get the point across by putting another one of my originals, "Right Now, Right

Now," on the B-side. At a time when the singer/songwriter was just beginning to be a force in the music business, I wanted to be up there with the best of them.

At the same time, I made my fashion stand on the cover, moving away from the tasteful tie and vest Willie had decked me out in for the photo on front of *Green Is Blues*. This time around, I complemented my new pompadour with a blue Edwardian frock coat trimmed in ruffled, fake fur and big silver buttons. I wanted everyone to see Al Green in all his glorious Technicolor.

But it didn't really seem to matter what I did, how well I sang or wrote or dressed. As was getting to be a regular occurrence, my ambitions far outran reality. "All Because" went the way of all of the other singles I'd released for Hi, and I'd be less than honest if I didn't say that, after it was clear the song was a stiff, I didn't start to get a little desperate. It had been almost three years to the month that I'd had my first hit, "Back Up Train," and I was seriously beginning to wonder if it was also going to be my last. When you start thinking like that, there's nothing stopping you from second-, third-, and fourth-guessing yourself, wondering if you've really got what it takes and, even if you do, whether that's enough in a business where blind luck and coincidence count for every bit as much as talent.

I'm sure Willie must have picked up on the gloom that hovered over me like a cloud. It probably was hard *not* to. I was fighting a losing battle not to feel bitter and betrayed by my lack of success, not to start pointing fingers and blaming folks and telling myself that all the DJs and promotion men and everyone else who could have made me a star all had a personal grudge against Al Green. Don't laugh. I've known more than one celebrity with a persecution complex.

I couldn't tell you for sure whether Willie saw a friend in need or an investment in jeopardy—or maybe a little bit of both. Whatever it was, he didn't waste any time: By late summer of that year, without even letting me know, he put "Can't Get Next to You" on the Hi Records' release schedule. I found out later that I wasn't the only one he'd kept in the dark. Joe Cuoghi, who had begun to wonder whether he hadn't been backing a loser with this one-hit wonder named Al Green, was ready to pull the plug on the whole partnership. It was as much of a surprise to him as it was to me when fresh-pressed copies of "Can't Get Next to You" started flying out of the one-stops.

But that wasn't the only surprise waiting for us. Willie went ahead and personally contacted the local and regional field staff of London Records, who had signed a deal to distribute Hi back in the early days of the label. I don't know what he told them, what he promised or threatened, but whatever it was, it worked. With a sack full of records to pitch, enough of those London guys took out my song and put it at the top of the stack that radio programmers began to take notice. Within a month, "Can't Get Next to You" was breaking big out of the Southeast. A few more weeks, and it had made its way up the Eastern seaboard and out across the Midwest. And by early October, just as the leaves were beginning to turn on the street outside my apartment, it reached the West Coast and we had a certified hit.

Before it was over, "Can't Get Next to You" had reached number 11 on the R&B charts. But more important to Willie and Mr. Cuoghi, it had also made a dent in the pop charts, getting up to number 60—not exactly a smash, but a good start for sure. Willie rushed to keep the ball rolling as the New Year turned by releasing a track called "True Love" that hadn't made the album. It didn't catch on, but the B-side, "Driving Wheel," did, at least enough to climb into the low 40s on the R&B charts.

Finally, after all those months of hard work and disappointment, we were off and running. Al Green was on the scene. And his life would never be the same again.

CHAPTER **26**

Now comes the part of the story everyone loves to hear: where the rags turn to riches, the rainbow ends in a pot of gold, and everyone lives happily ever after.

I hope I don't disappoint you. As a rags-to-riches tale, I would suppose mine measured up as well as any. I was a poor boy from the farm with a gift for singing who strove and struggled to reach the top until one fine day he saw his name up in lights.

Isn't that usually how it goes? Of course, what most of those show business fairy tales don't bother to tell you is that seeing your name up in lights is sometimes the last thing you are going to catch a clear glimpse of for a long, long time. Those stories never describe getting famous as a fast ride down a dark tunnel, where most everything looks the same and you don't know which way you're going and what you're going to do when you get there. The back of one limousine looks pretty much like another; hotel rooms, even the luxury kind, sooner or later boil down to a bed, a bar, and a television; and I've never been in a airport waiting room where the time passed quickly.

But those storytellers would like you to believe that it's all a dazzling, delightful joy ride, where the best of everything is yours for the taking, and there's always a line of fans who just want to shake your hand and a roomful of women ready to show you how much they love you. And that's true . . . no doubt about it. The only problem is, most times you're too tired, or confused, or scared of it all getting taken away from you to enjoy any of it when it finally comes around. You've got fans, but no friends. You've got money to burn, but you're living on borrowed time. You're sitting in the lap of luxury, but it's all rented accommodations . . . and you're paying the bills.

I've heard it said that it's lonely at the top. And I've heard it said that celebrities aren't like the regular run. Some people insist that you don't know what you've got until it's gone. Others will tell you can't give up what you never had. It's all confused and contra-dictory. The closer you get to what you think you're after, the less sure you are of wanting it. And the more you get of what you always wanted, the less you can remember why it was so important in the first place. I wouldn't presume to tell you that chasing after your dream isn't worth the race. Let's just say be careful what you dream about. Because it might come true.

The truth is, my rags-to-riches story *does* end happily ever after. It's just the road that led to the pot of gold took some unexpected turns, bringing me back to a treasure I had with me all the time.

But I'm getting ahead of myself. Naturally, having a number 60 pop hit off someone else's song wasn't anybody's idea of making the big time. But what happened next would measure up to just about anybody's description. After the middling success of "Dri-ving Wheel" on the R&B charts, we were faced with the decision of choosing another single. Despite the success of "I Can't Get Next to You," I still firmly believed that one of my songs could make it to the top. I was also more than a little leery that Willie was trying to turn me into a wind-up music box that he could set to singing any-thing he wanted. I suppose he must have picked up on my mixed feelings and knew that this was a crucial stage in both my career and our partnership. If either one was going to survive, we'd both have to pull together and, like anything else, that's a process of give-and-take.

So Willie gave and allowed that the next single should be "Tired of Being Alone," that song I'd written so early that morning over a year before. Looking back, I'd have to guess that he knew what all of us who'd put together the album were already sure of—the song was the strongest track we'd done, no matter who'd written it.

But for his part, Willie wasn't about to leave anything to chance. Taking the lesson he'd learned from prodding the London Records promoters to get behind "I Can't Get Next to You," Willie set off on a whirlwind cross-country trip, wining and dining radio station music programmers and DJs, and generally charming the record's way onto the playlist.

He came back with some very tall tales indeed. In Atlanta, he insisted, he drank a fifth of J&B every night with one influential female disc jockey for two straight weeks until he convinced her to give "Tired of Being Alone" a try. In New York, he was at it three weeks with half a dozen more big-time air personalities. In Chicago, he personally visited every record store on the South Side . . . or so he said.

Whatever he was doing out there, it was working. We released "Tired of Being Alone" in May of '71, and by the time Thanksgiving rolled around, we had our first million-seller. Now, by today's standards, seven months is a long time for one record to stay alive, but back in those days, it was different. People needed more then five minutes to hear a song, to decide whether they liked it, find out the name, and go down to the music shop and find a copy for themselves. Add to that the fact that "Tired of Being Alone" was a whole different sound from anything else that was being heard on the radio at the time, and it's no wonder that it was a slow but steady build.

And we used that time to our advantage. As well as the record did in the States, peaking at number 6 and staying on the charts for nineteen solid weeks, it did even better in England, where it topped out at number 3. Those were some impressive statistics because now, instead of the sound spreading from one region to the next, it was spreading from one country to the next and jumping clear across the ocean to get there.

Joe Cuoghi knew that Hi Records finally had a real star on its hands, the first one in the whole history of the little label. He didn't need a college degree to figure out that it was time to put the full resources of his company—and anything else he could pull from the deep pockets of London Records—behind me. So, working with London's British office, he put together some English tour dates in early December to capitalize on the still-growing overseas success of "Tired of Being Alone."

It was on that tour that I got my first real taste of that "tunnel" effect I was talking about. I'd spent a good amount of time on the road, of course, stretching back to the days of the Greene Brothers, but this was going to be my first time out of the country and, on top of that, England was about the coolest place on earth at that moment, still echoing to the great sounds of the British Invasion. I had visions of Big Ben, Buckingham Palace, and proper gentlemen in bowlers.

What I got instead was one damp dressing room after another, cramped hotel rooms with nothing familiar on TV, and quick glimpses of the countryside from the window of a speeding car. And most of the time, that window would be streaked with water. It probably wasn't the wettest, coldest, or most chilling season they'd had on record, but you couldn't have told that to me. I'd spent enough Michigan winters to know what miserable weather was all about, but even I'd never seen anything quite like that island. It was so soggy it felt like you were climbing underneath a washcloth when you went to bed at night and the smell of mildew was so strong that, these days, I'm still reminded of England whenever I catch a whiff of it. The people all had accents so thick I wasn't even sure we were speaking the same language, and the food . . . well, let's just say their cooking lived down to its reputation.

The shows were the one bright spot of the tour, especially the opening date in Manchester at a big old barn called the New Century Hall. The audience seemed to be as much black as it was white, which came as something of a surprise to me until I found out that England was home to lots of folks who had once been nothing but colonial subjects of the empire. But what was most surprising was how well they seemed to know my music. I could hear them singing along to most of the tracks from my albums and when I got to "Tired of Being Alone," some ladies up front actually started screaming, like I was the fifth Beatle or something. I almost stopped the performance when I heard it because I thought someone had gotten hurt, but it was a sound I'd be getting used to soon enough.

All in all, I was glad enough to get back on board a jet heading west, even though Hi Records had only sprung for a coach-class seat. What I didn't realize at the time was that I was heading right back into another career clash with Willie, our biggest so far, and one that, if I hadn't lost out on, might have changed everything.

One thing I've learned after all my years in the music business: If someone tells you they know what's going to make it and what isn't, they're lying to your face. And I include myself in that number. After "Tired of Being Alone," I worked up quite a high opinion of my own ability to write, sing, and pick a hit, so when I got back to Memphis, and the first thing Willie told me was that he and Al Jackson had been working on a new song for my next single, I naturally got more than a little uppity. I'd already decided that my new single should be another track off the album, a funky strutter called "You Say It," written, of course, by yours truly.

Willie was of a different opinion. As our work together progressed, he became more and more focused on the sound he wanted to get for me and from me, and that meant he was starting to put together music that would fit that description. As Hi Records' percussionist-in-chief, Al was becoming increasingly important to Willie's recording approach, since, as any halfway decent producer will tell you, a good drum sound is half the ingredients of a hit record at the very least. The two of them had come up with the skeleton of a song they thought had real potential and I hadn't been back in the country more than a couple of days when Willie approached me with a rough mix. He wanted me to write the lyrics, and I knew just why: If he could get me participating in the songwriting process, I'd be more obliged to cut the song and let them release it.

I could see right through his scheme, but for the moment I played along. "Give me fifteen minutes," I told him and went into the lobby of the Royal to write out the words right off the top of my head. Actually, it took more like five minutes, but I didn't want him to think I was being spoiled or spiteful, so I sipped a Coke and watched a few rounds of a boxing match on TV before I went back inside.

"Willie," I said as I handed him the sheer of paper, "I don't hear this song. I think I need something a little stronger."

Willie shot a quick look over to Al, then sat down at the piano bench like a banker about to tell you why he's about to turn down your loan. "Al," he replied, "you've got it all wrong. Not only is this song perfect for you, but if you sing this song the way it should be sung, you're never going to worry about being strong again."

"I don't think so," I said. "I think we got to come back with something that's got a little punch to it. Say like, 'You Say It.' Now, that cut's got some *fire!*"

"You put that out and we're right back where we started from" was Willie's answer, and I picked up an edge in his voice I'd never heard before. He was serious about this.

I didn't know *how* serious. We fought off and on for the next two days over that tune before I agreed to record it for him. Even then, I wasn't happy with what came out, partly because I was mad about being forced into doing the song and partly because I really wasn't convinced that it was the right direction to be heading in.

But once Willie had gotten me behind the microphone, he pressed home his advantage. "Softer, Al, softer," he'd say over the intercom. "You got to go lighter on it." We did take after take with him interrupting me right in the middle to coax more falsetto out, to get me to back off the beat and slide over the vocals. Finally, more out of frustration than anything else, I gave him exactly what he wanted just to put an end to the ordeal.

We finished late on a Friday night. By Monday, Willie had pressed up an acetate of the single and shipped it out. By Thursday, we'd gotten the word: We were coming onto the charts at number 8. Ten days later, we were at number 1 and we didn't budge for the next nine weeks.

"Let's Stay Together" was a certified smash.

With the almost overnight success of the song, it was time to get back in the studio to record a new album, my third in less than three years. Actually, we really didn't have get *back* to anything— we were pretty much living in the dark and gloomy studio space on a twenty-four-hour-a-day, seven-day-a-week music-making schedule. It was just another turn in the dark tunnel I was riding through, one that took me even farther from the natural light of day. If I wasn't in the studio, I was on a stage, and if I wasn't on a stage, I was in the back of a car heading for a stage, or in a hotel room after getting off a stage. I was beginning to lose track of time, unsure whether it was night or day at any given moment or where we were in the unraveling of a week or a month. Tuesday was the same as Sunday, midnight the same as noon, May the same as February.

With nothing else to think about and no other distractions, I had no choice but to focus fully on the music, and the tune stack on the album *Let's Stay Together* shows the advantages of that kind of merciless dedication. It was without a doubt the best album we'd done up to that point and, in my opinion, one of the best we *ever* did. The band never sounded stronger, my voice was as flexible and full of life as it had ever been, and for once, the song selections were a perfect reflection of the sound Willie had been working for from the moment we met. I'd finally gotten the message that I could get across more with a whisper than a scream, that less was better, and that there was as much music in the space between the notes as in what you sang. To my ear, *Let's Stay Together* was the first 100 percent Al Green album, a true reflection of who I was and what I was capable of doing.

By that time, the songwriting chores were spread out pretty evenly between me, Willie, and the mainstays in the band, mostly Teenie, Al, and occasionally Flick or Do Funny. Nobody had time anymore, least of all me, to get too worked up about where a good track came from and who got credit for it, and by then, Willie had a pretty good idea of what I would and would not tolerate as far as singing outside material.

On *Let's Stay Together*, he picked two gems: "I've Never Found a Girl," a nice simmering Stax standard that had been a hit for Eddie Floyd back in '68, and "How Can You Mend a Broken Heart," which had been a major hit for the Bee Gees, although they might just as well have given it right over to me and saved themselves the trouble. I'm not a bragging man, but I *owned* that song from the opening refrain, from the near-whispered pleading of my voice to the way I gave each word the weight and wisdom that would come from a sadder-but-wiser penitent on the far side of a once-in-a-lifetime love affair. To my mind, the Gibb boys had written a masterpiece . . . and it was up to me to make it immortal.

But you'll have to make up your own mind about such things.

CHAPTER 27

In truth, the performance I gave on "How Can You Mend a Broken Heart" was just that . . . a performance. I could imagine how a man might feel, pleading for the love of one good woman, but as far as firsthand experience went, I was just guessing.

Since the night I'd walked away from Juanita, music and only music had been my wife and mistress and jealous lover. It wasn't that I didn't want to find someone special to love and understand, or even that I didn't have the time. We all make time for the things that are truly important in our lives, and I guess that just goes to prove that for me, a successful career in music was my first, last, and only priority. What I didn't want was the distraction of another person, the responsibility for someone else's happiness, or the accountability that comes from being committed.

Commitment was the very last thing on my mind in the early months of 1971 when everything seemed to be going my way and the world with all its charms was laid out like a complimentary basket of fruit in a backstage dressing room.

I think you know what I'm getting at. My success was working on women like one of those ancient slave charms—the Mojo Hand or black cat bone. Like I said before—women like me. Some of them like me so much they forget their natural feminine shyness and Christian modesty and just come right out and tell me how they feel . . . and what they want to do about it. I don't blame them and I don't blame myself. We all know about the urges and impulses, the needs and desires that can turn the strongest man or woman into a weak and wanton creature. We read about it every day in the newspaper, but, more importantly, we read about it in Scripture. Anybody who thinks the Bible is just a bunch of holy commands and sacred rules and regulations most likely has never cracked the cover. The book is full of stories about folks like you and me, tested and tempted, and more often than not, falling way short of the mark. Samson gave up his God-given strength for a night of pleasure in wicked Delilah's bed. David turned from right-eousness by spying on Bathsheba, naked in moonlight. King Herod handed over John the Baptist when Salome danced her dance of desire, cursing himself for all eternity for one look at her swaying body. It's been that way ever since the world began, and I don't imagine it's going to change until Jesus returns.

In the meantime, we sow the wind and reap the whirlwind, ful-filling the desires of our flesh and bringing down upon ourselves the judgment of God. It's in our nature, from the moment of our birth to the hour of our death, and the struggle of every life is to break the bonds of sin and death, to crucify ourselves with Christ and be raised up again with Him a new creature.

But I guess I'm getting ahead of myself. I wasn't paying much attention to the laws of God and the wages of sin at the age of twenty-five, with a number-one single on the charts, my face on the covers of magazines, my voice on the radio from coast to coast, and my fans in a line around the block wherever and whenever I made an appearance. Not only was I pleased to make the acquain-tance of every young woman who managed to sneak backstage, or through the hotel lobby, or into the back of the tour bus, but I considered it my due, a fitting offering to my natural-born charisma, a reasonable expectation for a man of my intense attractions.

I know what you're thinking—that Al Green is a bragging fool, carried away with himself and the good fortune that came his way by the grace of God or a simple twist of fate. And you'd be right. There's an old saying in show business that says you know you're in trouble when you start believing what they say about you in the newspapers. But I'm here to tell you that you know you're in trouble the first time you step out onto a stage with the light shining down and the audience all hushed and ready and willing to believe anything you tell them. That's the moment when the devil steps forward, pulls out that parchment scroll and quill pen, and points to the dotted line.

There's no way in the world a man can stay humble and contrite beneath the blinding light of fame. And there's no way he can stay pure—if not in deed, then surely in his heart—when he sees firsthand how fame and fortune can turn a woman into a harlot, hungry for his power.

Did I taste of that power? Did I let myself be used as I used those who offered themselves to me? Did I sin and then sin again, with no thought to the consequences or the great and sure judgment I was bringing down upon myself?

Of course I did. You would, too. And if you don't believe me, read the Bible. The truth is there, for each and every one of us, when the prophet Jeremiah warns that the human heart is deceitful above all things and desperately wicked. "Who can know it?" he asks in sorrow and anger, and when I read those words, I tremble. And so should you.

I have had carnal relations with more women than I can remember or confess. Their names and faces, their bodies and voices have blended together long ago, one lonely form all blurred and transparent, like a restless ghost that wanders through my memory. And whatever she's looking for, I hope she finds. It's as much as any of us, lost in this fallen world, deserve.

I've been searching and seeking for one thing or another my whole life. Sometimes I thought I knew what I wanted, what would make me happy and bring me peace of mind. Other times, all that kept me going was the hunt, knowing that whatever I'd already tried hadn't worked and hoping that there was something still out there that would. And when you find out that one false treasure or another—sex or drugs or money or celebrity—isn't what you thought it was, it can be hard to accept the fact, being that you were so sure to begin with, so convinced that it was all you needed to make your life complete. I'd been hungry for the love of women my whole life. When I was finally able to get my fill, I didn't want to believe that too much of a good thing was still not enough.

I was on the road almost as soon as we put down the last note *Let's Stay Together* and it was out there, on that endless stretch of one-night stands, that I looked for the love I craved—one woman, sometimes two at a time. And if in my mind it's hard to remember or even tell the difference, one from another, I don't think they knew who I was at all. Al Green was a dream to them, a voice they heard on the radio, singing about all the romance and the passion that was missing from their own lives. I was nothing more than the sum of my songs, those three-minute pop tunes that could make them feel special by just closing their eyes and pretending it was them—and them alone—I was singing to. They were as hungry for love as I was—and just as ignorant about where to find it.

Those first days of real stardom, when I was music's hottest new commodity and a certified sky's-the-limit sensation, were some of the loneliest of my life. I believe I knew, even back then, that all the attention and acclaim could disappear as quickly as it had come. I was constantly surrounded by folks telling me how special and select I was, and there was hardly a night I spent outside the company of some sweet and willing thing who wanted only to bask in the reflected glory. But I learned real quick that, with those kinds of friends, you can never tell when they're giving and when they're taking.

All, that is, except for one. During those strange and unreal times, God gave me a true friend and boon companion, someone I could trust and who called on me to be trustworthy, maybe the most selfless and loyal person who ever crossed the path of my life. And I will always be profoundly grateful to Him for the gift of Laura Lee.

I met her first when we shared a bill on some Southeastern dates shortly after the release of *Let's Stay Together.* It was right around that time that I learned of the passing of my cousin Little Junior Parker, who had died of complications from an operation for a brain tumor up in Chicago. I'll tell you the truth: The news shook me. Herman had been the first person of my acquaintance to make a name for himself in music and I'd followed his career ever since I was a child, looking up to him from a distance as a model of what a man can do with a little music in his soul. Even later in his life, when the hits had stopped coming and my own star rose higher than his ever had, I kept in touch with him, trying to be an encouragement and letting him know that someone still cared. I think the truth was, his death put me in mind of my own destiny. Little Junior Parker had been a respected bluesman in his day, and in his passing had left behind a handful of great records like "Driving Wheel," "Mystery Train," "Next Time You See Me," and "Barefoot Rock."

But that was it. As far as most people cared or were concerned, Little Junior Parker could be summed up by the total time on a few 45s. I couldn't help but wonder if, in the end, all I'd have to show for myself would be a few songs that put people in mind of some fleeting moment in their own brief lives. I probably dwelled on my cousin's sad passage a little too much, but that's what the nearness of death will do to you: remind you that the bell will one day toll for you.

I guess all that preoccupation was beginning to tell in my performances, because one night after a show in Atlanta, Laura came
up to me, introduced herself, and as natural as you please, asked if
there was anything wrong or something she could do for me.

I must have given her a sharp second look, wondering if this
wasn't another of the bold propositions I got every night backstage
after the encore. But she just smiled and blinked her big brown
eyes and something about the gentle expression on her soft, round
face put my mind at ease. Laura was not a beautiful woman as
some folks count beauty, but she had another kind of comeliness,
an inner light that illuminated her face and shone forth in a smile
as radiant and warm as the morning sun. I was drawn to her right
then and there, trusting the instinct that told me she was on my
side, even though up until that minute the closest we'd come to
meeting was having both our names on the same theater marquee.

As it turned out, Laura and I actually had a lot in common,
especially the roots we shared in the church. Of course, the church
is a common link between lots of black people, but I couldn't help
but feel, as I got to know her better, that it wasn't just the Sunday
experience that bound us together, but a deeper connection to the
things of God and music as a means to praise and worship Him.

Laura was a year older than me, born and raised in Chicago,
where, from an early age, she had cause to give thanks for the
charity and compassion of God's people. She was nine years old
when her mother came down with a serious illness and was unable
to care for her little girl. Laura was taken in by her neighborhood
church and raised up by the pastor and his wife, Reverend E. A.
and Ernestine Rundless.

Now, anybody familiar with gospel music in the fifties should
spark to the name Rundless right away. More or less the first family of Chicago sacred music, the Rundless legacy can be heard in
many great songs and recordings of the era, and most especially in

the powerful and persuasive music of the Meditation Singers, an all-female quintet that at one time featured Ernestine Rundless, along with Della Reese before she launched her own career.

A natural-born singer, with a strong and earthy vocal style, Laura would naturally join the group as a young lady and, just as naturally, I suppose, decide to make a break for pop music as soon as she got the chance. Sound familiar? Like I said, Laura and I traveled down many of the same roads.

Signed to Chess Records in the mid-sixties, Laura made sure no one would ever mistake her for a gospel girl again, causing a sensation with her first hit, "Dirty Man." It was followed by a string of midchart singles for Chess throughout the sixties, all pretty much covering the same rude and low-down territory, many of them cut down at the hottest new studio on the scene: Muscle Shoals, Alabama. They included "Up Tight, Good Man," "As Long as I Got You," "Hang It Up," and "Need to Belong," which had earlier been a hit for Jerry Butler. In the seventies, she moved over to Holland–Dozier–Holland's Hot Wax label, and it was there that her music took on a change that put her way out ahead of her time.

On cuts like "Wedlock Is a Padlock" and "Women's Love Rights," Laura would break out of singing to deliver herself of long spoken sermonettes, mostly on the subject of female liberation. They might not have been the first "raps" on record, but they were sure the first *I* ever heard, and as far as I'm concerned, that makes Laura a genuine hip-hop pioneer.

By the time we met in Atlanta, Laura was working another one of her proud-and-loud declarations of independence, this one called "Love and Liberty." I'd caught her act from the wings a few times in earlier shows and, while I was impressed by the power and quality of her voice—as true a soul sister style as I had ever heard—I always felt that the rest of her act was just that: a lot of pretending. Now, understand, I personally didn't go for the up-front and outspoken type of woman. I liked my girlfriends meek, mild, and obedient. But in spite of all her strutting and bragging, it seemed to me that Laura could never quite get away from who she really was—a daughter of the church, gifted in song for the glory of God.

And there was nothing about her that evening when she finally introduced herself that changed my mind. The truth was, Laura Lee was as sweet and gentle, as kind and understanding exactly to the same degree that her public image was hard, hot, and high-handed. She may have wanted to throw off her past and renounce her upbringing in Pastor Rundless's stern but loving domain. But that's who she was and she just couldn't help letting it shine forth.

That first night I felt something tight and tired loosen up within me as I sat and talked with this warm-hearted young woman. I couldn't tell you what our conversation was about exactly, except to say it seemed we covered a little bit of everything and nothing in particular. All I know for sure was that, by the end of the night, I knew I had found someone I could trust totally and depend on entirely.

Did I fall in love with Laura Lee? The answer is yes, but maybe not in the way you might think. True, we were more than brother and sister to each other, but the bond we had was also different—and maybe stronger—than any romance. We were soul mates, birds of a feather, two halves of one whole. There was something pure about our love as it grew over the years that followed, something that remained as innocent and authentic as that moment when she first offered her hand in friendship.

And there was coming a time when I would hold on to that hand like a drowning man on his third time down.

CHAPTER 28

The year 1972 was a watershed one for Al Green, Inc. When I wasn't in the studio, cutting what now seemed to be like one endless album, I was out on tour, ranging all around the world, with return visits to Europe and England.

On one of those trips, when Willie came along to do a little business at the London home office, the two of us were invited over to the home of a cat named Sir Albert Lewis, who had made his money patenting the technology for radar and who owned Decca Records, the parent company of London. He was the richest man we were ever likely to meet, and both Willie and I were happily anticipating an evening spent in the lap of luxury. Except that it didn't quite turn out that way.

We hung around the hotel, waiting to be picked up in what we imagined would be Sir Albert's superstretch limo with his own personal liveried chauffeur. Instead we got a call from the front desk with directions to the house. That was it. No limo, no chauffeur . . . we might as well have been going to see some poor relation who even couldn't afford to take us out on the town.

Half an hour later, we drove up to the street number we'd been given, paid the taxi driver, and stood outside a small house on a block of small houses in a ordinary neighborhood on the outskirts of the city. I told Willie to check the address, then I asked him to check it again. Neither one of us could believe we'd come to the right place, but sure enough, there it was: LEWIS, written on a piece of paper under the doorbell.

That evening turned out to be one of the strangest—and most educational—evenings of my life. Sir Albert had a mousy little wife dressed in old print dress with an apron that was almost as worn down and faded as the smoking jacket and slippers he greeted us in. He was a big man with a fringe of frizzy hair around his bald head and small red eyes that made him look like he'd just woken up. Sir Albert seemed happy enough to see us. After all, we were his top entertainment investment, and we were selling a lot of records for him. But wherever that money was going, it sure wasn't being spent on rolling out a red carpet.

Willie and I kept looking at each other as Sir Albert and Mrs. Lewis sat across from us on their mismatched sofas and passed the time of day. Then from out of the blue, the old man asked us if we fancied a bite to eat. We were invited to dinner. I remember thinking to myself, *That's the whole idea.* But I just nodded and smiled and said I wouldn't mind if I did. Albert turns to the missus, who gets up and takes herself to the kitchen, returning twenty minutes later with a plate of fried steaks, some canned peas in a bowl, a couple of cans of Coca-Cola, and a bottle of ketchup. She sets it all down in front of us on some TV trays, and we all dig in like it's Saturday night at the old homestead.

Later, Willie and I shared a laugh on Sir Albert and his fried steaks, but on the taxi ride home, I began to wonder what a man like him had worked so hard for if it wasn't to enjoy the fruits of his labor. From there, it was a quick jump to asking myself what *I* was working so hard for. True, I never had to worry about food to eat or clothes to wear or a way to get to where I was going, but I couldn't help but think that I should have something more to show for all my efforts.

And when I got back to Memphis, I made sure that the first thing I did was to march right into the record company office and demand enough money from all my royalties and advances and wherever else they wanted to dig it up, so I could buy myself a house.

And not just some middle-of-the-road, Sir Albert Lewis house, either. No, I was determined to live in the style in which I hoped to soon become accustomed and looked around town for a place that would suit my new status, one that came with being a number-one hit artist—which, just before Christmas, I'd become when "Let's Stay Together" reached the top of the charts.

But the more I looked around at all the big Southern-style mansions that stood for class and breeding in Memphis society, the more uncomfortable I became. All those beautiful estates, with their three-car garages and magnolia trees running up the driveway, seemed like scenery in a movie starring someone else besides me. If I was going to spend my money for a house, it was going to be one *I* could call home, a place to come back to, where you knew you were settled and secure.

And the funny thing was, once I started imagining what such a place might be, what came to me was the home I'd left behind just over the river in Arkansas so long ago. That's not to say I wanted to find myself a shotgun shack on a sharecropper's lot. No, what appealed to me was the calm, serene beauty of God's creation. I wanted to be close to nature, someplace where the birds were singing sweetly and the scent of pine needles floated on the evening air like perfume, someplace where I could get away and get in touch, lose myself and find myself.

That's how I came to buy a lot of virgin land, sixty acres, on the very edge of a state park up beyond the city limits, where the suburbs and shopping malls turn into farm fields and forest stands. I had my own house built there, nothing too fancy or deluxe, but nice enough, with twenty-one rooms, for anyone to know that a man of means lived beyond its high hedge and big sweeping lawns. I borrowed a touch from Graceland with the musical notes I had worked into the wrought-iron design of the gates, and a taste of my own farm boy roots with the little herd of longhorn cattle I set to grazing in the backyard. The house itself was a modern split-level from the outside and something a little more elegant inside: red shag carpets and matching velvet drapes, a gilt-edge Louis XIV living room ensemble, and a knotty pine study with a upright piano, should I find myself in a musical mood.

Yet, even as construction on my dream home began, I found myself too busy to enjoy my new domain. The demands for the follow-up to "Let's Stay Together" meant a near-constant round of songwriting. Willie and I were working more closely with Al Jackson than just about anyone else, and Al had also taken over most of the drumming from Howard Grimes after Willie decided that Al had a softer touch. That was the way it was with Willie—always softer, lighter, smoother, simpler, as if his job was just to strip away every unnecessary note or word until the song shone in all its naked glory. And as we moved into the sessions for my fourth album, we came closer and closer to the perfection of our partnership.

Actually, *I'm Still in Love with You* was technically my *fifth,* if you count the fact that Bell Records decided that, since I was such a big success, maybe it was time to release the sessions I had done way back in '67 with the Soul Mates. They rushed out an album just called *Al Green* early in the summer of '72 and while I couldn't help but be embarrassed by that raw and ragged blast from the past, it seemed that my audience just couldn't get enough of Al Green. "Guilty," a single released from that Bell album, actually made it into the Top 40.

But that was nothing compared to the performance of *I'm Still in Love with You,* which we rush-released, hot on the heels of *Let's*

Stay Together. The album's debut single, one of our originals called "Look What You've Done for Me," reached number 1 in March of that spring, while the title track took over the top spot in July. But churning out hits wasn't as easy as it might seem.

Between recording and performing, our schedule had gotten so crowded that the only way we could get any concentrated song-writing done was to leave town and hole up where no one knew we were. In fact, that's how some of the best tracks on *I'm Still in Love with You* managed to get written in the middle of all the fury and fuss that was starting to swirl around the Royal. Without telling anyone, Willie, Al Jackson, Teenie, and I took a trip across the river up to a secluded lakeside resort in Hot Springs, Arkansas, to catch our breath and try and concentrate on new material.

Those three days we spent in the silence and serenity of that unspoiled spot gave us the peace of mind to concentrate on taking the sound we had developed to a whole new level. You can hear what we came up with on two key tracks from the album: the title song and "Love and Happiness." As different as night and day, "I'm Still in Love with You" was a sweet, sentimental song of pure surrender set like a jewel in Willie's gorgeous arrangement, seamlessly blending horns, strings, and backing vocals until the whole thing sounded like it might float away on a pink and gold cloud.

"Love and Happiness," which Teenie had written one morning between watching wrestling on TV and making love to his girlfriend, was an entirely different story. I wouldn't say it was a return to the old-style soul of my early days—it was too tightly wrapped and under control for that—but I definitely pulled it from the same source of raw and gritty need, laying it over with some of the sanctifying witness I'd learned back in Mother Bates's revival tent. The result was like a slow fever, building on the beat, pushing up the temperature with each breath of the staccato horns and pushing through to delirium as we came up on the fade. Recording

"Love and Happiness" was like mixing explosive chemicals—everything had to be added at just the right time and at just the right dose. The tempo was the most important thing to Willie and, if you listen close, you can hear Teenie counting it off with his foot on a cardboard box for the take that nailed it.

The rest of *I'm Still in Love with You* had us firing on all cylinders, making the best music of our lives, and knowing that we were doing it the whole time. A six-and-a-half minute version of Kris Kristofferson's "For the Good Times" totally summed up the cool and understated feel of the album, a feel that was reflected even on the album cover, with a white-on-white background accentuating my most stylish look to date. Willie and I had split the difference between being flamboyant and classy and, I must say, in my white turtleneck, white patent leather shoes with the stacked heels, and just a touch of diamonds and gold, I was as cool and in control as the music between that cover.

Creativity is a strange and fickle thing, sometimes flowing like a river and sometimes trickling down to a dry creek bed. For me, Willie, and the whole Hi Records' crew, a flood of pure music was pouring out of us all throughout 1972 and right into 1973. I can't account for it exactly, other than to say that, once we were in that particular groove, we rode it all the way, never knowing when we'd run out of inspiration and have to pull over to the side of the road.

We had our recording routine down cold. Usually Willie and Al Jackson would work out the fundamentals of a song, then give it to me to write the lyrics. Once we had something we were all happy with, Leroy and Al—or sometimes Bulldog Grimes—would put down a rhythm track. That's what I'd sing my vocals to, and Willie rarely altered the way my voice came through on his funky double four-track system. The most he'd add was a little echo chamber, and I never even heard of EQ until years later. After I sang the song, my job was pretty much done. Willie and the rest of the musicians would get to work adding their bits and pieces and when it was finished, it would be presented to me for approval. Once in a while I'd have a suggestion or a second thought, but by that time, I'd learned to trust Willie's ear as completely as my own and would let him have his way.

I've sometimes heard it said that Willie just made the same record over and over again. But I don't agree. Just like anybody else, we had a sound and, within that sound, we played around as much as we liked, changing things up and mixing them around. If some of it ended up sounding the same, it was because that was what naturally occurred when we came together. There was no use pretending to be something we weren't.

Especially when what we were was working so well. Within six months, we rolled right out of *I'm Still in Love with You* into my fifth album, *Call Me*, which would earn me my first Grammy nomination, and another number-one single, "You Ought to Be with Me," followed up in short order by the title track and "Here I Am (Come and Take Me)," both jumping into the number 2 slot on the charts. We had a sure sense that we could do no wrong by this time, and we were starting to play around with the musical formula that was serving us so well. I took on country music for the first time with a rendition of Hank Williams's "I'm So Lonesome I Could Cry" and Willie Nelson's "Funny How Time Slips Away." "Stand Up" was a tune I wrote by myself that gave me a chance to reflect my feelings about all the social and political upheaval that was going on at the time, while "Have You Been Making Out O.K." was one of those ballads we could now do in our sleep. In fact, the song itself has a sleepy, lazy feel to it, as if I was trying to describe a beautiful dream.

And in a way, that's what my life had become . . . a dream. After a lifetime of work, I'd become an overnight sensation, and in a little more than two short years, I'd racked up five million-selling singles, sold-out concert halls around the world, and sent soul music spinning off in a whole new direction.

God knows, I'm not bragging. It was just a fact. What was coming out of Hi Records was different from anything else the competition could put together and, as a result, some of the big hit-making factories of soul music in the sixties were starting to falter and lag. Stax, another staple of the Memphis music scene, couldn't keep its hard-core soul sound selling, and Motown was looking for a new formula once their big productions started getting a little top-heavy. In fact, some of the A&R ears from Motown came down to the Royal Studios shortly after we cut "Let's Stay Together" and threw down a bunch of cash to rent the place for a week. Willie was only too happy to oblige and turned the place over to them. They went through it with a fine-tooth comb, making notes on everything from the way he miked the drums to the crazy angle of that slanted floor. In the end, they brought in a dozen session musicians, just to try the place out and see if they couldn't get close to the sound we had. But what they couldn't duplicate or manufacture was the chemistry that Willie had achieved between me, his musicians, and that intangible asset that can only be called genius.

Who knows how long things might have kept up if they'd been allowed to run their course? *Call Me* was every bit as big a hit as what came before and there was no reason to expect that whatever came after wouldn't make every bit as big a splash. We were on a roll.

But God had something else in mind, and it was getting to be time for Him to make a move. I think I must have known that something was coming to an end and something else was about to start, even if I couldn't have put that feeling into words.

Yet, what I couldn't express one way came out another. The last cut on *Call Me* was a song I had written without even really knowing why. It was called "Jesus Is Waiting," and when I listen back to it today, I can clearly hear what was only a still small voice back then. Jesus was waiting. For Al Green. And the time had come to heed His call or turn away, one last time.

CHAPTER **29**

I've been a fool," I sang in "Jesus Is Waiting," "disregard-
ing your love . . ." I sang those lyrics with feeling, even
with conviction, but it was a fervor that I could only remember
once knowing. I could recite the words of repentance, the formula
for forgiveness, and the attitude of saving grace. But behind that
knowledge was spiritual ignorance. I had forsaken the faith and, in
the process, sold my birthright.

It had been a long time since I had felt the power of the Holy
Spirit move through my life and my music, a long time since I'd
given glory to God for the gifts He had bestowed. I had played out
the age-old drama of the prodigal son, turning my back on my
father's house to pursue the world and all its passing pleasures.
And while it's true that, in Scripture, there is the clear promise that
if you train up a child in the way he should go, he will not depart
from it when he is old, that's no guarantee that the road back
won't be twisted and curving and full of danger. I knew God was
real, knew it as well as I knew I needed air to breathe and water to
drink. But *knowing* is not enough . . . it's never enough. You've got
to believe and, believing, walk out your faith, one step at a time.
Somewhere down that road I'd traveled, I'd thrown away the map

God had given to mark my way. It's no wonder I found myself lost in a wilderness of my own vain imaginings.

So if I had fallen so far away from the love of God, how is it I could see my way clear to write and sing a song like "Jesus Is Waiting" on a album that was supposed to be about nothing more than flirtation and romance and the hot passions that spring up between a man and a woman?

I've asked myself that question and I've never found the answer. But if I had to guess, I'd say that the meaning behind the words of "Jesus Is Waiting" is somewhere between an invitation and a challenge, a test and a tease. A part of me, deep down inside, cried out, and the hunger I felt so powerfully I didn't even know it sought to be satisfied. Was it Jesus that was waiting or was it me? He says He stands at the door knocking, and for Al Green, the rhythm of that knock beat out a gospel tempo that I couldn't ignore.

If Willie and the band thought anything about us doing died-in-the-wool church music, they never said it to me. Of course, we all had a connection to the gospel sound and its message of Good News—you can hardly be a black man in the South playing music without having those songs stuck in your head. Still, while there was nothing unnatural about singing outright to Jesus, I'm sure most of them, Willie most especially, were hoping it was just a phase I was going through.

I never gave it a second thought. At their best, the songs I wrote and the music I sang were the expressions of what I was feeling at the moment they arrived. And at the moment "Jesus Is Waiting" arrived, I was in what you might call an expectant mood. After a trip to the top that pretty much took my breath away and more than I could imagine of the kind of success that was supposed to matter, I was already beginning to ask a question that has come to haunt more than one rich, famous and fabulously happy celebrity:

Is this all there is? And although I hadn't quite put it to myself in exactly those words, the uneasy feeling that followed me around like a hungry dog was getting harder and harder to ignore. Jesus *was* waiting . . . for the right time to make His move.

That time finally came in the summer of '73, in the middle of a nonstop tour to promote *Call Me*. At that point, I was booked up with solid shows for better than a year and, as a result, my life was suddenly no longer my own to control. I was answerable to promoters and producers and bottom-line box office numbers and in case I ever forgot why I was doing it all in the first place, all I had to do was look around the Hi Records headquarters, or the Royal Studios, or the office Willie and I had set up to take care of business. Everywhere I turned there were people who were depending on me to make their living, to keep the whole bandwagon rolling and meet the payrolls week in and week out. We had secretaries and accountants and janitors and engineers and bodyguards and roadies and publicists and . . . well, you get the idea. I wasn't just a singer, or a songwriter or even a star. I was an enterprise: Al Green and Company.

And most of the folks that worked for me I'd never met and couldn't call by name. And because I got tired of being surrounded by strangers all the time, I decided to add a few familiar faces to the entourage. I brought both my dad and my brother Bill out from Grand Rapids and put them on the security detail because that was the best way to have them next to me on a regular basis.

It was great having family around again, talking about old times and sharing that comfortable feeling you can get with kin. Bill and I had slept in the same bed growing up, and you just don't get much closer than that.

But it wasn't just family I had the yearning to draw close around me. More than anyone else, I wanted to keep Laura Lee close by. At that point in my life, I felt as if she was the only one who really understood me, knew where I was coming from, where I was going, and why it sometimes felt like I was stuck in between the two. It wasn't just that we both had careers in music and knew the pressures and problems that come with that territory. We connected at a deeper level altogether and shared a common longing to fill an empty place inside that we couldn't describe but only recognize, each one within the other. It was what bonded us as friends, but more important than that, it made us both pilgrims together, traveling down the same dark path.

As I said, we came to the crossroads of that journey in the late summer of '73 in a hotel room with the Matterhorn rising up outside the window. No, I wasn't in Switzerland. It was Disneyland and the spotlights that lit the fake snow on the ride shone into my room with a pale and ghostly light. I was feeling a little ghostly myself, as a matter of fact. Earlier that day, I'd met Laura at the airport in San Francisco, where I had an matinee scheduled at the Cow Palace. I hadn't seen her for a few weeks and, since we weren't on the same bill anymore, the only way we could grab any time together was when she was off the road, back home in Detroit, and I could send for her to spend a day or two with me while I was touring. For some reason, I felt a special need just then to see her, talk with her, and let her gentle presence soothe my mind, and she must have heard the urgency in my voice because she caught the next plane out, even though she'd just come off a heavy schedule herself.

We spent the afternoon hidden away in the hotel room until it was time for the show and rode out together in the limo. After the concert, we headed straight back to the airport. I was booked to play another date that same evening at Disneyland and had about three hours to get to the gig. It was all a blind rush, but, back then, *everything* was a blind rush until you actually got there and then, more often than not, they'd keep you cooling your heels backstage for no good reason. Whoever came up with the expression "Hurry up and wait" surely spent time on a concert tour.

It must have been about one o'clock in the morning before we finally got checked into the hotel the Disney promoters had reserved for us. I made sure Laura had her own room whenever we were together because it was important, to both of us, that folks on the tour understood that we weren't just in the middle of some hot and heavy love affair and that they should respect and honor her as much as I did.

We kissed good night and, after taking a shower to wash the stage sweat away, I got ready for some well-deserved sack time. I remember as I passed into sleep feeling strangely serene and at peace with myself and the world. In the midst of all the craziness that surrounded my life, I had Laura in the room right next door to mine and my father and brother just down the hall. It was a little like having a home on the road.

I couldn't have been asleep more than a hour or two when I was suddenly awakened by the sound of shouting. I sat bolt upright in bed, frightened that some crazy fan had broken into the room. The shouting continued and as I listened, I realized that the voice wasn't threatening so much as excited and happy, as if someone had just walked into a surprise party with all his oldest and dearest and friends in attendance. There was something oddly familiar about the voice, as well. Where had I heard it before?

It was then that I realized that the voice was my own! And while the words I shouted were of no earthly tongue, I immediately recognized what they meant. I was praising God, rejoicing in the great and glorious gift of salvation through His son, Jesus Christ, and lifting my voice to heaven with the language of angels to proclaim His majesty on high.

People who have had such an experience, when the power of

God and the presence of the Holy Spirit fall so heavily that they drip like sweet honey from the rock with the very oil of gladness, will tell you that their memories of the moment are always from the outside, looking in. And the same was true for me. There I was, rejoicing at the very top of my lungs, and yet at the same time, I could watch myself, hear myself, and wonder to myself, *Now, what is this fool shouting about? Doesn't he know folks are trying to sleep?* But as much as I understood that if I kept up all that hollering for too much longer I was sure to get arrested or worse, there was nothing in either earthly or spiritual realms that could have shut my mouth. A different spirit had taken charge, even while it left me free to watch and marvel at how the power of God can move a man with a sovereign touch. I believe to this day that two different events were coming to pass in that hotel room at the very same time. First, a man was being quickened and called to a new life in Jesus. Second, that same man was allowed to be witness of his own salvation, that forever after he could speak of the power of the Holy Spirit from firsthand experience. God didn't take away my mind. He gave me a new one, even as he left my senses free to marvel at the transformation.

Suddenly the shouting and celebration stopped and I heard a voice, calm and clear coming from inside me, but rattling the walls like a ten-point earthquake all the same. "Are you ashamed of Me?" was the question it asked and the words pierced me like a knife. I might have been ashamed of myself, for all the years I had let the love of God languish as I pursued my own lusts and desires. But ashamed of Jesus? Ashamed of the Lamb of God, the Alpha and the Omega, sitting at the right hand of the Father in glory and majesty. Never!

I began shouting out praises in tongues once again and, jumping out of bed, ran into the bathroom. The part of my mind that was still tethered to the world was starting to panic. If I didn't shut myself up pretty soon, there was sure to be an embarrassing scene, and then what would I tell the police: *I'm sorry, Officer, but I can't seem to contain the abundant grace of God within this mortal frame of flesh and blood.* I wondered how *that* would look on the arrest report.

I couldn't think of another thing to do but grab a armful of towels off the rack and bury my face in them. I remember biting at the cotton nap, trying to muffle myself when I suddenly heard that voice again, asking one more time, "Are you ashamed of Me?"

"Lord, no!" I shouted into the towels and threw them off myself, as if I was holding a fistful of poisonous snakes. "No!" I screamed again as I heard a pounding from the door connecting Laura's room to mine own.

"Al!" she was saying from the other side. "Are you all right? What's going on in there?"

I rushed back into the room and flung the door open. "I am not ashamed of the Lord Jesus Christ!" I yelled into her wide-eyed face. "I am not ashamed of His Gospel?"

"Al," she said, a look of fear clouding her big brown eyes. "What's happened to you. Should I call a doctor?"

For an answer, I grabbed her and half-dragged, half-pulled her with me out the hotel door and into the hallway. A little ways down the corridor another door opened and I could see Haywood Anderson, my chief security guard, rush into the hall, ready to take on whoever was assaulting his boss.

But no one could have overcome my attacker that night. Jesus Himself had laid in wait for me and picked that moment from out of all eternity to reveal Himself in all His glory and splendor. Whatever it was that I knew of God and His love up until that moment—all the sermons I'd heard preached and all the gospel songs I'd sung and all the times I seen folks weeping and wailing as they made their way to lay down their lives at the altar of Mother

Bates's revival tent—all that faded into insignificance. I was in the middle of a personal encounter, one on one with my Creator and now, at last, I understood what all the words and all the songs and all the tears had really meant.

As Haywood rushed up to me, he was joined by my brother Bill, who, as I recall, was still dressed in just his underwear. Other guests had started to poke their heads out to see what all the commotion was, but I didn't care. In fact, I wanted them all to know exactly what was going on. "I am not ashamed!" I shouted again and started hammering on my dad's door.

When he opened up, a robe around his shoulders and his eyes like saucers, I thrust out my hands right under his nose. "Look, Daddy!" I cried, wiggling my fingers at him. "Look at my hands!" I pointed down at my feet. "And my feet, Daddy," I said as tears began to drop from my eyes.

"What is it, son?" my daddy asked. "What's wrong with your hands and feet?"

"Can't you see?" I answered, the tears nearly blinding me now. "They're brand-new! All of me . . . is brand-new!"

Daddy turned to Laura with a terrified look. "What are we going to do?" he said. "What's wrong with him?"

But Laura just smiled and in that sublime moment I knew that she understood. "Nothing to do," she said softly. "Al's in God's hands now." She put her arm around me. "Come on, honey," she said. "Let's go back in the room and let these good folks get some sleep." She waved down the hall. "It's fine," she said to the bewildered guests. "Everything is just fine." And, along with Haywood, Bill, and Daddy, she led me back into my suite.

It took me the rest of that early morning to come back to myself, weeping and praying and holding on to my friends and family like a lost child found safe again. We all sang songs I remember, the old gospel gems I'd grown up with, and one by one

those around me offered up their thankgivings for so great a salvation of so great a sinner. And when dawn finally broke over the
Disneyland Matterhorn, the freeway began to fill up with morning
traffic and all along the boulevard, the shops and stores and little
souvenir stands that sold Mickey watches and hats with Goofy ears
began to open up, and I passed into a deep and untroubled sleep.
My head was cradled in Laura's arms. My daddy held my hand.
And my Savior dwelt within, never to leave me nor forsake me.

CHAPTER **30**

The more things change, some people will tell you, the more they stay the same. A man can go about being transformed from the inside out, his eyes open, his mouth shut, and his spirit reborn into eternal life and, when he wakes up after his long sleep, he's still got to wash his face, brush his teeth, and put his pants on one leg at a time. The world may look like a whole new place to him, but as far as everyone else is concerned, it's business as usual.

And when that business is all about you, it doesn't matter how different you may feel on the inside. You've got to meet your obligation, hit your mark, and show up for your dates: You've got to *perform*.

Now, the morning of my born-again experience in Anaheim, California, I was looking ahead to at least a solid year of concerts booked in advance. I had a multialbum recording contract to fulfill and a staff to support that now included members of my own family. Whatever else I might have felt like doing—such as basking in the warm glow of God's love for a few weeks while the world sorted itself out—was definitely going to have to wait.

Laura, my true friend and a woman who truly cared about

what was best for me, tried her hardest to convince me that I needed to take a break, if for no other reason than just to pray on what God had for me and what He wanted me to do next. Bill and Daddy went along with her urgings, even though I could tell that in the back of their minds was more than just a passing thought for what would become of their livelihood. I guess maybe if I'd listened to Laura and had been able to stay close by during those crucial first days after my encounter with the Holy Spirit, I would have found the strength to put first things first. It also would have helped if she'd been able to stick close as well, to keep me pointed in the right direction. But she had her own obligations, in this case a concert tour that would keep us apart for the next several weeks. In the meantime, I'd be on my own, trying to make important decisions by myself, about my future and the future of everyone who depended on my future.

Who can say why one man is born again and another stays dead in his sins? Who knows why God picks one and passes over the other? None of us can say what the plan of God may be for our lives, the number of our days, or the purpose to which they will be put. But I do know this: The choices we make follow after us, lifting us up or dragging us down. God may choose you or me or anybody He pleases. But we have to choose back, every minute of every day. Every time we say yes to Him, we climb a little closer to heaven. And every time we say no, we drop a little farther toward hell. In His mercy, He leaves it up to us.

I had a choice, too. I could continue to chase after the treasures dangled in front of my eyes like carrots before a donkey. Or I could turn aside, walk away, and begin again. And faced with those clear options, I did what most of us poor frail humans do. I tried to have it both ways.

Even that turned out to be easier said then done. The first sign of trouble came when I met up with Willie after the tour was over to begin writing and preproduction on a new album. I was just about bubbling over with excitement for all the changes I'd been through and couldn't wait to tell him all about it. Willie listened politely enough to my story, smiling and nodding when I got to the part about Jesus asking me if I was ashamed of Him. When I finished, my friend sat silent for a long moment, just stroking his chin and looking at me.

"Al," he finally said, "that's quite a story, and I can tell that you have really been changed by what's happened. You're a new man, that's for sure. But, Al, there's something you need to know."

"What's that?" I asked, puzzled.

"Well," said Willie slowly and deliberately. "I don't do gospel music."

Now it was my turn to stare at him, trying to figure out what he was getting at. I hadn't said a thing about music, gospel or otherwise. At that moment, singing was the farthest thing from my mind. But Willie, as usual, was thinking nine steps ahead of everyone else. He could see where this was going. If I was born again, then, sooner or later, it was going to start coming out in my music, and instead of songs about the love of a good woman, I'd be singing songs about the love of God, shed abroad in my heart. Willie wanted me to know, right up front, that he wasn't going to cross that bridge with me.

"Hey, man, what are you talking about?" I said, more than a little confused and concerned. Willie and I had been through a lot together. I wasn't ready to make a choice between him and Jesus. I didn't think I had to. "Nothing's changed. We can still do what we've always done. Besides, you and I've done gospel music before. How about 'Jesus Is Waiting'?"

"It's different now," Willie replied, calm but straight to the point. "You could have sung that song 'Jesus Is Waiting' or 'Judy Is Waiting.' Wouldn't have made any difference. Now it does." He stood up and put his hand on my shoulder. "You think about it, Al. I've seen this happen before. A man's got to make a choice. That's just the way it is."

The way it is. Willie was right, of course. A man *does* have to make a choice, between the things of the world and the things of God, but I've never been convinced that those things include music. Is God offended when we sing a song of love to a woman? Does he condemn us putting words and music to the longings and loneliness, the devotion and deep emotions that He made us to feel? Is there room in His world for songs about Jesus and songs about Judy? It took me a long time to answer those questions to my own satisfaction, and even today I can't say for sure that what I've discovered is true for anyone other than me. And for Willie, it was sure going to take some convincing.

The songs of my next album explain the dilemma better than I ever could. You'd think, what with the success of the three hit singles from *Call Me*, I'd have had a chance to step back a little and enjoy the fruits of my labors. After all, I was rolling into my fourth gold album and had just come off my seventh consecutive million-selling single. If ever there was a time to count my blessings, this was it.

But of course, the record company, the promoters, and the radio programmers didn't see it that way. They just wanted more of what was making them rich and it was up to me to deliver the goods, regardless of whether my spirit was in it anymore. And by the time the holidays rolled around, the last thing I wanted to was go back in the studio and cut another record.

But I didn't have much choice. The rule of what-have-you-done-for-us-lately was the law of my life, forcing me to prove myself over and over again. And when it came down to it, that's exactly what I did. *Livin' for You*, my sixth album, featured two more chart-toppers, with the title track and a cut I wrote by myself called "Let's Get Married." Making hit records was getting to be almost *too* easy, and with that attitude, something was bound to give.

You can hear the strain starting to show in some of the other songs on *Livin' for You*. Despite Willie's objections, we did record another gospel song, a version of the old standard "My God Is Real." And if you listen closely, you can hear echoes of my newly established faith in cuts like "Home Again," "Free at Last," and even "Livin' for You."

But it's on the last selection of the album that the tension between me and Willie—and between my old life and my new one—is right there for anyone with ears to hear. The track is called "Beware" and with it, for the first time, we broke out of the three-and-a-half-minute hit single formula and let ourselves stretch out a bit. I can't say the results were all that successful. My insistence on playing a guitar solo in the middle of the song didn't exactly enhance the results, and the sudden tempo changes back and forth only confused things more. I think at the same time, Willie was getting a little boxed in by his own formula, too. It was all there, the solid rhythm line, the tight horn section, the clear and simple arrangements, but it just never seemed to jell. It was like we were all looking for a groove that had slipped away without anyone noticing until it was gone. Another problem was that, increasingly, Al Jackson's time was taken up with his work for Booker T. and the MGs and other session gigs over at Stax Records. *Livin' for You* was the first time he wasn't around to either write or play and, although we had Bulldog Grimes sitting in, I think we all missed Al's rock-steady support.

But it wasn't the drumming that gave "Beware" its spooky, spacy feel. It was the words that I'd put to the music. Although I ranged pretty freely over the course of those eight-odd minutes, the message was clear enough. "The way people smile and say," I sang in the first verse, "using me in every way, it's okay/Time for changin'/life is upside down."

Life *was* upside down, even though I was doing my desperate best to keep it from tilting totally out of control. While "Livin' for You" was a big hit on the R&B charts, it never made the Top Ten in the pop listing and didn't end up selling enough for a gold certification. That was the first time that had happened since "Tired of Being Alone," almost three years before.

That shook me a bit and it shook Willie a little bit more. Even though, after our run of success, you had to expect a slight stumble now and again, we just weren't used to anything less than topping ourselves each time out, and Willie got right back down to business, writing and working up arrangements on a whole new bunch of tunes.

But chart numbers were only part of the problem. As it was turning out, Willie's warning about having to make a choice was starting to come true, whether I wanted it to or not. While I did nothing to change my act, singing the same songs people had paid good money to hear night in and night out, I did decide that regardless of where I might find myself, or in what condition, I would attend a church service every Sunday.

So it was that I came to visit churches, temples, and storefront houses of God from coast to coast and back again. For me, it didn't matter what the denomination was or the color of the folks in the pew next to me. I was hungry to hear the Gospel preached and, on occasion, I'd even end up with some Korean or Spanish congregation, where, even if I didn't understand the words, at least the Holy Spirit was there to welcome me. More than once, I almost missed a bus or a plane that was taking us to the next city and another gig on what by then was just one never-ending road trip, and it got to where those quiet and serene times I spent in churches were the highlight of my week.

But it seemed God wasn't entirely satisfied with me paying Him a visit once a week. He wanted to invade my *whole* life and He wasn't waiting for an invitation. All throughout the *Livin' for You* tour, the same thing would happen to me at the most unpredictable times. I'd be up in front of a sold-out crowd, singing "Let's Stay Together" or "For the Good Times," and suddenly, right in the middle of the number, I'd break out in a long and heartfelt passage of Scripture. The audience would kind of rock back all at the same time, like they were bowled over by a shock wave and their shouting and cheering would drop down to a silence so deep I could hear my own heart beating.

And it was beating as fast and as hard as a frightened rabbit. I didn't know what to think when those spells came over me, didn't even know where I had heard or remembered the Bible quotations I was spouting, and sometimes thought I was going crazy for sure. I don't know what the band thought, but there was a reason we were paying those cats top dollar: They were the best. Whenever I'd break into one of my spur-of-the-moment inspirational messages—talking about the tares and the wheat, the goats and the lambs, the Alpha and the Omega—the guys behind would slide into a long, slow vamp, keeping the music at a low boil until such time as I decided to come back and finish off the song.

Nobody ever said anything to me about those uncontrolled—and uncontrollable—outbursts. I was paying the bills and whatever I wanted to do was all right with them. And as long as the music kept playing, even the audiences didn't seem to care a whole lot. Once I got back to the hits, they were right there with me, maybe a little puzzled about the thee's and thou's, but willing to forgive me anything as long as I sang that particular song that they loved best of all. And of course, I always did.

But back at the hotel room, after the show and the inevitable party that went along with it, I'd cast my mind back to the moment when my voice was no longer my own, and a kind of despair welled up inside of me. Willie's words echoed in my head and I wondered how I had come to such a pass—a rich and famous entertainer compelled by a force far greater than him to proclaim the Kingdom of God. I didn't want my career to suffer any more than the people around me who depended on my success did. I didn't want to lose everything I'd worked so hard to achieve. But at the same time, I couldn't turn my back on the God who had come in visitation and asked with a voice that cut at my heart, "Are you ashamed of Me?"

Whenever I got a chance to see Laura, the only person I felt I could really trust, I'd tell her about what I was going through and her answers to me always made it seem so simple.

"Al," she'd say, "you've got to follow the leading of the Lord. No matter where it takes you." It seems that Laura was coming to a place in her own life where she would face that same decision. After building a career singing the downest and dirtiest roadhouse R&B, she was feeling the tug of the church and the prompting of the Holy Spirit once again as in the days of her childhood. God was preparing her for a such a time when He would lay claim to her gift of music, so it wasn't any wonder that she knew exactly what I was going through.

And of course, in the middle of all this struggle, deep in my spirit, there were still songs to write and albums to release, like punching a clock in a music factory. After the disappointing per-formance of *Livin' for You*, Willie went right back to fundamentals. No more eight-minute journeys through the whims and wiles of Al Green. We were back to cranking out the formula, and that meant locking down the hits.

On *Al Green Explores Your Mind*, we came up with what was the biggest record of my career. Written by Willie, "Sha-La-La (Make Me Happy)" was as pleasing a piece of pop candy as we'd ever come up with, and it bounced me right back into the million-sellers circle. But Willie wasn't taking any chances. He laid down the law about doing gospel material and the very best I could manage was to split the difference between the sacred and profane with a track called "God Bless Our Love."

Explores Your Mind had some other highlights, as well, including my version of "Take Me to the River," which another Hi artist, Syl Johnson, would get a hit off in '75. I could understand why; I always preferred Syl's version to my own. I also cut a tune called "One Night Stand," in which I talked up front and openly about the temptations of life on the road.

Altogether my seventh album was a pretty satisfying experience. It felt like we were back in the groove, a groove that would just keep unfolding as long as we did what we were supposed to. In four years, I had sold 35 million albums worldwide, 20 of those in the past two years. I had eight gold singles, ten Top Three R&B hits, and seven Top Ten pop charters. There was nothing going to stop us, nothing to even slow us down.

But it didn't turn out that way. God had other items on the agenda, events that would change me around and send me heading in a whole other direction, frightened for my very life and crying out to the heavens for a redeemer to come and rescue me from this sinful world.

CHAPTER **31**

It wasn't too long before "Sha-La-La" came out that I started doing some charity work, if only because after my encounter with the Holy Spirit, it seemed like I should be doing something besides just making myself rich and famous. I'd sing in hospitals and jails whenever I could grab a free day and the response of the audience in those places was always so gratifying.

Especially in the women's jails. They were always calling out for "Tired of Being Alone," which seems to have become the unofficial anthem of females behind bars. Sometimes those shows would get a little out of hand and it wasn't always because of the lady inmates. I can clearly recall at one women's facility when a security guard was assigned to take me up and meet the warden. She was a big, robust specimen, all spit and polish in her uniform, especially compared to little old me, about 110 pounds soaking wet in tight pants, a silk shirt, and fine Italian loafers.

We were riding up the elevator when suddenly I felt my butt getting pinched, good and hard. Not wanting to make a fuss, I tried to ignore it, but when it happened again, this time on the other cheek, I spun around and caught the guard right in the act. She had long nails with bright red polish that looked every bit as dangerous as the nightstick hanging from her belt and just winked at me with a sly grin. I probably would have been safer on the other side of the bars. I know my butt would have been . . .

It was at one of those prison concerts, for the inmates at the New York State Correctional Facility, that I first met Mary Woodson. She was the kind of woman that when you first saw her, you'd take a look, then a second look, and then a third, and then, after a while, your eyes would just become accustomed to turning her way. She was fond of wearing dusky colors like burnt orange, copper, sandstone, and ivory . . . warm and inviting tones that set off her flawless high yellow complexion, like Juanita. A radiant and ravishing woman, Mary had a classy way of carrying herself: statuesque and graceful and proud. She was there visiting a friend, she told me, although she never did say what her friend had done to land in prison. But Mary had all kinds of secrets . . . more than I could have imagined at the time.

Of course I always carried Laura around in the back of my mind but, after meeting Mary, that's pretty much where she stayed. I loved Laura and there were times, like in that Anaheim hotel room, when she was closer to me than any other human being had ever been. But there also comes a time when friendship isn't what a man is looking for, and a woman who's as loyal to him as a sister can't take the place of a woman who treats him like a man. And this was one of those times.

I casually asked Mary where she was heading after the concert, but I already knew the answer and it was "There's nowhere else you're going but home with me." But Mary didn't fall under my spell quite so easily. She begged off my invitation to come back with me to the hotel. It was late, she said, she had to get up early. It was probably best that she just get home and into bed. So I offered her a ride in my limo into the city, and on the trip back we just talked. I wasn't pushing anything. She was pretty and I liked having pretty women around me.

As I spent more and more time out on the road, I had begun to accumulate a certain type of girlfriend from one town to the next. It wasn't a romantic or even a physical thing, just a way to satisfy the fascination I've always had for beautiful women. I'd come into town and give them a call and they were always available to drop by and spend a little time. Like Tina, an old acquaintance from New York City, who was tiny and petite and used to dress just like a little doll. I'd invite her over after the show and we'd just gossip and pass the time until early in morning, when I'd finally wind down from the performance and fall asleep. And when I woke up, Tina would be sleeping at the foot of the bed, like a young child who had been up past her bedtime.

But Mary had other things on her mind, right from the beginning. Just to impress her after that first night, I invited her to fly out to San Francisco with me for another concert. Now, mind you, nothing had gone on between us yet, but I figured with all that free transportation coming and going, when we finally did get down to business, it was going to be something special.

In the meantime, I liked being around her and admired the way she kept and carried herself. She was a real woman, not like all the giggling girls who flocked around me on the road, and everything about her, from those rusty colors she wore to the smell of her perfume, was new and exciting. But there was something else about this gorgeous creature that I'd never experienced before—her moody times and the way she stared off into the distance like she was listening to someone else from very far away. To me, that just added to the mystery.

After San Francisco, I went back home to Memphis with Mary still on my mind. It wasn't more than a few days when I got a call. She was in town. Could we get together? By this time I'd kind of gotten used to women turning up on my doorstep. One dedicated fan had even taken an apartment down the block from the Royal Studios and would always be there in the morning, waiting at the corner. But Mary played it cool, and it was the way she held herself back, watching and waiting, that made me want to reach around her calm and collected manner to touch the cold flame that burned at her core.

It was an infatuation that blinded me to all the warning signs. I didn't care where she had come from or the baggage she'd picked up along the way. And when I finally got around to asking her about her past, we had gone so far along the path of our own destruction, I don't think she had any choice but to lie. It was as much my fault for not wanting to know as it was hers for not wanting to tell.

No, she'd never been married, she told me. And of course, she didn't have any kids. The truth was, Mary had left behind a whole family in New Jersey to come and be with me. But I'd only find that out later, after it was way too late. All I knew then, as the days we spent together turned to weeks, was that I wanted her around, right next to me.

But it wasn't just her beauty and bearing that drew me to her. She had a way of looking me straight in the eye and telling me things about myself that sent shivers down my spine. The first time it happened was on a beautiful spring day in a park outside of town, where we'd gone for a picnic, just the two of us.

"You know something?" she said with a sparkle in her eye. "You're going to be a magnificent star one day." I just laughed. As far as most people were concerned, I was *already* a star.

"No," she said, putting her hand over mine. "That's not what I mean. You're going to stand in front of great congregations. And you're going to preach wonderful sermons that will turn the hearts of many."

"Me? Preach?" I laughed again. "All the preaching I do is a lit-tle 'Love and Happiness.' " I joked about it, but I was starting to get a little nervous. She stared in that way she had, like she was looking right through me, then gave me a dreamy smile and turned away, up to the clouds like she was waiting for a sign from heaven. When she looked back again, tears were welling up in her eyes. "When you do that," she asked. "When you preach in your church, will you save a seat up front for me?"

It wouldn't be the last time she spoke about things to come as if they already were, and each time she did, I had a little more trou-ble shaking off the spooky feeling. Somewhere, deep down in my spirit, a voice was whispering a warning, but I was so wrapped up in the spell she was weaving, I didn't pay it any mind. I think I understood, without ever putting it into words, that Mary needed help. I just didn't want to admit it. And when I finally couldn't ignore it anymore, I wanted my care and affection for her to heal up the hurt. But it wasn't enough, it could never have been enough, and by the time I realized it, I was past the point of no return.

It wasn't too long after that picnic that things started to go wrong for Mary. Although I didn't know it at the time, her hus-band had come down from New Jersey to bring her back. She'd flat-out refused, but he wasn't going to let her go and made it clear that she belonged to him . . . and to her children. She was living out her fantasy on borrowed time and, sooner or later, that time was going to run out.

The night it finally did, I was in the studio, working on some new material, and at six that evening they put a call through for me. It was the Memphis sheriff. "We arrested a young woman down at the Peabody Hotel for smoking pot," he told me. "She says she's a friend of yours." I knew, without even asking, that it was Mary. Not that she was a big drug user . . . if anyone was nat-urally high, it was that woman. It's just when you have that stubborn feeling that something's going to go wrong, and you have it for long enough, you always seem to know all the details even before they happen.

I'd gotten to be a friend of the sheriff, thanks to my charity work, so I talked with him for a while until I convinced him that if I came down to the station to fetch her, he'd let Mary go. When she was escorted out of the holding cell, I could see right away that the humiliation and degradation of being arrested had taken its toll. She was pale and trembling and she hardly said a word to me, not even looking in my direction. It was as if she'd been robbed of all her natural grace and style and couldn't bear to let me see her so pitiful and hurting.

I wanted so much to make her feel better, to let her know I wasn't ashamed of her, and the best way I knew back then to lift people's spirits was with music. "Come back to the studio with me," I said. "I'll write you a song." She looked at me for the first time, up through her long lashes like a little girl, and it made me want to put my arms around her and protect her from anything bad ever happening again.

When we arrived at the studio, Willie and the musicians were still hanging around, waiting for me to get back and finish up the session. I grabbed a guitar and started working out a few chord changes, trying to put a song together that would turn Mary around. But I was nervous and upset by the events of the evening, so I ended up just riffing on "Sha-La-La," hoping the refrain would calm her down and soothe her anxious spirit.

And it did—or at least it seemed to. But the mood I'd worked so hard to create was shattered a moment later when the door opened and a good-looking woman rushed in and gave me a big hug. It took me a minute to recognize who it was—her name was Carlotta Williams, an airline stewardess I'd met on my travels who was in town on a layover. Right about then, having a party wasn't exactly at the top of my list. I was too concerned with Mary's fragile state of mind, but Carlotta seemed so happy to see me that I couldn't just turn her away.

It was getting late by this time and the day's hectic events had started to catch up with me. I closed down the session and suggested that Mary and Carlotta come back to the house, where we could relax and not be bothered, hoping that including them both in the invitation would send the message that we were all just friends, enjoying each other's company. I couldn't tell from the look in Mary's eyes whether she saw it that way or not, but she seemed calm enough, talking with Carlotta like the two were long-lost girlfriends. I made sure they understood I had lots of spare bedrooms where they could spent the night—the last thing on my mind right then was some kind of kinky encounter.

The three of us piled into the Rolls I had bought a few months before and, somehow, in the jumble of leaving, Carlotta ended up sitting in the front with me, while Mary was in the back. All the way home, I kept glancing at her through the rearview mirror, disturbed by the strange expression she had on her face, as if she had made up her mind about something, once and for all. Once she caught me looking at her and fixed me with a cold, appraising stare that set my nerves on edge. I turned away quickly, keeping my attention on the winding road leading through the thick forest back to the house.

Everything was quiet when we finally arrived, and as I pulled up to the house, one of my bodyguards let us in. After we got through the front door, the rest of the security staff shut everything up and double-checked the grounds. It was the same "lock down" routine they went through every time I stayed there and most nights it made me feel good to know that I was safe inside my own four walls.

But that night was different. It was as if being in the house itself was risky, that the danger had come right through the door with me. Carlotta must have sensed that something wasn't right, because she asked to be shown to her room right away, saying that she had an early flight the next morning. She sure had changed her tune, but it must have been obvious by then that there wasn't going to be any partying that night.

I showed her upstairs to a guest bedroom down the hall from my suite. After I made sure she was comfortable, I went back downstairs, still worried about Mary, with the image of her eyes through the rearview mirror still fresh in my mind. I walked into the living room, but she wasn't where I'd left her. I called her name and heard a soft answer from the kitchen.

Mary was standing at the stove when I came in, absent-mindedly stirring a big pot of water with a wooden spoon. She turned when she heard my footsteps and smiled, a wistful, sad smile. "Al, honey, have you ever thought of getting married?" she asked. It took me a minute to register what she was actually asking.

" 'Married'?" I repeated dumbly. "Maybe we should talk about this in the morning, baby."

She turned back to stirring the pot without a word. A long moment passed until, just to break the tension, I asked, "What are you cooking?" For some reason, I had it in my head that she was heating water for a bath, although all she had to do was turn on the tap. It all seemed so unreal in that moment, with the steam starting to rise up out of the pot and the tension so thick you could stick it with a fork: I guess my mind went back to those early days down in Jacknash when all the plumbing was outdoors and taking a bath meant heating water on the wood stove. I was worried and a little frightened, trying desperately to break through, make contact, and bring her back into the real world.

She didn't answer my question, didn't even acknowledge that I was there for what seemed like the longest time. Then suddenly she was in my arms, kissing my neck and hanging on like it was our last night on earth. "You know, Al," she whispered in my ear, "I would never do anything to hurt you."

The words sent another chill up my spine. "Hurt me?" I repeated, searching her eyes and trying to understand what was going on in their deep brown depths. But it was all distance and darkness and I guess she must have seen the confusion on my face then, because she kissed me again and told me everything was fine, that I should get ready for bed and that she'd find her own way up a little later. I left her there, still stirring that simmering pot of water, and went upstairs to take a shower.

Peeling off my clothes down to my underwear, I went into the bathroom. As I stood in front of the mirror, brushing my teeth, I suddenly heard a sound behind me, outside the door, in the bedroom. I turned around, but couldn't see anything, so I went on brushing. Bending down to rinse, I heard another sound. This time it was the door to the bathroom, opening slowly. I looked up just in time to see Mary's reflection in the mirror. She had the steaming pot in both hands.

In the next second, my world exploded into a thousand splatters of pure agony. Mary had added grits to the water, making a thick, boiling hot paste. With all her strength, she hurled it at me, splashing the bathroom walls and scorching my naked back. The pain was so intense that I wasn't sure what was happening for a moment before I heard screaming. Like that night of my salvation in the hotel room, for a moment I wasn't sure where the screaming was coming from until I realized it was coming from me. Only this time the joy had turned to horror.

What happened next was a red-washed blur as I squirmed and thrashed in searing anguish, trying to somehow get away from her and from the horrible burning on my back. I staggered into the bedroom and out into the hall, where Carlotta had just opened the door. "What in the world—" she started to say, but I pushed right past her and ran into her bathroom. Everything was spinning, revolving around the unbearable pain running all down my back like raking fingers. I slumped over on the floor and rested my head for a moment against the cool porcelain of the bathtub rim.

Carlotta burst in. "Al!" she screamed. "What's wrong?" It was then that she saw the egg-sized blisters rising on my burned flesh. She staggered backward and I thought for a minute she was going to pass out, but instead she grabbed my arm and pulled me up. "Come on," she urged. "Get into the tub." I climbed in and she turned on the shower, full-blast and freezing cold. I don't know what was worse: the pain of my back or that icy torrent. I screamed again, bent over, and started to black out when I suddenly heard, over the thundering spray of the shower, the sound of a loud bang.

I looked at Carlotta and she looked at me. It was as if we both knew that something terrible was unfolding around us and all we could do was stand in horrible, helpless witness. Then another bang, and the sickening, unmistakable sound of something heavy hitting the floor. I heard my own disembodied voice again, and to this day, I don't know whether I actually spoke the words or just caught them echoing in my head: "The woman has killed herself!" I jumped out of the shower as Carlotta tried to hold me back.

"Where are you going?" she shouted.

"Didn't you hear those shots?" I screamed back and ran out of the bathroom and down the hall, my back throbbing and the blisters beginning to ooze and bleed.

As I got to my bedroom, I began to slow down, suddenly realizing that I had no idea what might be waiting for me beyond that door. I peered inside, and through the open door I could still see the grits dripping down the bathroom walls. But there was no sign of Mary, so I went into the next bedroom: still no one. I made my way down the hall slowly and carefully until I got to the last bedroom. There, on the floor, was the lifeless shape of Mary.

Carlotta came up behind me and I could hear her whisper, "Oh, my God." But in that split second, all I saw, bigger than life, was the gun in Mary's hand. I could hear my security guards pounding down the hall behind me as I summoned all my courage and knelt down by Mary's side. There was no sign of blood. I put my fingers to her neck, feeling for a pulse. Nothing. I grabbed he wrist. It was limp. Then it was as if the earth opened up and swallowed me in darkness. Mary was dead.

CHAPTER 32

When the darkness parted, I was in a hospital, in a whole new kind of nightmare. The pain of those third-degree burns on my back made every movement torture, but what was worse was the constant interrogation by the police. One set of cops would come in and ask me to tell them what happened down to the smallest detail. I'd try to put my recollections together as best I could, even though it seemed so unreal, as if it had happened to someone else entirely. Then they'd leave and a whole other set would arrive and start the process all over again.

I could tell by the looks they traded between them that they were trying to decide whether or not I was telling the truth. There were lots of questions about the two shots that had been fired and I didn't really have an answer for them, although I've since heard it said that suicides sometimes shoot off a round to see if the gun works before turning it on themselves. Your guess is as good as mine, and while I never did find out what exactly the police thought was going on that night, I was only too happy to oblige when they asked me to take a lie detector test. I wanted more than anything to be left alone to try and pick up the pieces of my life.

I was on my way to the examination room when I saw my friend the sheriff in the hallway. I gestured to him and as he came close, I whispered in his ear, "Is any of this real?"

"It's real, Al," he said, "They took that woman out of there in a bag." It was at that moment that I finally let the tears start to flow—for myself, for Mary, for all that was dead and gone and never coming back.

Well, I passed the polygraph test and everything I said was backed up by Carlotta and the bodyguards. Eventually, the voices of the police faded and were replaced by the clatter of steel surgical instruments as they cut away the dead skin from my back and began the slow, arduous process of skin grafts. In all, I would spent the next eight months in convalescence, and, like most calamities, there was a bit of blessing in disguise. I was finally left alone: to rest, to knit back together the tatters of my life, to take the long view, and, most important, to try and find the answers to questions that so many people would ask me in the years to come.

Why had Mary killed herself? Why had she tried to destroy me? To this day, I can't say I really know. There were whole parts of her life she never let me into. Was she crazy for giving up her world for mine? I guess so. And was I crazy for letting her into my world? Maybe. And while I'm never going to be able to fully explain the events of that terrible night to everyone's satisfaction, I know first-hand that the famous thin line between love and hate is real, and for some people, what they can't have they've got to destroy.

Of course, those answers were never good enough for some folks. For years afterward, rumors and whispered gossip swirled around me and, while I guess I can understand the interest in scandals and celebrity, I can't say it didn't hurt to hear the lies that people told. Some said I'd murdered Mary. Others, that the bodyguards had shot her dead. Still others, that I had driven her to her desperate act by my neglect and abuse. It was also spread around that my religious "conversion" had come from almost getting scalded to death that night and being caught up in so disgraceful a mess that I had to do something to redeem my image. Of course, no one paid the slightest attention to the fact that I'd been born again almost a year before and had been preaching from the stage ever since. But that's the way things go when you're a public figure: that spotlight feels great until it starts cooking you like a bug under a magnifying glass.

I guess I could spent the next five hundred pages defending myself against such accusations, but what's the use? In such times, I lean on the Scripture that commands us not to make a defense for ourselves, but to let Almighty God speak and act on our behalf.

And God *did* shelter and protect his child, Al Green. During my long recovery, I was able to devote myself to reading the Bible, praying and spending time with Laura, just talking about the things of the Lord. It was during that time that I got closer to her than ever, partly because she was an ever-present help and friend and partly because I could see what she was going through in her own career. It had been almost three years since "Rip Off," her last major hit, and I could tell that the constant grind of touring, combined with the pressure of trying to come up with a musical formula that would bring her back to popularity, was all taking its toll. She talked increasingly about leaving it all behind, and while it made me nervous to hear such talk, I knew, deep down inside, it was because I was coming up to the same crossroads in my own life.

For the first time, I could clearly see that the world could go on without me and that even the folks who depended on what I did for their paycheck would somehow get by in my absence. I was able to finally put my career into some kind of perspective, placing my music on one side of the scale and my peace of mind and spiritual well-being on the other.

It was no contest. I'd been hitting it so hard for so long I'd lost touch with the simple pleasure of singing, not for money, not to top the charts, but just because the words fit into the melody so beautifully and from the abundance of my heart my voice would speak. Even as the flesh on my back slowly began to heal itself, so also did I begin to bind up all the different parts of Al Green back into something like wholeness.

In the meantime, Willie went ahead with some long-delayed plans to put together a greatest hits package. We certainly had enough material to fill two sides of a record and the timing couldn't have been better. I was still riding at the crest of my career and, since doctor's orders called for plenty of rest and relaxation, there was no better way to keep me out front of the public than to remind them of everything I'd done to date. Released in early 1975, *Al Green's Greatest Hits* was one of my best and fastest-selling records. I still had it, even when I wasn't around to pick it up.

But not all things stayed the same as they had been—they never do. While I was still in the hospital, Willie came by one morning with word that Al Jackson—the brilliant drummer and songwriter and one of my best friends in the music business—had been brutally murdered. We both sat in silence for a long time after he broke the news, listening to the soft ticking of the heart monitor I was hooked up to, and thinking back on all we had been through, and how much Al had been a part of it all. No question about it— Al Jackson was the foundation upon which rested most of the best of what came to be called the Memphis Sound. A quiet, gentle man, drenched in music and alive to the rhythm of life, his passing shook me as deeply as any of the events of those momentous months. Willie and I and the enterprise we had put together might be able to go on from where we were, recover our stride, and carry on carrying on. But without Al, it was never going to be the same, and without saying a word, we both knew it.

With all the turmoil and travail going on around me, you'd

think I'd just want to sit out on a porch somewhere, soaking in the sunshine and letting the world pass me by. And with all that I'd been through, it's hard to recall that, in 1975, I was still a year shy of my thirtieth birthday and nowhere near a ripe old retirement age. The fact was, toward the end of my burn therapy, I was starting to once again get restless, remembering my life on the road and in the studio with a rosier glow than I'd ever seen it in reality. Willie and the crew had been busy in my absence, writing up a storm, and, like me, were anxious to get back to work. And I was only too happy to oblige.

So for that matter, was the public. They welcomed me back with open arms on my eighth album, *Al Green Is Love*, by taking the single "L-O-V-E" all the way to the top. Another number 1, another million-seller. It was like the line to a song I once heard: How can I miss you when you won't go away?

With "L-O-V-E," which was written by Willie, Teenie, and me and brought in another Grammy nomination, all the trouble that had been brewing before the death of Mary over singing gospel or pop music kind of faded away. I found room in the song to sing about both earthy and heavenly love and Willie found room to lay in some of his best string arrangements. At that time, the work of Gamble and Huff, Thom Bell and the whole Philadelphia Sound was coming on strong and, although he'd probably get mad at me for saying so, I think Willie picked up on some of what was coming down from the City of Brotherly Love. Whatever the inspiration, though, we were making a happy, upbeat, and altogether joyful noise on both the song and the album that was a reflection of the good feeling we all had about being back on the block.

We followed up "L-O-V-E" with another Top Ten charter, "Oh Me, Oh My (Dreams in My Arms)," then headed right back into the studio to cut another album. *Full of Fire* was released in early 1976, just about the time pop music itself—and the Memphis

Sound especially—was starting to go through some heavy changes. In January of that year, Stax Records closed its doors after more than a decade of making music that defined a whole generation. The classic soul and R&B that we'd all cut our teeth on just couldn't compete with the disco fever that was sweeping the world, and while Willie and I might have imagined that the dance music sensation was a fad that would fade as quickly as it appeared, it was obvious that the rhythm-heavy boogie had gotten a hold of the public's imagination and wasn't about to let go.

Like so many other artists of that era, we had no choice but to try and keep up with the times. The title track of *Full of Fire* was another big hit for us, but it felt to me like one we hadn't really earned. If all that it took to top the charts was to crank yourself to 120 beats per minute, then any fool with a drum machine could be a star overnight and, if you look close at the disco era, that's exactly what happened. Another sign that things weren't what they used to be was that when Willie got around to cutting the track, he had to chase the backing musicians all over the country. Rhodes, Chalmers & Rhodes were out in Las Vegas, singing behind Paul Anka, and a lot of the cats in the horn section were up in Chicago, working with the Doobie Brothers. As a result, Willie had to cut tracks in both cities, put the song back together at the Royal, and bring me in to do the vocals. That was definitely *not* the way we were used to doing business.

But it was more than just the hassles and headaches of being in the music business that were beginning to wear on the two of us. Once I was out of the hospital, every step I took toward staging a successful comeback made me less sure of what I was looking to prove in the first place. The truth was, in the world of music, there *was* nothing left to prove. I was a star of international stature, the walls of my den glittered with gold discs, and anyplace I chose to perform would fill to overflowing faster than they could print the

tickets. More important, Willie and I had become one of the premier teams in pop music history. That's a simple fact. The sound
that we had created had sold millions upon millions of records,
revitalized soul music for a new decade, and defined a style that's
been echoed and imitated ever since. Folks have called me the Last
Great Soul Man and, if you describe the term as a singer who takes
a song and makes it his own, I wouldn't argue. What we'd accomplished in a few short years would go down in history. No one
could take that accomplishment away from us.

Unless we did it ourselves. Without ever saying as much, Willie
and I both realized that we were coming to the end of our partnership. I was more determined than ever to put pieces of the gospel
message in my music, and you can hear it in tracks off *Full of Fire*
like "Glory, Glory," "I'd Fly Away," and "Let It Shine." I still
hadn't sorted out in my mind and heart that age-old dilemma that
puts a poor man between singing for God and singing for the devil,
and was convinced that somehow, some way, I could have my success and still serve the Lord.

For Willie, just watching me try to walk that tightrope was
more than he could stand. He knew, sooner or later, that I'd have
to make that choice and, while he was hoping against hope that I'd
pick pop music and continue on down the same road with him, he
also knew that when God sets a man apart for His purposes, not
even the gates of hell will prevail against His plan. For Willie, it
was just a matter of time.

That time finally came in the summer of '76. We'd released
"Let It Shine" as the second single off *Full of Fire* and, though the
track didn't do so well, we still had a full slate of sold-out concerts
across the country. As usual, I was grabbing whatever time I could
to dash back to Memphis for the recording sessions Willie had set
up and we had already laid down some material for a new album,
including one standout selection called "Keep Me Cryin'." With

most of the record, which we were calling *Have a Good Time*, finished, we sat down and listened to the playback.

"Not too bad," Willie said when it was over. "I think I'd like to get a little more echo of Teenie's guitar, but we're a good ways there." He turned to me. "What do you think, Al?"

What did I think? It was a simple question, with nothing sad or serious attached to it, but for some reason, it stopped me cold in my tracks. What *did* I think? It was another record in a long string of records stretching out way behind me and, for all I knew, way ahead of me. What did I think? I tried to focus on the question, but I couldn't think of anything except how I felt. Tired. Discouraged. Lost in a puzzle of my own devising. I'd dreamed so long, worked so hard, to get to where I was, right then, sitting in a studio laying down one more song for my catalog of golden hits. Why didn't it feel like I'd arrived anywhere? Why was I still grasping for something just out of reach? What was this emptiness that I was still trying to fill?

I turned and looked at Willie and I guess the expression on my face told him everything he needed to know.

"Hey," he said softly, "we can go back, fix whatever you want."

"It's not that, Willie," I said and could hear the trembling in my own voice.

A long moment passed. "I know," he said at last. "I know it's not."

"Willie," I said. "I think it's time, maybe, you and me . . ." but I couldn't get the words out.

"I was thinking the same thing, Al," said Willie and in that moment I knew what a friend I'd found in him. He could see the pain I was going through. He was going through it himself. But no one had to say the words we both dreaded to hear. One of us wouldn't have to tell the other one, "It's over. We're done."

It was just understood.

CHAPTER **33**

No man, says the Bible, can serve two masters. And if he tries, he will end up hating the one and loving the other. When you see the truth, inspired by God and written for all the ages in black and white, it's easy enough to affirm the words with a "yea" and "amen." But when it comes to living them out, more often than not you run up against the wisdom of man and the ways of the world and end up thinking to yourself, *Somehow this doesn't apply to me.*

By parting company with Willie, closing out one chapter of my life, and making a fresh start, I imagined to myself that I was lining myself up with the Scriptures, that I'd be serving one Master now, and loving it. Ever since my moment of truth in Anaheim, I had ached to put the message of God's love into my music. Now I was finally free to be as open and out front as I wanted. But what I didn't anticipate was that being a messenger of God didn't come for free. I'd had to let go of one thing before I could pick up the other. And that, you can believe, is far easier said than done.

I started with high enough hopes and bold enough ambitions. My housecleaning extended beyond Willie to the whole of the Hi backing band that had been with me through so much music. I left the dingy expanse of the Royal Studios and set up my own eight-track facility in town, dropping half a million dollars in the process to improve a facility called the American Music Studios. I decided that I'd produce my own next record and recruited in a whole new lineup of musicians—mostly local cats with prime session experience—that included the rhythm section of Reuben Fairfax on bass and Johnny Toney on drums, James Bass on guitar, and a horn section comprised of Buddy Jarrett, Fred Jordan, and Ron Echols.

You might think it was hard saying goodbye to the people who I worked with so closely for so long, but the truth was, we never really lost touch. I think they all understood, just like Willie, that we'd had a good run and that the time had come to make a change . . . for all of us. Willie would go on to produce a whole range of artists for Hi and other labels and, as often as not, he'd call in the Hodges brothers or Bulldog Grimes to give him the certain musical touch that always set his sound apart. And if we didn't run into each other on the small but lively Memphis music scene, you can be sure we'd get together on birthdays and holidays to share a meal, a few good laughs, and a lot of treasured memories. They were all as dear to me as brothers, and every time we got back together, it felt like we were just picking up where we left off.

But the point was: We *had* left off. And having dropped one thing behind, I was anxious to pick up the next. Even as I began writing material for a new album I was putting together a business plan for a beauty care line—Al Green International Hair—to diversify myself and use the name I had built up for the endorsement of products I could stand behind. I had always believed in looking my best, so it seemed only natural to encourage others to let their own God-given beauty shine.

In early 1977, even as I was starting in on the early sessions for a new album—my first since leaving Willie and my debut as my own producer—Hi put out another single from *Have a Good Time*,

"I Tried to Tell Myself," and followed it up with the long-delayed release of "Love and Happiness," from clear back in '72. Even though Willie and I had parted company, I had stayed with Hi partly because I still had a contract to fulfill and partly because the company had always treated me fairly, which is a rare commodity in the music business. Both of the songs caused barely a ripple and I took that as a sign: I'd made my choice just in time. A change was due.

And I wasn't the only one who thought so. It was also right around that time that Laura decided she, too, could only serve one Master and left behind her R&B music career to return to the bosom of the church. She's always said she was inspired by my decision, but the truth was, I could never have made such a move without the constant love and encouragement of my dear and beloved friend. It felt good to know that she believed in me enough to follow me down that path, even though, for both of us, it was Jesus who was really leading.

I put out *Belle*, my eleventh album, late that year and there was no question but that for me, it was the most important release of my life. Musically, I was stepping out in faith, walking a tightrope without the old comforting net of Willie and the rest of the crew, but I have to say, from the very beginning, it felt good. I was long overdue to take a creative chance, and *Belle*, which had a sound that was more layered and textured than anything I'd done before, was a bold step in the right direction.

But more important than the sound was the message, which was pretty well summed up in the title track. The woman I'd been singing to might have been imaginary, but to me, she was every beautiful fan who had ever wanted to get next to me. The sadness you can hear in that song is real, too: I loved those women, loved their softness and sweetness and the way they gave themselves away for the chance to be lost and found in love. But those days—

and those ways—were past me now. God had called me to a higher place, turned me away from earthly to heavenly love, and while it hurt to say it, I had to leave the sensual for the spiritual. "Belle," I sang, "it's you that I want/but it's Him that I need." And I meant it. Each note and every word.

The song, my confessional in the truest sense of the word, was well received by the public, climbing into the Top Ten and giving me the comforting feeling that I could be a man of God and a man of the people, all at the same time. While the follow-up, "I Feel Good," didn't do as well, I still felt I was on the right track musically. But singing songs about Jesus wasn't enough for me. I needed another way to be of service, another way to show Him just how sincere and serious I really was.

That opportunity came a few months before we finished up *Belle* in the studio when I was driving through the outskirts of Memphis one spring afternoon on my way to work. Now, I'm not one to say that God guides my every step. I believe He gives me freedom of choice within His divine will, but that day, as loud and clear as a bell pealing on Sunday in a steeple, I heard Him tell me to turn off the freeway and head down a spacious boulevard toward a quiet, tree-lined neighborhood of small houses called Whitehaven.

I'd been down that road before. In fact, probably every visitor to Memphis has driven it at one time or another. It was Elvis Presley Boulevard, and as I passed by the white gates of Graceland, I couldn't help but wonder whether the Lord wanted me to stop off for the afternoon tour.

But no, He bid me drive on, down another mile or so, until I came to an intersection where, with the same unspoken conviction, I knew I was supposed to make a right turn.

As I drove down that shady street, not unlike a hundred other streets within the city limits, I saw children playing in their front yards, mothers hanging laundry, and old folks sitting on the porch, taking in the fragrant jasmine-scented air. It all seemed so peaceful, like an eternal picture of God's everyday provision and grace, that an ache rose up in my heart and I wondered, in that moment, what it would have been like to live that kind of life, humble and quiet, tending to a family and taking pleasure in the simple things. *What are you showing me, Lord?* I asked, almost out loud. *Why have you brought me here?* And at that moment I came to a stop sign.

Across the way, set back off the road on a rich green lawn that rolled off gently down a sloping hill, was a church. There was nothing special about it, nothing different from a hundred other A-frame houses of worship thoughout the South. It looked a little run-down, maybe, but nothing that a coat of paint and scrub brush couldn't take care of. I pulled the car onto the gravel driveway, past a sign that read FULL GOSPEL TABERNACLE, and shutting off the motor, climbed out and stood with the warm sun at my back and my long shadow stretching to the threshold of God's house.

I must have stood like that for a good fifteen minutes, listening to the birds in the trees and the faraway shouts of little children at play, and was taken back, in my mind, to my own childhood, standing on a Sunday outside of Taylor's Chapel or the House of the Living God and hearing the hymns rise up past the treetops and off into the clouds, borne away on a gentle breeze to the very ears of the Father. I recalled the great joy that flooded over me in such moments, the love of the music mixing with the presence of God in the midst of His creation and the sure comfort of my family all around me as we came up together to praise and worship. I remembered the peaceful feeling that swelled in my tender heart until it would almost break from the perfect harmony of life and the way my simple thoughts just drifted across my mind until there was only a blue horizon of God's greatness between my ears.

I remembered all that and wept, grieving for how far I strayed and rejoicing at how close I'd been, all this time. I walked across the driveway, the gravel crunching under my feet and through the glass double doors of the little church. I knew, in that moment, just what to do . . . clearer than I'd known anything ever before in my whole life.

"Hello," I said to the first person I met. "My name is Al Green and I'm going to preach in this church."

And sure enough, I did. I bought the Full Gospel Tabernacle—pews, pulpit, and hymnals—and applied myself to studying the Word and earning a degree as an ordained minister of the Gospel. When I was in town, I'd attended Bible classes, and when I was on the road, I'd taken along my correspondence. I had a strong, centered feeling at the core of my spirit that told me at last I was where I belonged. God had given me the Full Gospel Tabernacle in the Whitehaven district of Memphis, Tennessee, and the small but faithful congregation that came along with it. I was a shepherd with a flock, born to this purpose for such a time as this. And I knew from the moment I saw that church that I had come home.

Now, it's one thing to come home. And quite another to stay there. Becoming Pastor Al Green felt like the most natural thing in the world to me, just like preaching a sermon came as natural as singing a song. I can remember the first time I ever stood at the pulpit on a Sunday morning with my little message all written out for the congregation. My palms were sweaty and my knees were weak, and when I spoke, my voice cracked and quaked. But as the words rolled out of my mouth and filled the high ceiling of the church, I could feel all trepidation and timidity fall from me. As power surged up through my spirit right about then, a power to speak of truth with conviction, point to God with an upraised arm, and shout salvation with a mighty roar. Everything I'd ever learned as a performer I was able to bring to my preaching, but there was no formula, nothing fake about the sermons. I spoke like I sang, from a deep well overflowing, and when the folks heard, they rose up and were saved.

The ministry was my calling as sure as music was my vocation, but the demands of both those worlds would become more than I could bear. It wasn't long after I bought the Full Gospel Tabernacle that news came to me while I was on the road of the sudden death of my daddy of a heart attack. The grief I felt was only made worse by the distance between me and my sorrowing family. In that moment, I wanted nothing more than to be back at the church, where my parents and most of my brothers and sisters had joined the congregation, and share with them this passing of a good and giving man. The only comfort I could give myself that dark and lonely night in a hotel room as empty and cold as a tomb was that my daddy had lived to see me embrace God, as God himself had embraced him.

I can't say I ever completely got over the death of my daddy, but then again, I don't think any of us really do. We learn to live with the hole in our hearts and bear up under all the words we never got to say to them. My daddy was more than the man who fed and clothed and nurtured me. He gave me the strength of his own conviction—that God had given us the gift of music that we might lift His name before the nations. It was a lesson that took me a lifetime to learn, but maybe those are the ones that really stick with you in the end.

Even so, it almost took an act of God to bring me around one last time. In November of 1978, I released *Truth 'N' Time*, another collection of songs that I hoped would express my faith even more clearly than *Belle*. We took two singles off the album, a double-sided release with a rendition of "To Sir with Love," which I'd always wanted to do just because I loved the melody, and "Wait Here," a song with a message I took straight from the Book of Job.

I had my own reasons for feeling a little bit like Job during those early days of 1979. God had sure enough given me a church to pastor, but what didn't seem to be part of the package was enough time and energy to tend to the two halves of my life. The demands of touring and recording were as constant and time-consuming as ever, only now, any time that I might have taken to relax and unwind, I knew I had to give over to the endless chores of running a church. Something had to give.

And it did, in spectacular manner. I was on concert tour, promoting *Truth 'N' Time*, working a schedule that had me out for three or four days and then back home for the rest of the week. It was a grueling back-and-forth routine, and by the third week of the itinerary, I was so tired I could hardly see straight.

We got into Cincinnati late in the afternoon and I was able to make a dash for the hotel to get showered and catch a hour's nap before the show. There had been some problems at the church earlier that week, some fussing and feuding between a couple of ladies who really should have known better, but were looking to me to resolve their differences. It was weighing on my mind when I lay down on the hotel bed and closed my eyes and, an hour later, I was still worrying about it. Bleary-eyed and a little feverish from a cold I was trying to shake, I got up when the road manager knocked on the door and tried my best to work up the energy and enthusiasm I was going to need to give the audience the show they'd paid to see.

It was dark and raining when we arrived at the venue and from onstage, the crowd looked like a big, noisy beast spread out over the auditorium. A roar went up when I hit the stage and the band started cranking on "I'm Still in Love with You." I walked to the microphone, unhooked it from the stands, and moved toward the scrim of the stage. The footlights were blinding, especially against the darkness out front, and the audience was cheering so loud I could barely hear myself. I took another step toward them, squinting in the glare, and then, without warning, the world turned upside down.

For a sickening moment, I found myself tumbling out of control off the stage before I hit an instrument case and in a rush of pain and bright lights exploding in my head, lost consciousness as the screams of the crowd faded away.

I had fallen off the stage, out of the spotlight, and into the hands of the living God.

CHAPTER 34

One of my favorite stories in all of the Bible is the saga of Moses. Not that part where he see the burning bush, parts the Red Sea, or brings down the Ten Commandments, although all that is inspiring in its own grand way.

But the part I'm partial to is what you might call the interlude between the front half of Moses' life and the back half. The *long* interlude. You remember: Moses kills the Egyptian and leaves the land of his upbringing to wander in the desert wilderness. It's there that he comes upon the camp of Jethro, a priest of Midian, marries his daughter, and tends to his flock of sheep on the backside of Mount Horeb for forty years.

Forty years! Moses, who had tasted of all that the world had to offer as a prince of Egypt—a star, a celebrity—suddenly found himself a lowly shepherd, with no station or position, forgotten by the world, a man whose life and purpose had come to its conclusion. And it wasn't just for a year, or two, or ten that Moses lived that humble life. It was forty years: a lifetime or long enough, anyway, that he surely must have thought he'd die among the sheep he watched over.

I can relate. I know what it's like to leave behind the glitter and glamour of the world to seek out a poor and plain existence; what it means to give up all you have and cast your lot with the sick and needy. I too have walked through the wilderness to find my place at the base of the mountain of God. I too gave no thought to riches and fame, abased myself, and was brought low. And I too believe that, in due time, God will lift me up to do His purpose. It's my calling, my birthright, my divine appointment.

There's an expression I've never understood when people say that by *some* miracle such and such happened or didn't happen. Well, the miracle the spared my life in Cincinnati that night wasn't just "some" miracle—it was a *special* miracle, one that woke me up, once and for all, and set my feet on solid ground. Even though I came out bruised and bloody and had to spent the next two weeks in the hospital, recovering, I knew that I had been saved from death by a whisker's breath. And God had worked His will not for just *some* reason, but for one reason and one reason alone—to bring me to obedience.

Maybe you're thinking that God was a little harsh on His servant Al Green. After all, I'd all but given up my pop music career, bought a church, and studied for the ministry. What else did He want?

The answer is simple. He wanted *everything*. He always has and He always will. God, we're told, is a consuming fire, and whatever cannot stand in that fire will be burned away. For too long, I'd had one foot in the Kingdom of God and the other in the world. It was time for me to decide, and when that time came, the Lord was there to give me a little nudge . . . right off the edge of a stage. I guess it's a little ironic when you think about it—God had to push me off the stage in order to get me out of the spotlight.

When I rose up off that hospital bed and was wheeled to the curb for a taxi ride to the airport and a plane trip back home, I knew I was never returning to the places I had been. I didn't know exactly where I was heading or what I would do when I got there.

But I did know this: Whatever I put my hand and heart to from that moment on would be as unto the Lord. My career as a soul man was over. My life as a spirit man had just begun.

At that crossroads in my life, I would have happily given up singing entirely if that had been His will. But God knows me and loves me and wants to bring joy pleasure into my life and yours. He would allow me, in the years to follow, to keep singing, continuing to make records, and even, on occasion, experience the approval and applause of the public again.

All throughout the eighties, with straight gospel albums like *The Lord Will Make a Way, Higher Plane, I'll Rise Again,* and *Love Is Reality* and songs like "Going Away," "Everything's Gonna Be Alright," and "As Long As We're Together," I achieved what I was never able to as a pop singer—the Grammy award. It meant a lot that folks in the music business thought highly enough of my simple efforts in gospel music to give me that prestigious honor year after year and I took it as a sign from above that God was pleased with my music, too.

I even asked, and received on occasion, divine permission to perform outside the gospel arena. In 1982 I appeared for two wonderful months in the Broadway show *Your Arms Too Short to Box with God.* A few years later, I had the pleasure and distinction of meeting and singing with the gracious and lovely Miss Annie Lennox on a rendition of "Put a Little Love in Your Heart," which actually brought me back into the Top Ten for the first time in over ten years. I got a chuckle out of seeing my name one more time with a bullet beside it on the *Billboard* chart. It was as if the Lord was saying, "See, Al, it's something, but it's not everything."

I always prayed before agreeing to do anything that would put me back into the world, even temporarily, and so, when the opportunity came up again to cut a few sides with Willie Mitchell, I wanted to make sure I wasn't being presumptuous, even though nothing would have given me greater pleasure than to get back into the studio with my old friend and mentor one more time. Well, even before I finished that prayer, I heard a strong and clear confirmation in my spirit and I knew then that God was giving back, renewed and transformed, what I had given up to Him. And along the way, He accomplished the impossible, just to show me that it could be done. Willie, who had told me he would never make a gospel record, produced what I think is one of my finest spiritual releases, *He Is the Light*. It was like God was getting the last laugh . . . but then again, He usually does.

And I joined in the laugh when I made it back onto the R&B charts again in 1990, this time on my own with a song called "As Long as We're Together," also produced by Willie and another Grammy winner. The same thing happened a few years later with a rendition of a song I'd first done years before. "Funny How Time Slips Away" was a duet with country singer Lyle Lovett, and we picked up one more Grammy with it. It's funny what comes to you when you stop running after it.

The truth was, I'd stopped running after music to give me the meaning and purpose for my life. I still love to sing a good song, gospel or pop, but it's not a matter of life or death now. Music is woven into the fabric of my days, sure enough, but the tapestry is rich and varied with many hues and patterns.

And the loom on which that cloth is woven is the Full Gospel Tabernacle of Memphis, Tennessee. God delivered me from the Egypt of my own vanity and pride and delivered me to the humblest of circumstances, a place where I could discover, for the first time in my life, the spiritual rewards of sacrifice and service. Like Moses sitting on the slopes of that rocky old mountain, carefully watching over Jethro's flock, so too I was brought to a lowly station to minister to the needs of the poor of spirit, those called blessed in the Beatitudes.

Where before my days were spent in bringing my name before crowds of strangers, either chasing after fame or trying to hold on to it, now the seasons rolled by in rituals of baptism and marriage and funerals and the hundred other simple milestones that mark the lives of ordinary folks.

It's here that my story settles down, mixing and blending into the lives of my congregations, lives not unlike your own, I imagine, simple in every way but unique to each of us. You might say that the best part of my life was over—the most exciting and glamorous and dramatic part—but I'd have to say that it's only the first chapter that's come to an end and that the work I put my hand to these days has as much of the miraculous and unexpected as anything that came before it. But all that'll have to wait for another time . . . another book.

In the meantime, let me just leave you with this. In the life of Moses, when he reached a ripe old age, God called him again, off the mountain and back to Egypt to do a mighty work. For Al Green, that day may be coming too, when the singer and preacher, the entertainer and the evangelist, the man of the world and the man of the spirit come together to do a wondrous thing and call many to His name.

And won't that be something to see?